EDUC
ANSWERS

The Daily Telegraph

John Clare's
EDUCATION ANSWERS

ROBINSON
London

Constable Publishers
3 The Lanchesters
162 Fulham Palace Road
London W6 9ER
www.constablerobinson.com

First published in the UK by Robinson,
an imprint of Constable & Robinson Ltd 2001

Copyright © Telegraph Group Ltd 2001

All rights reserved. This book is sold subject to the condition that it shall not, by way of trade or otherwise, be lent, re-sold, hired out or otherwise circulated in any form of binding or cover other than that in which it is published and without a similar condition including this condition being imposed on the subsequent purchaser.

A copy of the British Library Cataloguing in Publication Data is available from the British Library

ISBN 1–84119–258–9

Typeset by WordSpace, Lewes, East Sussex
Printed and bound in the EU

Contents

Introduction *ix*

General *1*
Finding the right school *1*
Education policy *10*
Grants, fundraising and scholarships *18*
Education standards *29*
Being involved: governors, bursars, etc. *32*
Teachers' viewpoints *34*
Home tutoring and support *39*
Learning and behavioural difficulties *44*
Bullying *53*
Rules and discipline *56*
The parent–school relationship *63*
Gifted pupils *66*
Foreign languages *67*
New technology *72*
Attendance *77*
Finally ... *78*

Primary education *93*
Ready for school? *93*
Choice of school *95*
Education/school policy *99*
National tests and league tables *101*
Grants, fundraising and scholarships *107*
The parent–school relationship *108*

Contents

Learning and behavioural difficulties   *111*
Rules and discipline   *114*
Literacy   *117*
Writing   *121*
Teaching aids   *124*
Gifted pupils   *126*
Extra-curricular lessons   *128*
Home tutoring and support   *130*

Secondary education   *131*
Choice of school   *131*
The future of grammar schools   *140*
Ofsted reports and league tables   *142*
Education/school policy   *147*
Education standards   *147*
Examinations – particularly GCSEs   *153*
Subject choices   *157*
Gender differences   *159*
The parent–school relationship   *166*
Teaching approaches   *166*
Behavioural problems   *169*
Rules and discipline   *171*
Gifted pupils   *171*
Home tutoring and extra help   *173*
Vocational education and educational holidays   *174*
Extra-curricular lessons   *176*
Finally ...   *176*

A-level education and alternatives   *179*
Choice of learning institution   *179*

Contents

League tables 185
Alternatives to A-levels 187
Teaching standards 191
Subject choices 192
The syllabus 199
Examinations and revision 202
Home tutoring and extra study 204
University entrance requirements 207
The next step? 208
Finally ... 208

University and other further education 211
Which institution and which subject? 211
University and FE college performance 246
Gap years 255
Application and entrance requirements 263
Selection procedure 273
Foundation courses 277
Costs and funding 280
Student life 298
Dropping out and other problems 305
Degree results 310
Studying abroad 313
Post-graduate study 315

The next step 321
The only route to a career? 321
Graduate job prospects 326
Expected salaries 335
Careers advice 338

Contents

Teaching as a career 347
TEFL (Teaching English as a foreign language) 355
Career changes 356
Work experience 360
Lifelong learning 361

Useful contacts 365
Index 369

Introduction

Education is a complex subject that bears directly on everyone's lives, initially as pupils and students and later as the parents and grandparents of those going through the system. What makes it particularly awkward is that the way the system is organised and operated is in a state of perpetual change, which is confusing for people whose interest naturally waxes and wanes according to their stage in life.

Parents who left school or university 10 or 15 years ago and now have young children embarking on their own educational journey cannot rely on what they remember of how things worked then – because they don't work like that any more. Confused, too, are those who experience education most directly: pupils trying to come to terms with the new A-levels; students struggling to pick their way through an increasingly diverse university system; and, of course, those who teach them, for whom constant change represents constant pressure.

All, I am happy to say, have bombarded me with questions ever since I started writing the *Any Questions?* column in *The Daily Telegraph* in January 1997. What follows is a selection from the one thousand questions and answers published in the column's first four years.

They cover the whole range of the educational experience, from pre-school to post-graduate. Many of the questions are the fundamental ones about how to choose the best school, select the right course, identify and get into the best university, where to spend a gap year and how to find a graduate job.

Introduction

The issues that come up most frequently include literacy and numeracy, standards, league tables and Ofsted, state versus independent schools, single-sex versus co-education, national tests, educating children at home, how to study effectively, bullying, dyslexia, providing for gifted children, computers in the classroom, teaching as a career, where best to learn a language, the quality of university courses, and how to raise money and track down scholarships.

My answers are based on what I have learnt in nearly 20 years of reporting on education for the BBC, *The Times*, and, latterly, *The Daily Telegraph*. In that time I have visitied hundreds of schools, colleges and universities, plagued thousands of teachers and scores of politicians with my questions, and read everything I could lay my hands on.

In the process, I have acquired some understanding and a few strongly held opinions, but the real virtue of this book is that whenever my understanding lets me down or my opinions don't stand up, readers have been quick to set me straight. Here, then, is the collective wisdom of two million *Daily Telegraph* readers distilled into as few words as I can contrive.

Fortunately, the questions still keep rolling in by letter, fax and, increasingly, e-mail. If you would like to add yours, may I draw your attention to the paragraph that appears at the end of every *Any Questions?* column:

"Write to John Clare, Education Editor, *The Daily Telegraph*, 1 Canada Square, London E14 5DT; fax 020 7538 6268; e-mail john.clare@telegraph.co.uk. Questions cannot, alas, be answered individually."

General

This chapter includes advice on home tutoring, learning difficulties, choice of school, educational policy and bullying.

Finding the right school

Frustration

" All my efforts – including making an official appeal – to get my 11-year-old into the only decent school in the area have failed. Am I alone in my frustration? "

> No. Nationally, 20 per cent of parents fail to secure a place at the school of their choice. It is worth remembering, though, that 10 years ago 90 per cent of parents had no choice at all.

Parental choice

" I keep reading about parental choice. How do I exercise it if the only decent school locally is full? "

> Are you sure it is the only "decent" school in the area? Parents have always needed to be wary of schools' word-of-mouth reputations, which may be out-dated, wrong-headed or based on criteria irrelevant to their

General

child's needs. Now, many are learning to question what the local league tables seem to show. A school half way down may be doing just as good a job for a wider range of abilities than one higher up serving a more favoured area. If the school you wanted is full, go and look around some of its competitors with an open mind. Parental choice is more real now than it has ever been, but it will never guarantee a chosen place.

Choir schools

" Leaving aside financial considerations, if you had a seven-year-old grand-daughter with a sweet singing voice and several singers in her family, how would you advise her parents best to nurture any musical talent? "

Cathedral choirs offer the best training. Of the 10 that admit girls, four have excellent choir schools: Salisbury, Exeter and Wells, which all admit boarders, and York, which does not. Further information from: the Choir Schools Association, The Minster School, Deangate, York YO1 2JA (01904 557230).

Withering on the vine

" Will bad state schools be forced to close by parents deciding to send their children elsewhere? "

Not yet. The Audit Commission says such schools tend neither to close nor recover but "wither on the vine". As they lose pupils, so they lose money, making it harder for them to address their failings. At Harborne Hill comprehensive in Birmingham, for example, numbers dropped from 500 to 350 after a critical Ofsted report. The budget deficit rose and the school was forced to cut staff. Now, Ofsted says it is incapable of teaching the national curriculum to the pupils that remain and has condemned it as a failing school.

An excellent preparation

" My husband and I have full-time jobs and are thinking of sending our 11-year-old daughter to boarding school. But her grandparents and many of our friends are quite disapproving. How can we persuade them we're not being heartless? "

The newly formed Boarding Education Alliance would say your critics owe their ideas more to Tom Brown and St Trinian's than to modern-day reality. Boarding, it insists, is no longer about isolating children from family life, and is an excellent preparation for adulthood. The alliance, which represents nearly 200 schools, runs an information line: 0020 7798 1553.

"Life isn't fair!"

" From September, Greycotes, my daughter's prep school in Oxford, will become the junior department of Oxford High, having been acquired by the Girls' Day School Trust. Because our fees are higher than the trust's, we will then be paying

General

£900 a year more than those whose daughters join for the first time. Can it be fair that parents should be charged different amounts when their children are sitting next to each other, being taught by the same teacher and using the same facilities?"

"Life", observed Michael Oakley, the trust's secretary, "isn't fair. We can't afford to reduce the Greycotes fees, though we've frozen them since 1996, which means a saving to parents of about 10 per cent." From 11 your daughter will enjoy a splendid education at Oxford High – at very modest fees.

State boarding schools

" I've heard that some state schools offer boarding for their students. Where can I find out more?"

The Department for Education and Employment has just published a *Parents' Guide to Maintained Boarding Schools*, which describes the 36 such schools in England and Wales. Tuition is free; boarding fees range from £4,000 to £6,000 a year. Copies can be obtained free from: DfEE Publications Centre, Sherwood Park, Annesley, Nottinghamshire (0845 6022260).

No current guide

" Could you recommend any guides to the best primary and secondary schools?"

Finding the right school

Since the last edition of the *Daily Telegraph Schools Guide* was published a couple of years ago, I am afraid there is no current, reliable and objective guide to the state sector. There is a solution, but it is available only on the Internet. Go to the "School Search" box on the Department for Education and Employment's excellent website, www.parents.dfee.gove.uk/ Having typed in the first part of your postcode, you will find a list of all the schools in your area and be able to compare their exam results and read their Ofsted reports. The site also covers Wales and Scotland.

Appealing

" We are appealing against a school's refusal to offer our daughter a place. What are our chances of succeeding? "

Last year, 29 per cent of primary and 24 per cent of secondary school appeals were decided in parents' favour.

Do they all do a decent job?

" As my husband is in the Army and based abroad, we're entitled to receive help with our son's school fees. The Ministry of Defence has sent a list of boarding schools, some of which are relatively inexpensive. Can we assume they all do a decent job? "

No – and I wish the Ministry would stop publishing the list. For example, one school named is Falcon

General

Manor, near Towcester, Northants. Sixty-one of its 97 pupils have their fees paid either by the MoD or the Foreign & Commonwealth Office, at a cost to the taxpayer of nearly £500,000 a year. Last week, Ofsted reported that it had been concerned for some time about the welfare of the pupils, who are aged six to 18, and there were "considerable weaknesses" in the quality of teaching and management. The school, which is privately owned, has had five heads in two-and-a-half years.

The case also demonstrates that the quality of a school cannot be judged by its architecture – Falcon Manor is based on a 17th-century mansion "set in attractive and extensive grounds" – or, I regret to say, by its membership of the Independent Schools Association. Many good state schools offer boarding for around half the fees payable at Falcon Manor. For details, phone the State Boarding Information Service on 020 7798 1580.

State boarding schools

" Is it true there are state boarding schools and that they charge much less than the independent ones? "

There are 36. As state schools (grammar and comprehensive), they do not charge for teaching. Boarding fees are between £5,000 and £6,000 a year, compared with an average of £12,500 in the independent sector. A booklet – *Parents' Guide to Maintained Boarding Schools* – is available free from the DfEE Publications Centre,

Sherwood Park, Annesley, Nottinghamshire NG15 0DJ. The State Boarding Information Service has an informative website at: www.stabis.org.uk/.

How much will private education cost?

" My wife and I have settled in north London, where we hope to raise a family. The local wisdom is that the state schools are poor and that we'll have to pay for private education. Is this true and, if so, how much will it cost? "

Although not entirely true, it is the case that there are not enough good schools (nationally) and finding a place at one is difficult. Start by consulting the primary school league tables, theoretically available from the local council but more easily located on the Department for Education and Employment's website: www.dfee.gov.uk/perform.htm/. This will enable you to identify the schools in your area with the best results in English, maths and science (or, in the case of secondary schools, GCSE and A-level). Then go to the excellent website for parents – www.parents.dfee.gov.uk/ – and call up the Ofsted reports on those that interest you. Having drawn up a shortlist and contacted the schools, you will probably find that most are heavily oversubscribed. You will need to be either very persistent, or prepared to accept second best. The alternative costs about £6,000 a year.

General

The role of the crow in admissions policy

" How did crows come to play such a big part in school admissions? Our son has been refused a place at his chosen school because we live too far away 'as the crow flies'. Yet the bus journey is shorter from our house to the school than it is for children who've been offered a place because they live closer 'as the crow flies'. "

> I am afraid it is easier for local education authorities to draw concentric circles on a map than calculate (unreliable) travelling times. Some, though, do go to the trouble of measuring the shortest safe walking or cycling route, which seems the fairest solution.

Aren't we supposed to know?

" I have discovered by accident that the comprehensive to which we were intending to send our son has been condemned by Ofsted as 'failing to provide a satisfactory standard of education'. Apparently, the report was published two months ago but I have seen nothing in the local paper. Aren't prospective parents supposed to know? "

> Schools are required by law to send current parents the official summary of their Ofsted report. However, they are only "advised" to make copies available to the media, libraries and local employers, so they may not do so when the report is unflattering. All reports are published on Ofsted's new, user-friendly website – www.ofsted.gov.uk/ – but there is nothing to draw par-

ents' or the media's attention to schools judged to be failing. I have suggested to Ofsted that it should post a monthly list of such schools, balanced by those deemed to be outstanding. Watch this space.

The best starting point

" Although our daughter is only five months old, family and friends are already beginning to panic us with questions about our plans for her education. We're keen to explore the state sector but don't know where to start. Aside from the league tables, which offer valuable but rather bald information, what would you recommend? "

The league tables – especially as presented online at www.dfee.gov.uk/perform.shtml/ – will remain the best starting point until we have a credible measure of the value that schools add. The league tables list all the primaries in each local education authority, give their latest results in English, maths and science, and enable you, by clicking on the name of the school, to compare its results over four years with those of others in the area and nationally. Having identified half a dozen possibles, you can read Ofsted's reports on them at: www.ofsted.gov.uk/reports/index.htm/. If you do not have a computer, take these web addresses to your local library or Internet café.

Chances of success

" We're thinking of appealing against our preferred school's

refusal to offer a place to our daughter. What are our chances of success? "

> Last year, 29 per cent of primary school appeals succeeded, as did 24 per cent of secondary school appeals. However, the proportion dropped to 16 per cent in the case of those secondary schools with foundation status (formerly known as grant maintained).

Education policy

Increased spend

" *Is it true, as the Government claims, that spending per pupil has increased in real terms by more than 50 per cent since 1979?* "

> Spending increased by 52 per cent between 1979 and 1992, largely because pupil numbers were falling. Since then, spending per pupil has dropped by seven per cent, largely because numbers are rising.

Raising morale

" *Every year, the Farmington Institute for Christian Studies, which I run, enables 50 primary and secondary teachers of religious education to spend a term studying and doing research at a university or college. The scheme, partly funded by the Millennium Commission, has proved highly effective in stimulating, refreshing and encouraging religious education teachers. If the Government really is serious in wanting to raise the morale of teachers, and the standards of teaching gener-*

ally, why doesn't it consider funding similar teacher fellowships for all subjects?"

An excellent, if expensive, idea. Since someone has to cover for the absent teacher, each fellowship costs the institute £10,000.

Who should decide?

" Why is the Government so determined to restrict the right of schools to decide which pupils to admit?"

Is it a "right"? Schools are publicly funded and should act for the greatest good. On the other hand, research, most recently carried out by Edinburgh University, shows that allowing parents to choose schools – which is the other side of the equation – leads to a substantial increase in segregation between the social classes. This, naturally, further harms the prospects of those who are already disadvantaged.

An alternative to higher taxes

" Bedfordshire County Council is planning to introduce a charge of £75 per term for post-16 pupils who have previously qualified for free transport, because they live more than three miles from the nearest school or college. Isn't this another sad example of councils pursuing policies inimical to country living?"

Paul Brett, Bedfordshire's director of education,

says the council has to cut spending. Post-16 transport, which it is not legally obliged to provide, costs nearly £1 million a year. Rather than being an attack on country living, the charge is an alternative to higher taxes.

Teacher's Day

" I think that, as well as a Mother's Day and a Father's Day, we should have a Teacher's Day. I sent my idea to David Blunkett at the Department for Education. He said it was excellent and wrote: 'Teachers are often under a great deal of pressure and your idea would provide a good way that we could all recognise their hard work and dedication.' He also said I'd have to get some publicity, so please would you put it in your column? "

With pleasure. The letter is from Vyvyan Evans, 10, a pupil at Arundel C of E primary school, Arundel, West Sussex. To get off the ground, a National Teachers' Day would need to attract a good deal of support. Postcards, please, to Vyvyan or to me, and we shall see how far we can take it.

" You published a letter last month from a 10-year-old asking if anyone supported the idea of an annual Teacher's Day. Was there much response? "

Between us, Vyvyan Evans and I received about 50 letters and postcards – not enough, I am afraid, to launch a national campaign.

Education policy

It's "policy" to use school buildings

" The Warwickshire infant school of which I am a governor will close on May 6 and June 10, so that it can be used as a polling station; this will deprive the children of two days' schooling. There is a public hall nearby that would serve the purpose equally well but the district returning officer says it's his 'policy' to use schools. What can I do about it? "

> The Representation of the People Act requires a polling station to be somewhere familiar to the community and within walking distance. So your local hall clearly fits the bill, and you should take up the matter with Ian Caulfield, chief executive of the county council. A more direct solution would be to designate the polling days as two of your staff's five statutory in-service training days. Then the pupils would not lose out. However, the Local Government Association tells me that is never done. I wonder why not?

The use of schools as polling stations

" The use of schools as polling stations is an even more serious issue than you suggested. The local government elections on May 6 2000 will coincide with the national maths test for 14-year-olds, and the European elections on June 10 fall in the busiest week of GCSE and A-level exams. So secondary schools can't close on polling day – which underlines the point you made about the reluctance of district returning officers to seek alternative venues. At Slough Grammar, where I am head, we have to find space for two polling stations on both days,

General

even though there's a perfectly acceptable public building in the park nearby. Why?"

The only reason Ian Bell, Slough's returning officer, could give for not using the park building was that it might not always be available, and continuity was important. John Dunford, general secretary of the Secondary Heads Association, said many of his members would find polling day very awkward, partly for lack of space – they will need their halls for exams – but also because of worries about security with, as he put it, "people wandering in off the streets to vote". The long-term answer is probably Sunday voting. In the short term, returning officers must be more willing to look elsewhere.

Government propaganda

" I enclose a copy of an article from the current issue of Education Journal, *a monthly magazine. It is by David Normington, who is described as 'director general, schools, Department for Education and Employment'. Does that mean he is a civil servant? If so, should he be writing government propaganda? "*

Mr Normington is a senior civil servant. At the end of a lyrical account of the Government's education policies (including the abolition of grammar schools and the assisted places scheme), he concludes: "It is not an option to proceed on some points but not on others, for it is the carrying through of the whole programme of reform which will deliver the ultimate prize of higher education standards for all." Implementing the Government's policies is certainly his job; proselytising for them is not. I hope Michael Bichard, the Permanent Secretary, takes note.

Why so hostile?

" Why are headteachers so hostile towards the Government's plans for introducing performance-related pay into the classroom? You would think that, as managers, they'd welcome it. You'd think most teachers would, too. "

The main problem is that few heads yet think of themselves as managers. Historically, they have relied on local education authorities to take the tough decisions, leaving them to make common cause with their staff.

As for teachers, we don't know their views – only those of union activists. And they know that if pay became a matter between individuals and their managers, the union's role would be greatly diminished.

Futile

" How is it that I, as deputy head of a large Midlands comprehensive that never opted out of council control, can still see no sign of the Government's promised extra billions for education? "

It is not surprising. Despite all the huffing and puffing, Labour spent less on education, after allowing for inflation, during its first year in office than the Conservatives did the year before, and less in its second year than in the first. Last year [1998–99], spending on each secondary school pupil fell to £2,380, the lowest level for 10 years. Furthermore, millions of pounds that ought to go to schools are still being wasted on local education authorities and futile government initiatives such as Education Action Zones.

Fobbed off with platitudes

" As a teacher and parent, I felt incensed and patronised by the Department for Education and Employment advertisement in your newspaper recently. Under a photograph of a woman standing on a man's shoulders and peering through a window, the caption read: 'There is an easier way to find out how your children are doing at school.' The advertisement went on to extol the virtues of testing children at seven, 11 and 14, the implication being that were it not for the tests, teachers would keep parents in the dark. I think it's typical of the way the Government belittles the status and professionalism of teachers. What are your view? "

I think the Government is doing what it can to improve the status and professionalism of teachers. Perhaps only parents who are not teachers can understand the frustration of being fobbed off with platitudes, as they generally were before the tests were introduced.

Sterile

" As president of the Cambridge Union Society, I'd like to invite you to speak in our forthcoming debate: 'This House believes a back-to-basics education creates basic minds.' Knowing of your position outside the educational establishment, I'm sure you are qualified to speak with a fresh perspective on this question. "

> I am sorry to hear that the Cambridge Union is planning to waste time on such a sterile debate. No one argues that mastery of the basics is a sufficient preparation for life, and no one, as far as I know, denies that it is a necessary preparation. I am afraid that I shall be washing my hair that night.

Single-sex schools

" Whatever happened to single-sex schools? "

> Thirty years ago there were more than 2,000. Then most were merged in the rush to comprehensive education. Now there are 227 girls' schools and 197 boys'. About a third are grammar schools.

Good little Europeans

" How much pressure are schools under to turn their pupils into good little Europeans? "

> Jack Lang, the French education minister, has just been

outlining the programme for the current six months of the French presidency of the European Union: "It is our responsibility to secure the psychological and intellectual foundations of political Europe. It is up to each member state to create within its frontiers a new state of mind which will make our citizens, from their most tender age, European citizens." So if schools (and nurseries?) are not under pressure yet, it looks as if they soon will be.

Grants, fundraising and scholarships

A good use of funds?

" Hereford and Worcester, where I am the governor of a hard-pressed comprehensive, is having to cut £3 million from its education budget. At the same time, the Government is paying out £3.7 million through the Assisted Places Scheme to support 900 children at local independent schools. Yet there are 100,000 children in state schools here being educated at half the cost of an independent school place. As a local head remarked recently: 'Never was so much taken from so many on behalf of so few.' What do you think?"

I think state education is badly underfunded and that we are all worse off the wider the gap grows between what the state thinks should be spent on each child and what the independent sector thinks is necessary. However, I also think clever children from less affluent homes should have the opportunity to go to independent schools, and the £120 million a year spent on the scheme would make little difference to the funding of state education.

Charitable aid

" I'm told a lot of charities – not all of them well known – make grants for children's education. Where can I find out about them? "

Details of 1,200 trusts that together give away £40 million a year are contained in the current edition of the *Educational Grants Directory*. Some are restricted to people living in a particular parish, others to the children of parents in specific occupations. The grants are generally not large but are available for such items as books, equipment, clothing and travel. The directory (£19.95 plus £2.50 p&p) is published by the Directory of Social Change, 24 Stephenson Way, London NW1 2DP; (020 7209 5151; www.dsc.org.uk/).

Show them the heavens

" Could I enlist your help in our effort to raise funds for an observatory we're planning to build in the grounds of Bedford School? Showing young children the heavens through a powerful telescope is one of the best ways I know of enthusing them with the joy and excitement of science. The observatory, which will be open to all local schools as well as the community at large, will cost £120,000, a third of which has been pledged by the Harpur Trust. "

A worthy cause. Dr Philip Evans, headmaster of Bedford and the author of the letter, is a scientist and government adviser on education. He himself became interested in astronomy as a young boy.

"My strongest desire ..."

" *We write to you, as two veterinary surgeons, on behalf of Endalk Abebe, a young Ethiopian park warden, who is desperate to help halt the deforestation of the Simien Mountains National Park, where he works. This is one of the world's unique landscapes and habitats, home to the Walia ibex, the Simien red fox and the Gelada baboon. Endalk, an intelligent young man and devout Christian, already has a diploma in forestry from Addis Ababa University but needs to further his education with a degree from Bangor, which has an international reputation in natural resource management. Would your readers help us raise the £35,000 the course will cost over three years?*

Endalk Abebe says: 'My strongest desire is to improve my knowledge about the protection, utilisation and conservation of natural resources so as to help my people use their land appropriately and sustainably.' "

I shall be happy to put readers in touch with the two vets.

" *I am one of the two vets who wrote to you in January on behalf of Endalk Abebe, a young Ethiopian park warden desperate to help halt the deforestation of the Simien Mountains National Park, the place where he works. We told you that he already had a diploma in forestry from Addis Ababa University but needed to further his education with a degree from Bangor, which has an international reputation in the field. We asked if your readers would help us make this possible. I would like to thank you and them for the £5,500 raised through your column. Endalk has begun studying for an MSc in tropical environmental forestry. He has settled down well and is extremely grateful."*

Warmest thanks to all who responded.

Free to EU pupils

" Can pupils from other EU countries study free at British state schools?"

Yes. It is a particularly popular option for German pupils, who are allowed to take a year out. Those interested in state boarding (fees are about £4,750 a year) can obtain a list of schools from the Boarding Schools Association (020 7798 1580; www.boarding-association.org.uk/).

A guide to fundraising

" I've just been put in charge of fundraising at our comprehensive. I have some ideas but don't really know where to begin. Has anyone written a guide to the subject?"

A Handbook of School Fundraising by Harris Rosenberg, published by Kogan Page, should tell you everything you need to know. Unfortunately, it costs £19.99

(01903 828800 to order). I shall be glad to donate my review copy to whoever makes out the best case for receiving it.

" *Exford is a school in the middle of Exmoor national park, with two teachers and 56 pupils, aged four to nine. One classroom is in the original Victorian building and the other in a dilapidated 'mobile' hut. This structure is so damp that it is too dangerous to use electric equipment such as computers. Ofsted said our accommodation was preventing us from delivering the national curriculum. Somerset County Council has turned down our bid for £130,000 to build two new classrooms, so we've decided to raise the money independently. So far, we've been promised £27,000. We think the book you were offering could help us raise the rest.* "

This was the winning entry in my competition for a copy of *A Handbook of School Fundraising* by Harris Rosenberg (Kogan Page, £19.99; 01903 828800 to order). Many wrote in frustration about their unsuccessful attempts to raise money by running jumble sales, bingo nights, Sixties discos, fashion shows and summer fairs. "The ticket sales were always slow/The profit made ever low", explained one entry, entirely in verse. Among so many worthy causes – not least a school for children with severe learning difficulties anxious to raise £6,000 to retain its music therapist – I was particularly impressed by the business-like way Exford's PTA had identified its needs and set about meeting them. As a consolation prize, Mr Rosenberg offered entrants a half-hour's free telephone consultancy on their fundraising queries. I shall put the others in touch with him. *(And see p. 29)*

Ex-service funding

" The Royal British Legion Women's Section has launched an award scheme offering £25,000 a year in scholarships and grants to help ex-serving families with young children and ex-servicewomen wanting to retrain for a new career. Please could you draw it to your readers' attention? "

> The legion is offering 15 £1,000 scholarships for children aged nine upwards and 20 £500 grants for adults. Qualifying applicants include ex-servicewomen, wives and widows of ex-servicemen and dependants of ex-servicemen or women. Details: Royal British Legion, 48 Pall Mall, London SW1Y 5JY (020 7973 7200).

£1m-a-year award

" The government says that it would like to award one of its next £1 million-a-year Education Action Zones to a group of parents. Is that realistic? "

> I am not sure, but it is an attractive idea. Having identified an area that meets the official criteria (details from Angela Overington at the DfEE, phone 020 7925 6338), prospective bidders would need to secure the support of local school governors. They would also have to identify business partners prepared to contribute £250,000 in cash or in kind, so it is no small

General

undertaking. However, I shall be happy to act as a clearing house and put interested parties in touch with one another.

What a marvellous idea

" We run a scheme that provides clockwork radios for rural primary schools in South Africa to help teach black children English. The half-hour programmes, which are backed up by teachers' notes, have been devised by us – the Open Learning Systems Education Trust (OLSET) – and are broadcast daily by the South African Broadcasting Corporation and community stations.

Typically, the audience is a class of 50 or more children sitting on the ground under a tree, with the wind-up radio hanging from a branch. Known as the Freeplay, the radio is built by disabled workers in a Cape Town factory opened recently by President Mandela.

So far, we've distributed more than 2,000 to schools in remote areas where there are few batteries (and little money to buy them). However, more radios are urgently needed and we wondered whether your readers might like to help. Each Freeplay will make a big difference to many children. "

I think this is a marvellous idea. The teaching programmes, 'English in Action', are well written and enlivened by stories, songs and games. The radio is a rugged machine with a generator powered by a carbon steel spring. It takes 25 seconds to wind and will deliver distortion-free sound at a high volume for an hour.

The Freeplay costs £27 and I am taking the liberty

of setting readers – including, I hope, primary schools – the target of buying 100. For each radio, *The Daily Telegraph* will contribute £5 and OLSET £1 – so I am asking for £21 a radio. Primary schools that pay for a Freeplay will be put in touch with the school that receives it. Smaller donations will, of course, be gratefully received and pooled.

> *" I thought your appeal last week for clockwork radios to enable primary school children in remote parts of South Africa to receive English language lessons was a brilliant idea. Here's my cheque for £21. Please keep your readers posted. "*

Thank you. The response has been overwhelming. My tentative target of 100 Freeplay radios was exceeded the day after the appeal was published. We already have enough for 465 machines and the cheques are still coming in. Some schools keen to contribute – and to be put in touch with the recipients of "their" radio – have asked for more time. The Open Learning Systems Education Trust, which devised the 'English in Action' lessons, says it can distribute as many radios as we can provide.

I will report in more detail on the outcome of the appeal in two weeks' time. Meanwhile, warmest thanks to everyone who responded.

Some weeks later ...
Over the past three weeks, marvellously generous readers of this column have donated more than £23,000 to my clockwork radio appeal. The Freeplay radios, man-

ufactured by disabled workers in Cape Town, are to enable schoolchildren in remote areas of South Africa to receive daily English lessons from the Open Learning Systems Education Trust.

"This was the first appeal ever", wrote G L Eddis, "that had me reaching for my chequebook as soon as I read it." "My wife and I are suffering from charity fatigue," wrote Dr Nigel Clark, "but this enterprise struck us as particularly worthy because donations were likely to be used practically and efficiently." "One of the best charitable schemes I have felt compelled to contribute to in a long while," wrote Audrey Bowes, adding that she worked at a primary school that was constantly struggling for funds, "but at least our children have the essentials for a good education". Dr Elizabeth Begley agreed: her own children attended a school that had everything and it made her sad to think of those who were eager to learn, but lacked the most basic equipment.

Some readers wrote cheques for £210 to buy 10 radios. Others sent £5, explaining that a pension stretched only so far. One even sent a £1 coin taped to a card.

Benjamin Lloyd, seven, and his five-year-old brother, Sebastian, sent a week's pocket money; trainee history teachers at Bristol chipped in some of their "weekly beer money"; and the staff of Cansfield Community High, Wigan, collected £74.30. Among many similar events, a cake sale at St Edward's Middle School, Berkshire, raised £85.53; a harvest festival collection at North Marston first school, Buckinghamshire, produced £69; and Form 10W at Denmark Road Girls' High, Gloucester, collected £68.

"Your article tied in beautifully with the assembly theme of 'Neighbours' that I used this week," wrote Keith Blackwell, head of Churchill primary, Kent. "We held a sale of elephant and giraffe biscuits which raised enough for three radios. The children are looking forward to hearing where they go."

Some readers said they would like to continue helping "their" school. As soon as I can arrange it, all will be sent the necessary information. Some who contributed said they had visited or lived in South Africa and the subject was close to their heart. Others had even more personal reasons. Janet Eatough wrote on the day that her grandson, Joseph John Eatough, would have been five. He died of cancer when he was two. She said: "I was wondering what to get him for his birthday. Something more lasting than flowers. Please buy a radio in his memory."

The Daily Telegraph, having initially promised £500, has kindly donated £3,500. To all, my very warmest thanks. Normal service will be resumed next week.

" Please tell us the result of your appeal to buy wind-up radios so that pupils in rural South Africa can listen to broadcast English lessons. "

Thanks to the readers' generosity, we have sent nearly £32,000 to the Open Learning Systems Education Trust in Johannesburg, enough for more than 1,100 radios. About 100 primaries have been put in touch

General

with the grateful receiving schools.

Charities

" Where can one find out about charities that give money for educational purposes? "

The Educational Grants Directory 1998/99 describes 1,200 charities that give away £40 million a year. Some are small and have a specific purpose. The Betty Martin Charity, for example, makes grants towards the costs of clothes, tools, instruments and books to people in need who live within 15 miles of the parish church in Midhurst, West Sussex. Others, such as the Professional Classes Aid Council, are national. It distributes up to £100,000 a year to the "dependants of people of professional background who are in financial distress". The directory is in libraries or can be bought for £19.95 plus £2.50 p&p from: Directory of Social Change, 24 Stephenson Way, London NW1 2DP; phone 020 7209 5151.

Many thanks

" Two years ago you kindly presented our school with a copy of A Handbook of School Fundraising *by Harris Rosenberg after we'd told you about our struggle to replace the damp, dilapidated hut in which half our 56 pupils are taught. After much hard work, and thanks in part to the book, we've raised £95,000 and have persuaded the Government to match it with an equivalent sum. Work on the new classroom will begin*

in the summer. Many thanks for your support. "

The letter is from Dr Brian Martin, a governor of Exford First School in the Exmoor national park. The handbook, published by Kogan Page, costs £19.99 and is also available from www.amazon.co.uk/. A sign of the times is the appearance of *Practical Fundraising for Schools*, a monthly newsletter full of information about how to make ends meet. If subsequent issues are as good as the first, the annual subscription of £49.50 could be a useful investment. Details from Step Forward Publishing, 01926 420046.

Education standards

No mystery

" I'm a governor of a primary school where about 40 per cent of the children fail to reach the expected level in reading at the age of seven. Apart from voicing my dismay, is there anything practical I can do about it? "

You could start by asking the head and your fellow governors to join you in watching "Literacy Matters", the video published by Ofsted. It shows five excellent teachers in three primary schools, using a range of highly effective techniques to teach young children to read. The video should convince parents and teachers alike that there is no mystery about literacy – and no excuse for children not mastering it. Literacy Matters (£11.75 incl p&p), Euroview

Management Services, PO Box 35, Wetherby LS23 7EX (01937 541010).

Hopeless

" One of our son's teachers is absolutely hopeless. Now that the school is about to be inspected by Ofsted, how likely is it that she will be found out? "

Inspectors sit in on each lesson for about 30 minutes and may observe a teacher for up to half a teaching day. Ofsted says: "A key component of the evaluation of teaching is the contribution it makes to what pupils achieve. Teaching cannot be satisfactory unless pupils are learning and making at least satisfactory progress, are well-behaved and have a reasonable attitude to learning." Lessons are graded on a seven-point scale: excellent or very good (grades one and two); good or satisfactory (three and four); less than satisfactory (five, six and seven). Inspectors are required to tell teachers their grades, explain the reasons for them and pass the information on to the head. However, an unsatisfactory mark cannot on its own be used to justify disciplinary action.

Saving her from embarrassment

" As we know from our grand-daughter's delightfully worded letters, her spelling is appalling and punctuation random. Now that she has started university, what can we do to save her from embarrassment? "

Odd though it may sound, send her a copy of *Good English for Canadian Students*. It is a pointed but charmingly written guide to the errors most commonly committed by students at Edinburgh University's centre of Canadian studies. The booklet costs £3 (including postage) from 21 George Square, Edinburgh EH8 9LD. Cheques should be made payable to the University of Edinburgh.

" Recently, you were kind enough to recommend our booklet, Good English for Canadian Students, *as a 'pointed but charmingly written guide to the errors most commonly committed by students at Edinburgh University's centre of Canadian studies'. I thought you would like to know that your readers have bought more than 450 copies and sent us many suggestions for inclusion in the next edition. Thank you. "*

Chutzpah

" One of your correspondents asked recently what to do about the appalling spelling and grammar in his grand-daughter's thank-you letters. Our practice is to return the letter politely with corrections, which seems to be much appreciated. "

I am not sure which to admire more: your chutzpah or your grandchildren's tolerance.

Exam results/free meals

" Is there really a connection between schools' exam results and the proportion of pupils entitled to free meals? "

It is so strong that the Department for Education and Employment divides primary schools into five entitlement bands – ranging from 8 per cent or less qualifying for free meals to 51 per cent or more – and publishes the median scores in English, maths and science of children aged seven and 11 in each band. At 11, for example, the proportion of pupils who reach the expected level in English declines across the bands from 84 per cent to 50 per cent. In secondary schools, the department uses seven free-meal bands. In maths, the median proportion of 14-year-olds who reach the expected level of attainment declines remorselessly from 80 per cent in schools where 5 per cent or less qualify for free meals, to 32 per cent in schools where the majority are entitled to free meals. Very few schools – all with outstanding heads – succeed in breaking the link.

Being involved: governors, bursars, etc.

Inquisition

" As a long-standing governor of a primary school in Essex, I've had a letter saying I must declare any membership of secret societies 'including the Freemasons'. I have no intention of doing so. In my 45 years of public service, my integrity has never been questioned. Besides, the demand seems to me to be tantamount to an inquisition. What's your view? "

The letter, from Quilters school in Billericay, says its policy "follows that of the county council". In reality, it goes further. Labour-controlled Essex decided in November to require members of staff to disclose membership of secret societies but made the declaration voluntary for councillors. Clearly, the same concession should be extended to school governors, who give their time voluntarily. I would be interested to hear from others who feel similarly persecuted.

How to become a bursar

" Your page often carries advertisements for school bursars. Please could you tell a 50-year-old Oxford graduate with 30 years' business experience the qualifications required for such positions? "

A recent survey of 360 bursars found that 94 per cent had come from "another walk of life", 45 per cent had been in the Armed Forces, 30 per cent were graduates and 14 per cent were accountants. Their average salary was £39,000. The National Bursars' Association – tel 01460 65628 – runs a national registration scheme.

How to become a school governor

" I work full time but I would like to be involved in the community, perhaps as a school governor. How should I go about it? "

The Technology Colleges Trust is looking for people who work in industry, the professions or the Civil Service who have commercial and administrative experience and

General

are interested in being co-opted on to the boards of secondary schools. Write to Mrs Christine Prentice, TC Trust, 37 Queen's Gate, London SW7 5HR.

A guide to Edspeak

" Having just become a school governor, I'm quite baffled by all the jargon and, especially, the acronyms. Where can I find help?"

I recommend *What does it Mean? A guide to Edspeak* by Barbara Bullivant and Elizabeth Wallis. A brisk 35 pages, it will enable you to tell an AWPU (age-weighted pupils unit) from a SENCO (special educational needs co-ordinator).

Teachers' viewpoints

Bring back textbooks

" You were wrong to suggest that teachers aren't bothered by the shortage of textbooks because they see them as a threat to their professionalism. Textbooks were banished from classrooms by 'progressive' educationists who favour 'text-based learning', which forces us to devise our own courses and waste time producing endless worksheets. We do need some freedom in what we teach and how we teach it, but we'd like our textbooks back."

I think every pupil should have a core textbook for every subject. Schools should set up a textbook fund and ask parents to contribute. Chris Woodhead, the

Chief Inspector, is on our side – as he was when phonics and whole-class teaching were scorned. This Government has shown itself amenable to raising standards. Let us make textbooks the next frontier.

Repeat after me ...

" Why does your newspaper persist in attacking teachers and state education? 'Repeat after me,' read a recent Daily Telegraph *headline, 'our state schools are a disgrace'. Repeat after me, Mr Clare: most of your readers send their children to state schools and, while they might wish for better resourcing, are reasonably content with them. "*

I deplore generalised attacks on teachers and state education. I also think it important to keep up the pressure to raise standards, which are generally too low.

Now is not the time to give up

" Your report about a new government scheme for teaching reading filled me with despair. In nearly 30 years as a primary school teacher, I've been 'guided' by subject advisers, classroom inspectors, teacher trainers and educational theorists. As the bandwagons have rolled by – the Initial Teaching Alphabet, Real Books, Look and Say – I've tried to take the best from the new, combine it with the best from the old and, drawing on common sense and experience, find out what works and what doesn't. Most recently, my colleagues and I – vilified as we are for our perceived 'incompetence' – have thrown ourselves wholeheartedly into introducing the national

General

literacy strategy. Now you tell us it's to be replaced by a 'rigorous phonics programme': another new initiative, yet more millions wasted. Why? I just can't wait to retire – and the same goes for many of my younger colleagues."

> I strongly sympathise. You have been through 30 years of almost continuous revolution and the results have not been particularly encouraging. But now is not the time to give up. The national literacy strategy was a big step forward. It established a clear strategy for teaching reading. A rigorous phonics programme was the missing component. Now the Department for Education and Employment's standards and effectiveness unit has supplied it. Read the four modules entitled Additional Literacy Support – they should be in every primary school by now (if not, order them by calling 0870 001 2345) – and you will surely be convinced.

The inevitability of change

" I work in a very unhappy primary school where the management methods are ruthless and uncaring. We older, experienced teachers are victimised and made to feel inadequate while the younger, favoured ones are repeatedly praised. We've had to abandon set books and whole-class teaching in favour of group teaching and daily worksheets. The paperwork and hours of unproductive meetings leave us too exhausted to teach effectively, and standards are certainly not what they were. Some older teachers have suffered breakdowns and left but the rest of us are not old enough to take early retirement. What can we do?"

I publish this not because I have an answer but because many teachers feel the same. For the past 10 years, education has been in constant change, to which younger teachers find it easier to adjust. Change, though, is inevitable: better to embrace it than take it personally.

" *I wonder if your readers understand what it is really like being a teacher and why so many of us are fed up with our jobs? I am seriously considering giving up mine, and would like to try to explain why.*

I am 27 and since qualifying six years ago have been teaching in a successful comprehensive on the outskirts of London. I have a degree in geography from Manchester and a postgraduate certificate from the London Institute of Education. My career – about which I am passionate – is going well. The quality of my teaching has been praised by Ofsted and I am head of the humanities department, responsible for six staff. However, I stay on top of my job only by working six days a week from when I get up until I crawl into bed. The school day runs from 8.15am to 4pm. Before and after that, I plan the lessons I teach each week to 250 pupils aged 11 to 18 – holding their attention for 50 minutes every 50 minutes takes some doing – and mark their tests, essays and homework. Then there are after-school revision lessons, classes to be taken for absent colleagues, staff meetings, parents' evenings, residential trips and termly reports to write. My day off is Saturday. I have no social life (I am not married). Although teachers do have generous holidays, by the end of term I am physically and emotionally exhausted. For this I am paid £27,000 a year, which bears little relation to the effort and time I devote to the job. I have achieved middle-management status and ex-

cellence in my field yet I struggle to pay the rent on my flat. My contemporaries in other fields – accountancy, computing, journalism – reap far greater financial rewards and enjoy a much higher social status.

In short, committed as I am to teaching as a career, I cannot cope with teaching as a way of life. What would you suggest?"

> Teaching has never been well paid but the battering it has taken over the past 20 years has undoubtedly damaged its standing as a vocation. However – paradoxical though it may seem – thanks to Ofsted, the literacy and numeracy strategies and league tables, primary education is improving rapidly, secondary schools have never been better run and parents' confidence is beginning to be restored. Now is not the time to quit.

" I was infuriated by last week's letter from the 'fed up' teacher who is 27, earns £27,000, has a secure job and a quarter of the year off. Like many in her profession, she seems to know nothing about the world beyond school. My daughter, who is 28 and has a PhD, is doing research into ovarian cancer for a salary of £18,500 and four weeks' holiday a year. Her boyfriend, who is 32 and also has a PhD, has been researching breast cancer at Cambridge for six years and has yet to earn £20,000 for a 60-hour week. Your correspondent should stop moaning and get on with her job. "

> The letter (and my response, variously described as "glib, unhelpful, insulting") aroused strong emotions. Non-teachers tended to share the view that teachers

would feel less hard done by if they knew more about the "real world". Some, like the husband of a staff nurse who has 20 years' experience and earns £15,950, said the vocational aspect of the job was more important than the financial reward. However, all the teachers who wrote flatly rejected vocationalism, many adding that my correspondent should get out while she still could.

Home tutoring and support

Which CD-Rom?

" There are so many supposedly educational CD-Roms on the market: how can one judge their worth and choose between them?"

Most leading retailers offer reasonably well-informed advice and some will let you run the software on in-store computers. More helpful is PIN (Parents' Information Network), an independent organisation that publishes *Software Evaluations*, tried and tested by parents, children and teachers, and a regular newsletter containing reviews of CD-Roms. Write to PIN, PO Box 1577, London W7 3ZT (www.pin.org.uk/).

Bringing writers together

" My 12-year-old grandson says he wants to be a poet. How can I put him in touch with others of a similar bent?"

General

Through *Young Writer*, a lively (and unpatronising) magazine written for and by children aged about 10 to 16. Published termly (£7.50 a year; also available on audio cassette at £17.50 a year), it runs a pen pal scheme to put children in touch with one another. Young Writer, Glebe House, Weobley, Herefordshire HR4 8SD (01544 318901).

Where do I start?

" *My husband's job is taking us to Malawi for two years. Although I'm not a teacher, I shall be responsible for our eight-year-old's education. Where do I start?* "

Worldwide Education Services (WES: 01869 248682; www.weshome.demon.co.uk/)) offers a complete educational programme – including curriculum, timetables and backup – to expatriate parents who have no teaching qualifications or experience.

Advice on teaching at home

" *My six-year-old grandson suffers from Attention Deficit/Hyperactivity Disorder, which is partially contained by drugs. My daughter wants to teach him at home. Where can she get advice on how to go about it?* "

Two organisations run helplines for home educators: the Home Education Advisory Service (01707 371854; www.heds.org.uk/) and Education Otherwise (0800 7300074). They do not specialise in the needs of children with disorders but may be able to put your daughter in touch with other parents in a similar position.

Arranging an educational holiday

" Our two grand-daughters, aged six and eight, live in somewhat deprived circumstances: their father is unemployed and their mother a semi-invalid. We'd like to arrange some sort of educational or adventure holiday for them in the summer. Could you advise? "

I recommend Active Training and Education (ATE), an organisation that offers children busy and well-supervised residential holidays in castles and country houses. A week costs about £185; call 01684 562400. Eight is the minimum age. Your local authority should help you find a summer playschool for the six-year-old.

Brush up your grammar

" Having retired, and with time on my hands, I have agreed to help the 10-year-old grandson of a friend with his English grammar. His teacher is apparently illiterate. Although I remember how well I was taught, I would be happier with a textbook to refresh my memory. Could you suggest one? "

A book that has just reached me is *Brush Up Your Grammar* by Michael Cullup, which covers the ground in a clear, straightforward way. It costs £4.99 from bookshops (cheap enough to buy the boy's teacher a copy) or £5.94 (incl. p&p) from the publishers, Elliot

General

Right Way Books, Kingswood Buildings, Brighton Road, Lower Kingswood, Tadworth, Surrey KT20 6TD; tel 01737 832202.

"A no nonsense textbook"

" I enjoyed Latin and would like my children to have the opportunity of learning it. However their primary school doesn't offer the subject and nor does the local comprehensive. I am happy to teach them myself but the modern textbooks I have looked at – such as the Oxford Latin Course *– seem more concerned to make the language 'relevant' than set out a convincing way of learning it. Any suggestions?"*

So you really want to learn Latin, by Nick Oulton MA (Oxon), is the answer. "This is a no nonsense text book", the preface declares. "Learning Latin is not the easiest thing to do – it involves a good memory and loads of discipline." Reassuringly, the book begins with amo, amas, amat followed by mensa, mensa, mensam. In three volumes, each equivalent to a year's work, the course progresses in lucid and manageable stages up to GCSE. Highly recommended (not just by me but by the head of classics at Winchester).

No shortage of material

" My two sons aged 13 and 16 are both unable to attend school because of post-viral problems. They feel unwell much of the time. Could they study via the Internet?"

There is no shortage of material on the Internet but textbooks and CD-Roms are much less confusing. Bear in mind that study – especially self-study – by any medium requires application of a kind that will make real demands on your sons. Three websites on which to find resources and advice on home education are: www.educate.co.uk/; www.education-otherwise.org/; and www.heas.org.uk/.

It's possible he will be better off

" My six-year-old grandson is very bright and also hyperactive. He is an only child and has no playmates. Somehow, my son has gained permission to teach him at home, though neither he nor his wife has a teaching qualification. I believe my grandson should be at school with others of his age, where the staff could cater for his needs. Unfortunately, I cannot discuss this with my son or daughter-in-law. What do you think? "

It is quite possible that the boy you describe will be better off taught at home, as the law allows. If his parents are not already in touch with a network of home educators (who often bring their children together), you could point them to Education Otherwise: emergency helpline, 0870 7300074; www.education-otherwise.org/. You could also offer to be responsible for part of your grandson's curriculum.

Learning and behavioural difficulties

The wrong programme

" *Four years ago, an educational consultant advised us to send our son, who is quite severely dyslexic, to an expensive independent school that claims to specialise in dyslexia. We've never been very happy with the provision they've made – there seems to be more emphasis on extra-curricular activities than helping our son keep up – but now that he's doing A-levels (he scraped through GCSE) things are much worse. They're making him do Italian when he has a struggle to write English. What can we do?* "

> The "farming" of dyslexics by schools that have little or no expertise in the subject is a scandal. As it is probably too late now to move your son, you should ask the British Dyslexia Association (0118 966 8271; www.bda-dyslexia.org.uk/) to assess him and draw up a programme for the remaining 18 months of his A-levels. Then, as is your right in the circumstances, insist the school sticks to it.

Dyslexic? Or not?

" *Our 10-year-old son is dyslexic, but we're having a dreadful battle getting his school to recognise it. I gather we're not alone. What should we do?* "

> It is a depressingly common problem. Some teachers still regard dyslexia as a myth – an attempt by parents to secure an unfair share of resources for children who

are not as academically able as they would like to think. Other teachers resent any suggestion that (despite lacking specialist training) they cannot deal with the problem themselves. Local education authorities often oppose the formal identification of dyslexia because, once a statement of special needs has been agreed, they are legally bound to meet its requirements, whatever the cost. You will find a clear, authoritative account of what to do in *The Dyslexia Handbook* (£9.50 inc. p&p) published by the British Dyslexia Association, 98 London Road, Reading RG1 5AU; phone 0118 966 8271.

"Doing fine"?

" As we live in Alaska, where schooling is often inadequate, we sent our daughter, then aged eight, to Windlesham House, a boarding prep school in West Sussex. During her three years there she seemed to fall steadily behind, but the school kept reassuring us she was 'doing fine'. We've now discovered she is severely dyslexic, a condition Windlesham House failed to diagnose. We feel angry and cheated. Can we take legal action against the school or claim compensation or a refund of fees? "

Philip Lough, the head, admitted that the school took nearly three years to identify the severity of your daughter's dyslexia. "No one wants to give up on a child – you try your best," he explained. When he finally realised that the school could not offer her the necessary help, he waived the requirement for a term's notice of withdrawal.

45

General

I am astonished that a school claiming to cater for dyslexia, as Windlesham House does, should have been so slow to appreciate your daughter's needs. Parents should always treat such claims with caution. It is difficult to pursue a successful claim against an independent school, but possible if the child sues in his or her own name.

What can we do?

" My 10-year-old grandson is severely deaf. His mother was determined that he should go to mainstream schools and learn to speak, not sign. Reluctantly, she sent him to a special unit for deaf children, attached to a local primary school. At first, he spent most of his time in ordinary classes, but then things began to deteriorate. He was often left on his own in the unit and was temporarily excluded for aggressive behaviour. He has a violent streak when crossed and finds it hard to integrate with other children. Now he's been permanently excluded. As grandparents, we could help financially, but doubt any school would have him. What can we do? "

It is not clear from your letter whether your grandson's parents are now reconciled to sending him to a special school (many of which are as opposed as your daughter-in-law to signing). Certainly, no special school would blame him for his aggression. Among the best for deaf children is Mary Hare (01635 244200); others are listed in *Special Schools in Britain*, which costs £8.99 from Network Publishing (01527 834400).

Learning difficulties: a local initiative

" *To help meet the needs of parents whose children have specific learning difficulties such as dyslexia, we have compiled a directory of appropriately qualified teachers in mid-Anglia who offer private tuition. I enclose a copy and wonder if you would be interested in encouraging similar local initiatives elsewhere.* "

> This is an excellent idea. In addition to listing more than 50 tutors in areas that extend from Bedford to Ipswich and Peterborough to Chelmsford, the 48-page booklet has details of local and national organisations covering a range of special needs.

Is he dyslexic?

" *My husband and I are extremely worried about our eight-year-old son. He's hyperactive at home and can't concentrate at school. What little work he does is untidy and usually incomplete. His primary school teacher dismissed the suggestion that our son might be dyslexic, even though he is behind in reading, spelling and arithmetic. Two prep schools have rejected him. What do we do now?* "

> If you have not had your son tested by a good educational psychologist, you should do so at once. Pay no attention to his teacher: your son clearly has problems and they won't simply go away. You should also obtain a copy of *The Dyslexia Handbook*, which costs £9.50 inc. p&p from the British Dyslexia Association, 98

General

London Road, Reading RG1 5AU (0118 966 8271).

Keen to encourage

" How unusual is it for a child with a formal statement of special educational needs to be placed in a mainstream school? "

This year, 58 per cent of such pupils are in ordinary schools, up from 48 per cent five years ago – a trend the Government is keen to encourage. Nearly 250,000 children have "statements".

Who can help us?

" We are nearing despair over our son's learning difficulties. His school is reluctant to recognise them; the education authority has failed, after more than a year, to issue a statement of his special needs; we're paying hundreds of pounds for extra tuition; and yet he seems destined to leave school with only one or two GCSEs. Who can help us? "

I have passed your letter to Patience Thomson, who has written so lucidly on this page about the needs of dyslexic children. Formerly head of a special school, she has also taught young offenders and has a wide and sympathetic understanding of youngsters who fail to thrive, and of the burden this puts on their families.

Very flimsy grounds

" Looking for an independent school for our son, who is quite severely dyslexic, we've been dismayed to find that many claim to offer specialist help on what seem very flimsy grounds. Is there a list of schools that have been officially approved? "

Yes. It is published by the Council for the Registration of Schools Teaching Dyslexic Pupils, which is supported by the British Dyslexia Association and the Dyslexia Institute. Only schools that pass a rigorous inspection every three years are included. For a copy, send a 31p sae to: Christine Manser, Greygarth, Littleworth, Winchcombe, Glos GL54 5BT. The information is also available on www.crested.org.uk/.

It's not worth it

" My dyslexic son's school is encouraging me to buy him a DreamWriter, a robust-looking laptop that costs £100. It seems cheap but is it worth it? "

Not if a 13-year-old who wrote recently to the TES is to be believed. He is trying out one for his local education authority and complains that carrying it around the school – it weighs 4¾lb – gives him sore shoulders. Even more seriously, he says that its reliability is poor because if it is accidentally knocked ("even gently") all the work on it is lost.

General

The "statementing" process

" We are unhappy with the provision being made for our autistic son and plan to appeal to a Special Educational Needs Tribunal. We've had plenty of advice but much of it is confusing and we'd be grateful for an authoritative source of information."

> *Sent Ahead* is an excellent guide published by IPSEA, the Independent Panel for Special Education Advice. Besides explaining how to appeal, it describes the whole "statementing" process with admirable clarity. The guide costs £7.50 (including p&p) from IPSEA, 6 Carlow Mews, Woodbridge, Suffolk IP12 1DH (0800 0184016 or 01394 380518).

Is this "dyscalculia"?

" Our son, who is mildly dyslexic, has severe problems with maths. He can't seem to learn his times tables, uses his fingers for the simplest calculations and becomes hopelessly confused. Could this be what is known as 'dyscalculia'? What can we do?"

> Dyscalculia has much in common with dyslexia, though the two conditions do not overlap exactly. (To learn more, type the word into any Internet search engine.) Your best starting point is *Dyslexia and Mathematics*, a leaflet just published by the British Dyslexia Association. It explains the difficulties dyslexics may have with maths, outlines strate-

gies for overcoming them and includes a useful reading list. The leaflet costs £1.50 (including postage) from the BDA, 98 London Road, Reading RG1 5AU; phone 0118 966 8271.

A guide to special schools

" Is there a guide to special schools for children with emotional and learning difficulties? "

Special Schools in Britain gives details of 1,500 schools (and 20 further education colleges) catering for children with a range of disabilities. It costs £10 (including p&p) from Network Publishing, 01527 834400.

Liable for damages

" Does last week's House of Lords ruling – that local education authorities may be liable for damages if they are negligent in providing for children with special needs – extend to all pupils? "

Yes. Heads and teachers are now accountable in law for failing to measure up to professional standards. As one leading firm of solicitors puts it: "The implications are as great as if the law of medical negligence had only just been recognised." All those who think they under-achieved at school through no fault of their own but because of the school's "failure to act appropriately" might now have a potential claim. However, they will have to prove negligence and that they suffered financial loss as a result.

General

Left-handed

" Rather late in the day, our eight-year-old daughter has been diagnosed as left-handed. Where can I find out more? "

Everything you could possibly want to know can be found in *The Left-hander's Handbook* by Diane G Paul. Approved by the BMA, it is published by the Robinswood Press and costs £9.95. (It is, however, currently out of print, so check your local library.)

" I take exception to the parents who wrote last week to say their daughter had been 'diagnosed' as left-handed, as though it were a disease or disability. I'm surprised you didn't correct them. "

I was surprised by how many left-handed people took offence, though I am sure none was intended.

www.iamdyslexic.com

" I am an 11-year-old dyslexic and have produced a website to try to help other children with the same problems. Please would you tell your readers about it? "

The letter is from Barnaby Blackburn. His website – www.iamdyslexic.com/ – is both helpful and charming.

Bullying

Tackling the bullies

" What advice would you give parents who know or suspect their children are being bullied at school? "

Take it very seriously. As most heads privately admit, some children in every school are bullied, verbally or otherwise. It is one of the worst things that will ever happen to them and they may well be ashamed to talk about it, believing it must be their fault. In primary schools, you have two points of contact: the head and the form teacher. Arrange to see both or, at the very least, talk to them on the phone. Tell them what you know (including names of the suspected bullies); emphasise your concern; ask how they are going to deal with it; don't be fobbed off; and arrange to speak to them again so that you can check on developments. In secondary schools, talk first to the head, who will pass you on either to the deputy responsible for pastoral care or to the head of your child's year. Again, tell them what you know or suspect and leave them in no doubt about your concern. Every secondary school should have a strategy for dealing with bullying, and that does not just mean a formal statement of being against it. The most effective method is to bring the problem out into the open by, for example, showing an anti-bullying video and encouraging the children to talk about the issues it raises. If your school does not do that, suggest they get in touch with

General

Kidscape, 2 Grosvenor Gardens, London SW1W 0DH (020 7730 3300).

" Having recently become governor of a comprehensive, I've been given convincing evidence that bullying is a significant but unrecognised problem. What should I do?"

First, read *Bullying: a Practical Guide to Coping for Schools* by Michelle Elliott, director of the Kidscape charity. Aimed principally at teachers, and written by experts, it describes the circumstances in which bullying flourishes and what schools can (and should) do to tackle them. As the Department for Education circular 8/94 puts it: "School staff must act – and, importantly, be seen to act – firmly against bullying whenever and wherever it appears. Governing bodies should regularly review their school's policy on bullying." If yours has not, it is time it did. The guide is published by Pitman, 128 Long Acre, London WC2E 9AN (020 739 7383).

" Friends of mine have just withdrawn their son from Lancing because he was being bullied. On one occasion, boys in his dormitory hit him about the legs with a hockey stick. His ankle was severely bruised and he was on crutches for a week. The school said he had to learn to stand up for himself. Are these attitudes and practices still common?"

Surveys suggest that bullying – both verbal and physical – is distressingly common, not least because it is so rarely exposed. Sir Patrick Cable-Alexander, bursar of Lancing, said the incident was a "misguided prank which went badly wrong". It led to one boy being suspended and others being given a severe warning.

They don't take it seriously

" We think our eight-year-old son is being bullied at school. His teachers say the right things but we are not convinced they're taking it seriously. We don't feel we know enough about the issue to challenge them, which leaves us feeling helpless. What's your advice? "

> I urge you to read *Bullying – The Early Years* by Delwyn and Eva Tattum. It explains clearly and sympathetically what bullying is, how it arises, the damage it does (as much to the bully as to the victim) and what teachers, parents and children can do to stop it. Parents who suspect their own children may be bullying will find the pamphlet particularly helpful. It costs £3.90 (including p&p) from Countering Bullying Unit, University of Wales Institute, Cyncoed Road, Cardiff CF23 6XD; cheques payable to UWIC.

They won't pay for transport

" Our grand-daughter, who has an official statement of her special educational needs, has been so severely bullied at her local primary school that the council has agreed she should be transferred to another school, where she will feel safe. However, the new school is some distance away and the council has flatly refused to pay for transport. What can we do? "

General

I suggest you contact the Local Government Ombudsman, who investigates complaints of injustice arising from maladministration by local authorities. The ombudsman for your area – southern and central England – is Mr J R White; phone 024 7669 5999. For full details, see the website: www.open.gov.uk/lgo/.

Disturbing development

" *As a headteacher, I'm becoming increasingly concerned about the new attitude to bullying. Bullying is evil but anyone now accused of it is almost automatically assumed to be guilty, especially if race is involved. Recently, I've come across a number of false allegations made by adolescents who are either seeking to excuse their own bad behaviour or are simply oversensitive (girls being particularly prone to the latter). I think we're unwittingly encouraging a new form of bullying. Do you agree?* "

Have readers come across any evidence of this disturbing development?

Rules and discipline

Drugs – is expulsion the answer?

" *My son, who'll be taking his GCSEs in the summer, was recently expelled by a leading independent school after being caught smoking cannabis. Another school, equally eminent and equally hostile to drug taking, has now offered him a place, knowing all the circumstances. I certainly do not condone drugs, but I cannot understand why schools insist on expelling pupils for taking them. Aren't they just shuffling the problem around the system instead of addressing it?"*

In a word, yes – as an increasing number of heads are coming to recognise. Although they are still reluctant to talk about it publicly, a number have adopted a new strategy. Instead of expelling pupils for a first offence, they ask their parents to agree to the introduction of random urine testing accompanied by compulsory drugs counselling. Only if that fails do they resort to expulsion. Heads say the response has been very encouraging. Other schools should be urged to follow suit.

Expulsion – the *real* reason

" My 17-year-old son has been expelled from his Catholic independent school in the final year of his A-levels because, according to the head, his grades aren't good enough and he 'can go no further with his education here'. My son, who's been at the school since he was seven, has never been a great academic but he's an excellent sportsman. With the school's encouragement, he's played hockey and tennis for the county. The humiliation of being expelled has had a devastating effect on him and he's given up studying altogether. It makes me so angry. Is this how they improve their league table positions?"

Fee-paying parents should read the school's small print carefully. It effectively entitles the head to give notice of dismissal for any "reasonable" cause, which can include a pupil's failure, in the school's judgement, to work hard.

General

It is also true that improving – or simply maintaining – their league table positions has become very important to schools. In the extreme case you describe, a school that accepts responsibility for a child for 10 years and then ditches him without good cause is guilty of shabbily irresponsible behaviour. You should appeal against the decision to the governors. I shall be interested to hear of any similar cases.

A prank that backfired

" Less than six months before taking her GCSEs, my 16-year-old daughter has been expelled from her grant-maintained school. The head claims she put 'faecal matter' on a teacher's desk with the deliberate intention of shocking her. My daughter says it was a mouldy piece of chocolate cake that she'd found in a locker and she only meant to play a silly prank. I believed her and paid a solicitor £1,200 to represent us before an 'independent' appeals committee. We lost. So now my daughter, who has learning difficulties, is stuck at home and fast losing heart. She'll probably fail her GCSEs. Even if the head was right, should he have expelled her? How independent are schools' appeals committees? What can I do? "

I have talked to the head, who was adamant about your daughter's guilt. In his view, your daughter exceeded the bounds of what any school should tolerate. The appeal committee, though it agreed with him, has overturned his decisions in the past. He added that he would have no objection to any of his teachers helping your daughter with her work if they wanted to.

Provocative

" When I took my 13-year-old son to boarding school, I was shocked to see provocative posters of unclothed women stuck to the walls of the boys' sleeping and study areas – and this in a co-educational school that prides itself on the 'maturity' of the relationships between girls and boys. Am I just being prudish? "

> I don't think so. When I quiz schools about the phenomenon – which is widespread – they usually say they permit nothing a mother would find disturbing. So you should make your feelings known to your son's housemaster, and ask other mothers (and fathers) what they think.

" I sympathise with the mother who wrote to you recently about the provocative posters at her son's school. I'm a house matron at a boarding school, and here, the decision about what is acceptable is left to me and the female domestics. Most parents don't like to intervene, but we have to look at the pictures every day. Banning them isn't realistic, but the boys can be taught to be considerate of others' feelings. "

> A good solution: other schools please note.

A perfect life

" When I was at boarding school 25 years ago, the regime provided a perfect life for a slightly rebellious teenager. We were closely monitored and cared for. Rules were enforced, television was rationed and smoking and drinking resulted in

instant expulsion. Looking now for something similar for my rebellious daughter, I find everything has changed. In the new, laissez-faire world of boarding, there seems to be little or no supervision. The children watch television whenever they want, appear to go out when they please and do as they like. The emphasis is all on five-star comfort, not security, discipline or care. I don't want Tom Brown's Schooldays, just a moral code, rules and the will to implement them. Please could you advise?"

> Boarding is certainly more diverse than it was, though I think you exaggerate even the liberal end of the spectrum. However, strictness (tempered with kindness) can still be found.

A real insight

" I am considering applying for a job in a school for children with emotional and behavioural difficulties (EBD) but would like to know more about what it's like to teach in such an environment. Any suggestions?"

> Ofsted has just published an admirable report on the subject. Called *Principles into Practice*, it draws on inspections of 40 EBD schools judged to be good or very good and provides a real insight into how they work. Compassionate, practical and full of good advice, it deserves to be read by every teacher who struggles to cope with difficult children. To order the report, which is free, phone 020 7510 0180.

Appalling behaviour

" *I have just returned from Tyne Cot, the Commonwealth War Graves Commission cemetery at Ypres, where I was appalled by the behaviour of some British school children. They were running up and down the graves shrieking and laughing. What is the point of taking children on such visits if they don't know how to behave?* "

Surely this is unusual? Or have other readers had similar experiences?

" *We were at Tyne Cot, the Commonwealth War Graves Commission cemetery at Ypres, the week before you published the letter from the reader who was appalled by the behaviour of some British school children there. My husband, whose father fought in the First World War, remonstrated with a group who were climbing on the memorial cross and generally causing a disturbance. Later, our visit to the Flanders Field exhibition was spoilt by another party of children who were racing about making it impossible to hear the commentary or appreciate the atmosphere. The final straw came at Sanctuary Wood, where pupils from a girls' school were using the trenches as an adventure playground. In each case, the teachers were either indifferent or nowhere to be seen. Your correspondent's experience was far from unique.* "

Dozens of readers, I am sorry to say, wrote in similar terms to Delia Shelley, of Solihull. "The pupils rushed around screaming and chasing each other," reported Hermione Wynn, of Malton, North Yorks. "They were a great embarrassment and I wondered why they had come." "The Last Post ceremony at Tyne Cot was ruined by a group of yelling school children," wrote Beryl Teed of Maidstone, Kent. "Some people on our trip had gone to find their grandfathers' graves and were very distressed by the children running wild," said Jean and Richard Noake of Kings Heath, Birmingham. "There were Cub Scouts at Sanctuary Wood rushing and screaming along the trenches," reported Enid Crossland, of Sandhurst, Berks. "A deeply shaming experience," concluded Sheila Baseby of Banbury, Oxford. However, many insisted such behaviour was not the norm. "Why are people so negative?" asked Lesley Cook, a history teacher at Fullbrook, Surrey. "I have taken hundreds of pupils aged 13 and 14 to Ypres over the last 10 years. We've had the occasional few who have had to be reminded of their behaviour but the vast majority are very moved, especially by the Last Post ceremony at Tyne Cot." "I was heartened and impressed by the excellent behaviour of several large groups of British (and other) school children," wrote Bill Butt of Lowestoft, Suffolk, who recently spent three days at Ypres. "Every British school party I have encountered has behaved impeccably," reported Pat Mortlock, who visits Ypres every year with Tonbridge Girls' Grammar School.

Some readers took a different view. "We encountered high-spirited British, French and German school children at Tyne Cot," wrote Laurie Auger of Porlock, Somerset, whose three uncles died in the First World War. "Our initial reaction was distress but, on reflection, we wondered whether those buried there, many only a year or two older than the children we saw, would have been so perturbed. Or would they feel delight that, through their sacrifice, children of the previously warring nations were free to run and laugh there?" Brenda Collins, an English teacher at St Maur's, Weybridge, Surrey, said she often had to remind her pupils not to walk around in reverential silence. "The young soldiers buried there would, I am sure, be delighted to hear the sounds of youthful chatter and laughter, to know that they didn't die in vain and that they are still remembered by a generation lucky enough not to have experienced the horrors of war."

One lesson seems clear: teachers who take pupils to war memorials should be at pains to ensure that they understand their significance.

The parent–school relationship

Long-winded clichés

" Having a grandson in primary school and a grand-daughter at a comprehensive, I wonder if I'm alone in my dismay at the blandness of their school reports. Year after year, their teachers repeat the same long-winded clichés. Couldn't they do better? "

Teachers are required to report in detail on pupils' progress through the national curriculum, which tends to make for exceptionally stodgy reading. But what are other readers' experiences? Do you find school reports enlightening or incomprehensible, waffly or well-judged? Are they accurate? Wounding? Politically correct? Do they appear to be written by a teacher or a computer? Do you treasure them or bin them? Examples would be welcome, and anything received will be treated in confidence.

A scandalous system

" You wrote that parents are dissatisfied with school reports made up of computer-generated sentences. As the husband of a teacher, I can assure you the staff derive no benefit or pleasure from them either. Having decided what she wants to say about a pupil, my wife has to select the computer phrase that 'comes closest'. Then she enters a four-character code, which someone else uses to generate the report. The result is completely meaningless to her. It also takes longer and prevents her from saying what she means. We think it's a scandalous system. "

So do I. The best way for parents to put a stop to it is to send the reports back with a note saying they do not think bland, mechanical statements do justice to their children.

Speeding up the process

" I sympathise with your hostility to school reports made up of computer-generated sentences. However, writing them out by hand is laborious and time-consuming and, like most teach-

ers, I type slowly. Do you know of any other way to speed up the process?"

"CyberTranscriber", a program developed by Speech Machines, a Midlands-based company, uses speech recognition technology to enable teachers to speak their reports into a telephone. The written version is e-mailed back to them a few hours later. The system, which is also being used by lawyers, has been tried out by Putney High School, West London.

Surely there's a better way?

" *Do any of your readers share our frustration about parents' evenings? You hang around for hours only to have a series of hurried conversations with your child's teachers that must leave everyone feeling thoroughly dissatisfied. Surely there's a better way?* "

I agree. There is never enough time. If there is a problem, both sides tend to be defensive and believe the other is failing to acknowledge or deal with it. As a demonstration of "partnership", the occasion leaves a lot to be desired. We are planning to explore the subject in more detail and I should be glad to hear the views and experiences of parents and teachers.

We fear she may be victimised

" *We are unhappy about aspects of our daughter's school but are reluctant to complain for fear she may be victimised. Can you offer any advice?"*

Schools have a duty to ensure that parents know how to raise concerns or lodge a formal complaint without incurring ill will. Leaflets explaining the procedures – and reassuring parents that their children will not be penalised – should be freely available. If this is not the case, ask a parent governor to obtain a copy of the excellent "model general complaints procedure", published by Rise (Research and Information on State Education Trust), 54 Broadwalk, London E18 2DW. It costs £6.75 but can be downloaded free from the Internet at: www.mandolin.demon.co.uk/model.html/.

Gifted pupils

An initiative

" I understand there's to be a government initiative identifying high-ability pupils and providing them with a more challenging curriculum. I am interested because my five-year-old urgently needs to move forward from her isolated and stationary position, but I can't find any hard information."

There is none: an "initiative" is what it is likely to remain, so you must make your own arrangements. A starting point is the National Association for Gifted Children (01908 673677; www.nagcbritain.org.uk/).

Not selected

" David Blunkett, the Education and Employment Secretary, says that selection by ability is bad for pupils, parents and schools. Yet his department has just announced master-classes for the 'most able' children. Aren't they going to be selected? And, if so, won't that be bad for them? "

> Mr Blunkett says they won't be selected but "put forward" by teachers and parents. So there will be no test – or guarantee – of their ability.

Foreign languages

When to introduce a second language

" My daughter is about to give birth to her first child. She is fluent in Italian, married to an Italian and is going to live in Italy. To become fully bilingual, should the child be exposed to English and Italian from the start or should the second language be introduced later? "

> The evidence is that children learn languages quickest when they are youngest and that the first two years are the most important. However, it is more complicated than that. To combat the effect of being surrounded by Italian, the child would ideally need to hear only English at home. But what if the parents feel happier conversing in Italian? What if the father prefers talking to the child in Italian? What if he speaks English with a strong Italian accent? True, your daughter could

counter most of that by speaking to the child only in English – but will she feel easy doing so? The only rule is to do what comes naturally: it is, after all, a home not a language centre.

" Your recent advice to the Italian–English parents who would like their child to be bilingual was unnecessarily cautious. Our experience – my wife is Greek, I am English, we live in England and have three fully bilingual sons – is that each parent should speak to the child exclusively in his/her native language. There are times when one wonders whether it's all worthwhile – but I assure you it is. "

Many parents and grandparents of bilingual children have written in similar vein. Thank you for putting me right.

Did it confuse the child?

" My husband and I are expecting our first child in October. As a graduate in French, I am considering the possibility of talking to our baby in French, in the hope that he or she will become fully bilingual. I wonder if any of your readers have conducted this educational experiment without being a native speaker of the other language? Was it worth the effort? Or did it merely confuse the child? "

Replies would be welcome. I should add that my correspondent works for the Foreign Office and so cannot predict the wider language environment in which the child will grow up.

" *You requested help recently in advising a woman expecting her first child who asked whether she should consider speaking French to the baby in the hope that he or she would become fully bilingual. Being in a similar position, I'd be very interested to know the response.* "

The question generated much interest. Tony Woodcock, who used to run a primary school in Brussels, said bilingualism was by no means trouble-free. "Even within the same family, one child may pick up the language easily but another may not and become disturbed, experiencing what is known as 'anomie' or rootlessness." Kate Atkins, like my correspondent a graduate in French, said that whenever she spoke French to her daughter "she would wail and flail her arms about, stopping only when I returned to English". However, she had delayed introducing the language until her daughter was eight months old, which many others said was a mistake. Joyce Holden said that in circumstances similar to my correspondent's – her nephew took a degree in French, married a French girl and settled in England – the child became confused when he went to nursery school, where the other children could not understand him when he spoke French.

They, though, were very much in a minority. Edward O'Keefe said his son had married a Norwegian and emigrated to Norway. "Although he is fluent in Norwegian, he spoke to his three children in English from birth. Their mother speaks to them in Norwegian, and the parents converse 50–50 in English and Norwegian. The children accepted it quite naturally and are totally at ease in either language." Novello Noades, a former French teacher, said she had conducted the experiment with complete success, but added a warning: "I spoke to our son, Ryan, only in French from the moment he was born and he was certainly never confused by it. However, my husband is not a linguist, and became frustrated many times during the first few years, particularly when Ryan would be crying and speaking to his father in French: 'My own son, and I cannot understand what he is saying!'"

"Press ahead", was the advice of Glyn Davies, who learnt Welsh as an adult and pointed out that in Wales many children are brought up bilingually without one or both parents being a native Welsh speaker. "Between birth and 36 months is the only period in a person's life when he or she can learn two or more languages as easily as one. At this stage, children absorb languages rather than learn them, but it is crucial to introduce both languages at the very start."

Beate Werm, from Frankfurt, added a note of caution. She and her husband are both German but she has always spoken to their daughter, Maureen, in English. "I believe it has been worthwhile, although there have been fights when she wanted to force me to speak German with her. It took many years before Maureen, now 18, told me it had been a good idea to bring her up in both worlds – because that is what it comes down to: two worlds, not just two languages."

To all who responded, many thanks.

A plea from China

" I am e-mailing you from China in the hope that you can give me some advice. My son's English is still very poor even though he has been studying the language for eight years. The problem is that he is supposed to read a passage aloud every day and then listen to the tape of the text. But he does not like doing it. What should I do? "

Do any readers know enough about how English is taught in China to advise? What, for example, is the point of the exercise? It seems unlikely that this old-fashioned-sounding method aids comprehension.

" You asked recently for help in advising a reader who had e-mailed you from China saying that his son, who had been studying English for eight years, still couldn't speak the language and was objecting to having to read a passage into a tape recorder every day. I was intrigued and wondered what the response had been. "

Surprisingly large. Many readers noted that Chinese students often had difficulties pronouncing English and rarely had access to native speakers (though apparently some Chinese cities have an "English corner" in a public place where students and visiting native speakers can gather). Others pointed out that it was only recently that we started teaching foreign languages as if they were meant to be spoken. The best advice was that the boy and a good English speaker should both record passages from the English-language *China Daily*, allowing the student to compare pronunciations. Edward Coomber wrote to say that his company (www.coomber.co.uk/) produces a two-track recorder for just such a purpose.

Which are reputable?

" There are so many language schools offering courses abroad for teenagers. How does one tell which are reputable and give value for money? "

There is no British-based regulatory body and none abroad that commands general respect, so it is best to use the large, well-established schools. These include: EF International Language Schools (020 7401 8399, www.ef.com/); Euro Academy (020 8686 2363, www.euroacademy.co.uk/); and International House (020 7491 2598; www.international-houselondon.ac.uk/). If the package includes travel, look for membership of ABTA.

New technology

Is shorthand obsolete?

" I think my daughter's job prospects would improve if she learnt shorthand but she says that new office technology has made it obsolete. Who is right? "

You are. A recent survey based on 5,000 office vacancies found that directors, in particular, want a secretary/PA to whom they can dictate work. Last year, the national average salary of PAs – now regarded as an "integral part of a busy executive structure" – rose by seven per cent to nearly £16,000.

Is it really necessary?

" In common, I would guess, with the majority of your readers, I do not have access to the Internet and find your frequent references to 'websites' and 'www' addresses increasingly irritating. Is it really necessary? "

As a relatively late convert, I sympathise. Indeed, it was only when *The Daily Telegraph* lent me a laptop, which enabled me to experiment in privacy, that I began to understand how useful the Internet could be, particularly for navigating the education system. A mass of information, from pre-school to post-graduate, on results, courses, policy documents, statistics, curriculum materials, prospectuses and inspection reports can all be found with a couple of clicks on fewer than 30 websites (many of which lead seamlessly to others). In fact, education has become so thoroughly computerised that I am convinced every parent ought to have a machine, and so should every college and university student. My guess is that one third of my readers – including many grandparents – are there already. Why not pop along to an Internet cafe and join us?

Computing in the classroom

" I share your scepticism about the educational value of many

of the uses made of computers in schools. Couldn't more be done to identify what does work in the classroom so that teachers would waste less time (and money) on what doesn't?"

Yes, and Research Machines, one of the biggest players in the field, has been asking schools to help. The first results, based on the responses of 100 secondary schools, show that many of the most widely used applications – including the Internet and e-mail – are judged to contribute least to children's learning. Similarly, software such as Smile in maths, Fun with Texts in modern languages, Encarta in geography and English, Corel Draw in art and World of Sport Examined in PE are all much used but poorly rated. Word (i.e. word processing) emerges as one the most popular programs in PE, modern languages, design technology, IT and English, and there are gold stars for Crocodile Clips in science, SuccessMaker in maths and English and Cubase in music. Also, digital cameras, where they are available, are a big hit in design technology and art. I urge teachers to contribute to this important database of good and bad practice by calling up the website: www.fischertrust.org/.

Computers: the right direction?

" The headteacher of the excellent Nottinghamshire primary school of which I am a governor wants us to buy 20 laptop computers at a cost, including the central server, of £30,000. That's a huge sum to meet out of a school budget and, as there seems to be little government help available, we're having to

consider a major fund-raising effort. But is this the right direction to take?"

No. The facts are these: on average, primary schools have 18 computers each; nearly all are desktops; nearly half are more than three years old; the cost works out at £8,300 per school, 40 per cent of which comes from school budgets, 30 per cent from the Standards Fund, and much of the rest from parents. The subjects in which they are used most are English and maths, the aim being "to enhance learning". In my view, primary school pupils should be introduced to computers; the machines can be especially useful for teaching remedial literacy and numeracy; otherwise, they are an elaborate distraction. You should encourage your headteacher to scale down her ambitions.

Laptop computer suppliers

" My daughter, a university student, has convinced me she needs a laptop with up-to-date software. How can I keep the cost down? Are there any specialist suppliers to the student market? And have universities thought of negotiating bulk purchase?"

In answer to the first question, my colleagues on "Connected" recommend a firm called Morgan, which sells surplus and end-of-line computers (without software) at competitive prices. It has showrooms in central London, Birmingham and Manchester and a website: www.morgancomputers.co.uk/. However, others, less technically experienced, say Morgan expects customers to know just what they want and is not for beginners. Instead, they recommend second-hand machines through www.loot.com/, where the choice is wide and the ambience that of a car boot sale. My colleagues do not know of any specialist student supplier and share your surprise that no university appears to have thought of negotiating bulk purchase.

Are laptops a health risk?

" Are laptops a health risk? From September, pupils at my 14-year-old daughter's school will be required to use laptops. The machines will be networked by radio waves. I'm worried that not enough research has been done on the effect these might have on health. Can you advise? "

The Stewart Committee, a group of independent experts set up by the Department of Health to investigate whether mobile phones posed a threat, has published its carefully worded findings, recommending "a precautionary approach". The full report is available at www.iegmp.org.uk/.

" Could I reassure your reader who was worried about the laptops at his daughter's school being networked by wireless technology that the link is made by infra-red waves. They are the same as those used in remote controls for TV sets and are no risk to anyone. The only reason the Government is so cautious is the impossibility of proving a negative. "

Thank you.

Attendance

School phobia

" I am deeply concerned about my grand-daughter who, at the age of 10, refuses to go to school. Where can one get help? "

> The causes of school phobia (which is different from truancy) are complex. Referral by a GP to a family therapy team is usually the first step in unravelling them. An information sheet (£1.50 plus 50p postage) is available from the Advisory Centre for Education, 22 Highbury Grove, London N5 2DQ (advice line: 020 7354 8321). Pam Stevenson runs a school phobia helpline: 01304 210997.

" Could we add a word of warning, based on our own distressing experience, to your recent note about school phobia? Having never heard of the condition, we struggled for years to get our youngest son to primary school. On some days, it would take two hours of coaxing. He became increasingly depressed and fell behind in his work. Yet we could never convince anyone that we – or he – needed help. The educational psychologist said we should keep forcing him to school, and we were threatened with legal action by the education welfare officer, who insisted that our son's behaviour was 'just defiance'. Finally, we saw a child psychiatrist, who diagnosed a severe degree of school phobia. Since then, we have been educating him at home. We're all gradually recovering from the experience, but feel we were not given the support we needed and that there is too lit-

tle recognition of the problem."

Thank you.

School trips in term-time

"*I read in* The Daily Telegraph *that 40 pupils and four teachers at a secondary school in Lancashire had spent the first week of term on a skiing trip. Aren't they supposed to be in school? Why don't they go skiing in the holidays? What about those whose parents can't afford such luxuries? Is it a common practice?*"

Increasingly so – to the dismay of many. Schools say that the trips are cheaper out of holiday time and, anyway, they are "educational". Parents who disapprove should make their views known to the head and the chairman of the governors, who are on very weak ground.

Finally ...

Coping with a move

"*Our eight-year-old daughter has gone into a sad decline since we moved six months ago from Manchester to Essex. She was really happy at her previous school – a bright button academically and socially with lots of friends. Now she's become quite withdrawn. She seems to have lost all her confidence and hasn't any friends. What can we do to encourage her?*"

Please, as soon as you possibly can, talk to her class

teacher, remembering that he or she knows your daughter only as a quiet little girl who does not seem to socialise much. Moving to a new school can be traumatic for a child. Her teacher, once she knows the background, will be able with care and sensitivity to help her make one or two friends, after which she should soon begin to blossom again.

" Further to the advice you gave last week to the parents of the little girl who was so unhappy after moving from Manchester to Essex, my experience of working for Childline is that such children's lives are often made miserable because they are taunted ceaselessly about their accent. Please could you draw this to parents' and teachers' attention? "

Thank you.

Empire building

" As a 14-year-old schoolgirl, I am writing to complain about the heavy load of books we have to carry around all day. I'm sure it's bad for our backs, but our teachers don't seem to care. For example, for one 35-minute lesson we have to bring a textbook, an exercise book, a vocabulary book, an oral book and a writing book. Why can't we stay at our desks and let the teachers come to us? "

I agree. Teachers say they need their "resources" around them. But I wonder whether it isn't more a matter of creating empires. What do others think?

General

" As a modern languages teacher, I can't understand why you were so sympathetic last week to that wimpish 14-year-old who complained about the heavy load of books she has to carry round school. How could I, or my science colleagues, take the resources of our labs to her? Anyway, the walking is good for her and she probably lifts heavier weights working out in the multi-gym. "

Readers' sympathies were divided. An 18-year-old who calculated that she had carried a seventh of her weight through secondary school described her back problems; a mother of two girls weighed their daily load and found that, including sports gear and lunch box, it averaged 25lb; a therapist wrote of the damage done to spine, shoulders, arms and hips. Others pointed to the sense of dislocation that comes from not having a permanent base, of the time wasted commuting between lessons and of the increased opportunities to play truant. On the other hand, a reader who was at school during the Second World War said carrying around a gas mask and a greatcoat, as well as her books, had done her no harm; many others pointed out that if classes stayed put, pupils could not be divided by ability for different subjects. The two most popular solutions were a locker for every child (which many schools cannot afford in terms of money or space), and a well-designed backpack with strict instructions to use both shoulder straps. Pupils, it seems, are doomed to remain pack horses.

Personal security

" To reach school, my 12-year-old daughter has to cross London by Underground, changing twice. I'd like her to carry a rape alarm, but haven't been able to find one. "

Boots sells a "personal security alarm" at its larger stores.

Advertising

" Is commercial advertising common in schools? "

No, but it is about to become so. A body called Imagination School Media Marketing claims to have signed up 350 schools for what "promises to be a rewarding partnership between commercial organisations and education establishments". Ten posters, each measuring 24sq ft, promoting breakfast cereals, fashion clothing, footwear and soft drinks, are to be hung in corridors, stairwells, canteens or reception areas, producing an annual income of £5,000 a school. "We need the money," explained David Hunter, head of Norton Canes, a comprehensive in Cannock, Staffs. "We'll have the final say over which ads we accept and where they're hung." At Warwick, a comprehensive in Redhill, Surrey, Diana Perry, the head, said: "The money would buy five computers. But it makes me uneasy. Should we be targeting youngsters like this?" Answers on a postcard, please.

General

Dismayed

" *I was dismayed to discover that my son's secondary school exercise books contain advertising for soft drinks, sports clothing and 'spots cleansers'. How long has this been going on?* "

> They are called "JazzyBooks". Nearly two million have been distributed free to 2,000 primary and secondary schools since May last year, saving schools an estimated £250,000. Apart from commercial sponsors, advertisers include government departments, the Royal Mail and the Prince's Trust. All adhere to an ethical policy and the advertisements are vetted by an independent panel of parents and teachers. I see no harm in the books. Schools wanting to know more can phone JazzyBooks on 020 7323 3223 (www.jazzybooks.co.uk/).

Anorexia: the need for guidance

" *I am dismayed by the way a leading independent boarding school reacted to my daughter's anorexia. She had started term fit and healthy but was sent home near its end (after getting drunk at a dance), a shadow of her former self. It emerged that, on most days, she had survived on a bowl of porridge and the occasional apple – and the school didn't even notice. When the anorexia was confirmed, the head showed little sympathy or understanding. He banned my daughter from the campus until she had regained weight, adding considerably to her stress. Members of his staff, including a counsellor, who were said to be 'highly trained' in dealing with the condition, offered contradictory and ultimately unhelpful advice. I am writing this as a warning to other parents."*

I have decided to suppress the name of the school because I am not convinced it is wholly to blame. For example, you knew at half term that your daughter's weight had fallen drastically. Also, it is impossible not to sympathise with the head's view that her appearance (5ft 11in tall, weight 92lb) was having a profoundly disturbing effect on her friends and other pupils. However, parents and schools (pupils as well as staff) do need guidance on how to recognise and deal with anorexia, which can affect as many as one in a hundred young people.

Clearly, significant weight loss is the first sign to look out for. A BMI (body-mass index – weight in kilograms divided by height squared in metres) of less than 20 should also set alarm bells ringing. So should: a preoccupation with weight; attempts to conceal weight loss; constantly going to the lavatory after meals (self-induced vomiting or purging); paying obsessive attention to food; and, more generally, increasing secretiveness and withdrawal from close relationships.

In such a constellation of circumstances, the proper procedure is to seek medical advice from a GP, which should lead to a referral to an NHS child and adolescent service. Schools, of course, should be supportive and sensitive but should resist the temptation to pretend that they are expert or able to cope on their own. Finally, anorexia often reflects some disturbance in the family and certainly has a major

General

impact on it. So families, no matter how far away they live, should be involved in their child's treatment. I am glad to hear that your daughter is fully recovered and has settled down happily at her new school. The Eating Disorders Association helpline: 01603 621414 (www.edauk.com/).

An increasing problem

" As a teacher responsible for personal, social and health education, I wondered if you could recommend something suitable for 15-year-olds to read about anorexia, which I fear is becoming an increasing problem. "

My wife, who runs an NHS eating disorders service, says *Finding out about Eating Disorders* by Hilary Tunnicliffe is clear, accurate, engagingly written and suitable for the age group. Her only concern is that it tends to underestimate how serious anorexia can be: people do die from it. The booklet is published by Hobsons (01223 507360) and costs £4.99.

Under threat after 75 years

" The uniform worn by the girls at our school since it was founded 75 years ago is under threat. It is a dress made of white cotton with red spots, which our supplier can no longer find. Would your readers know of an alternative source? "

They are not often stumped. The appeal is from

Margaret Allen, a prep school in Hereford, which – unusually – is owned by the parents of its 125 pupils. Details from Lady Mynors, the headmistress, on 01432 273594.

(Editor's note: the headmistress of Margaret Allen School is now Mrs Anna Evans.)

" *The response from your readers to our school uniform problem has been brilliant. We've now found a supplier of the necessary red-spotted white fabric.* "

Thank you. The solution came from School Shop, a mail-order company in Maidstone, Kent. The firm sells directly to parents and reckons to be able to meet any school clothing requirements.

Dispiriting

" *The* Telegraph *article suggesting that independent schools could make their lavish sporting facilities available to children from the state sector failed to explain that any such scheme can be frustrated by local residents. Caterham School in Surrey recently built a £2 million sports hall and indoor pool. Bowing to neighbours' pressure, Tandridge Council has restricted use of the hall and pool to present or past pupils, which means they are virtually empty in the holidays. Do you know of other examples?* "

I don't – but what a dispiriting story. By contrast, the King's Trust, a Christian educational charity, wrote to say that it uses the facilities of 25 independent schools to run summer sports camps for children of all ages and backgrounds. For details, phone 0845 141 0800.

Honours

" Is it true that, among the many teachers who have been awarded honours since the Government came to power, none has been from the independent sector? "

Yes – oddly enough.

Of one mind

" I read your column with interest but I am struck by the similarity of thought and style between the questions and the answers. Can it be that you are writing to yourself on some occasions? "

I find that my readers and I are frequently of one mind.

Beyond recognition

" Your column has grown in interest for me since the birth of my son 12 months ago. My problem is that it is more than 20 years since I had anything to do with schools, and the system seems to have changed beyond recognition. Could you recommend a guide that would bring me up to date? "

Your Child's Education by Niki Chesworth, part of *The Daily Telegraph*'s "lifeplanner" series, offers an admirably lucid introduction. Published by Kogan Page, it costs £8.99.

Unwanted textbooks

" Now that our three children have left school, we have a pile of unwanted text books and revision guides. Is there a charity that can make use of them? "

If there is, I would be pleased to hear of it.

" You asked last week if there was a charity that could make use of unwanted text books. There is and I enclose the details. "

Thank you. Last year, Book Aid International (020 7733 3577; www.bookaid.org/), a registered charity, dispatched some 700,000 school and university textbooks, children's books, vocational manuals, dictionaries and encyclopaedias to Third World countries. About half were collected as a service to the community and delivered to Book Aid by Rotary International (01789 765411; e-mail, secretary@ribi.org/) which has 1,700 branches in Britain and Ireland. Books must be in good condition and not more than 10 years old.

Up to speed

" Now that our four-year-old has started school, my husband and I are discovering how much education has changed in the past 20 years. How can we best bring ourselves up to speed? "

General

Letts Educational has just published eight booklets under the umbrella title of *You and Your Child*. Five of them provide a general introduction to pre-school and primary education, the national curriculum, successful learning and learning difficulties, while the others are more tightly focused on literacy, numeracy and ICT and computers. They give lucid, accurate answers to the questions parents are most likely to ask and offer sound advice about how to help a child get the most out of primary school. The content of the booklets (£4.99 each from large bookstores) overlaps so you will need to choose the areas in which you are particularly interested.

"Where dreams are made"

" How can we find a good ballet teacher for our son? "

For a list of registered teachers in your area, write to the Royal Academy of Dancing, 36 Battersea Square, London SW11 3RA or, better still, consult its website ("The place where dreams are made"): www.rad.org.uk/.

Whistling: out of fashion?

" When did you last hear a child whistling on the way to school? "

Oddly, the self-same question is asked by the Bishop of St Albans in the current issue of his diocesan newsletter. "It doesn't happen, because children are harassed and harangued and pressured to perform", he says. "Not only are they not whistling. A good proportion of them have given up hope even before they get to reception class." My own view is that whistling – like keeping a sense of proportion – has simply gone out of fashion.

" You suggested last week that children no longer whistled on their way to school because whistling had gone out of fashion. Could that be because pop songs no longer have whistleable tunes? "

That was one popular explanation. However, teachers reported that boys (but rarely girls) could be heard whistling at the start of lessons, and mothers noted a high incidence of back-seat whistling on the school run. Perhaps it is still prevalent but the sound is drowned out by bus and car engines.

They all arrive by car

" All 183 pupils at my infant school – Valley End, Chobham, Surrey – arrive by car. We have no public transport and no school bus service. There's no pavement, either, yet the speed limit outside our door is 60mph. Children have twice been hit by cars. The county council's response to our request for a 20mph limit was dismissive. Do your readers know of other schools in a similar situation and the way they dealt with it? "

Surrey County Council's response to Sue Jane, the

General

headteacher, is worth recording: "During the hours when pupils are being dropped off or picked up at the school, the extent of local parental parking has a much more dramatic impact on vehicular speeds than any Traffic Regulation Order." Can readers offer any advice?

" Please tell the head of Valley End infant school, Chobham, Surrey, who wrote to you about the county council's dismissive response to her plea for a 20mph speed limit outside the school, that every council's highways department is part of the problem, not the solution, and has to be circumvented. To do that, she must start a campaign by contacting her local councillor and enlisting the support of parents, political activists and the local media. In my experience, it shouldn't take more than nine months to persuade councillors to change the highways department's mindset. "

That stirring advice came from Barry Walters, the leader of North Somerset Council, who could probably be persuaded to map out the entire campaign. Others reported similar experiences to Valley End's and said councils seemed terrified of creating "precedents" by agreeing to traffic-calming measures. However, St Matthew's, Downside, another Surrey village school, said it had persuaded the council to install hazard warning lights, though the speed limit is still 60mph. The best news came from Broughton-in-Furness, Cumbria, where Lowick school has won electronic signs that reduce the limit to 30mph at the start and end of each school day.

Duty of care

" Did you know that, although buses taking pupils on school trips have to be fitted with seatbelts, those that are hired by local education authorities to take pupils to school do not? Our two children's journey to their village school in Northamptonshire is along twisty, narrow lanes. Only last week, two school buses in a nearby village collided and 18 children were taken to hospital. Yet the county council has awarded the contract to a company that does not fit belts. Don't you think it is failing in its duty of care? "

> I do. Northamptonshire County Council said it was obliged to accept the lowest bid. However, the Department of Transport says the council has the power to require contractors to fit seatbelts. It should do so without further delay.
> *(Editor's note: the contractor later did fit seatbelts.)*

Guardian families

" I have friends in China who are thinking of sending their children to independent schools in Britain. I understand it is possible to find guardian families who will take care of the children at half term and keep an eye on them at other times. How is that done? "

> Until recently, this was an area fraught with difficulty, not to mention legal complications. However, a number of reputable guardianship organisations have come together with schools such as Eton and Cheltenham

General

Ladies to form Aegis, the Association of Educational Guardians for International Students. Its aim is to "safeguard the welfare and happiness of the children under guardianship and, in conjunction with the educational institutions, to act on behalf of the parents". Details from: Margaret Banks, 3 Morland Avenue, Leicester LE2 2PF; fax 0116 210 9894; e-mail mrb@webleicester.co.uk/.

Poems on the Underground

" Decorating the walls of my classroom are some delightful London Underground poster poems which I obtained a few years ago through your column. Is there any chance of another set? "

Poems on the Underground is about to celebrate 1,000 years of poetry in English with 12 poems. They start with the seventh-century Caedmon's Hymn, include Shakespeare's sonnet 116 – "Let me not to the marriage of true minds/Admit impediments" – and Blake's Jerusalem, and conclude with Jo Shapcott's delightful Quark:
" 'Transcendental,' said the technician,/'to stumble on a quark that talks back.' " For a set of posters, send your name and address with a cheque or postal order for £5 payable to London Transport Museum to: Georgina Davis, London Transport Museum, Freepost, London WC2E 7BR.

Primary education

Topics in this section include national tests, admittance, and the use of computers in classrooms.

Ready for school?

The choice is yours

" Our son is due to start at primary school in September when he'll be just four. However, he was born three months prematurely and we feel that, physically and mentally, he will still be very much a three-year-old and could lose confidence among more advanced children. What can we do to delay his start in education? "

> Despite what infant schools may tell you, compulsory education does not begin until the term after a child has turned five. Until then, the choice is yours.

Now or later?

" We have just started looking for a school for our three-year-old son, who will be starting in September next year. We have enough money to pay fees for five or six years. Do you think it's better to spend money in the early years so that he gains a solid

grounding, or later to ensure good GCSEs and A-levels?"

> It depends on how good the local state schools are. Consult the primary school league tables and ask to see the Ofsted reports on the highest scoring ones in the area. If that points to the independent sector, consider the secondary schools to which your son would transfer. How awkward would that be, educationally and socially? I believe it is a lot easier for parents to compensate for deficient teaching when their children are younger.

A simple test

" Is there a simple test for determining whether our four-year-old son is ready for school?"

> I know of two: can he draw a circle in both a clockwise and an anticlockwise direction (necessary to form letter shapes); and can he touch his left ear with his right hand, or his right foot with his left hand (indicating whether essential connections have been made in the brain)?

At least two points of entry

" The primary school we chose for our son admits children only in September. If we hadn't sent him when he was just four, he'd have had to wait a year – and the head said she couldn't guarantee him a place then, anyway. Although he seems to be coping (in a class of 30), we still don't think he's ready for school and would far rather have kept him at the

nursery (in a group of about 10). We resent having our hand forced. What's your view?"

> The Government's code of practice on admissions says there "should be no question of schools putting pressure on parents to enter their child early in order to secure a place". Parents, it adds, are "well placed to judge when their child is ready". But that, I am afraid, is as far as it goes. Schools ought to have at least two points of entry, in September and January. The law does not require attendance until the beginning of the term after the child's fifth birthday.

Don't fear she will be left behind

" Is our daughter, who will be four this month, too young to go to school in September? Will she have trouble catching up if we don't send her until Easter?"

> She is not too young if you think she will enjoy it, but you should not send her out of fear that she will be left behind. She will still be learning if she stays at home and will cope just as well when she goes to school.

Choice of school

A sensible move

" Please could you give us the names of some good primary schools in Derby and the surrounding area? Our granddaughter is only two but her parents are moving and it seems

sensible to choose an area with good schools."

Indeed it does. You should consult the official primary school league tables [published in *The Daily Telegraph* on December 2nd, and available at www.dfee.gov.uk/]

Look before you leap

" We are thinking of moving to the country for the sake of our two young children, but hear quite contradictory reports of the effectiveness of small rural schools. What's your view?"

"Pupils in small schools," says Ofsted, "are not disadvantaged in comparison with those in larger schools simply because of the size of the school. Small schools are capable of providing an effective education, and many are among the most successful schools in the country. At the same time, a disproportionate number of the smallest schools have serious weaknesses or require special measures." So look before you leap.

Two nations

" Two years ago, we moved our elder daughter, then aged eight, from her state primary, which had not been a success, to an independent school, where she has excelled in every way. Her sister, now eight, is at another primary school, doing well, has lots of friends and is very happy. Should we move her to join her sister or leave her where she is?"

I see no reason to move her now, but if your elder

daughter is remaining in the independent sector, you may want to think again when the younger one finishes primary school. Unless you can find a good comprehensive, a strong sense of "two nations" may begin to emerge, both socially and academically.

A sorry tale

" We are one of nine sets of parents who have just been through the charade of appealing against the local primary school's refusal to admit our children. It was a farce because the appeals panel made it clear that it had no power to compel the school to create an infant class larger than 30 and no power to compel Warwickshire, the local education authority, to appoint an extra teacher. Indeed, the panel chairman told us we were there only because the Government, having decided to limit infant class sizes, had apparently forgotten to deprive us of our right of appeal. So this is the downside of New Labour's headline-grabbing pledge to reduce class sizes: it bears not on schools nor on local education authorities but on parents. Our two children will now be going to primary schools miles apart. "

A sorry tale – but thank you.

Parents' anxiety may be unnecessary

" Our local parents' grapevine suggests that if we don't put our baby son's name down now for the right prep and senior schools his educational future will be blighted. I'd hoped to wait and see how he develops. What's your advice? "

It is true that in some areas – London particularly – there is a heavy demand for places at some prep schools that are successful at getting children into a small number of highly selective senior schools. But even the most elite institutions draw from a wide range of prep – and primary – schools, so parental anxiety can sometimes be unnecessary. If you can find a junior school that will enable your son to give a good account of himself in the entrance exams at 11 or 13, he will almost certainly secure a place at the senior school that is right for him.

The best trad preps

" Which are the best traditional prep schools for a really able boy? "

Success at winning scholarships to Winchester and Eton is a good indicator. This year, the Dragon, Oxford, took the first place at Winchester as well as the 10th, 11th and 20th, and the 13th at Eton. As always, another strong performer was Milbourne Lodge, Esher: second, 9th and 16th at Winchester, plus two scholarships to Eton. Summer Fields, Oxford, took the fourth and seventh places at Eton and the 15th at Winchester. Other successful schools included Pilgrims', Winchester; Packwood Haugh, Shrewsbury; and Dulwich College Prep, London.

Education/school policy

Mixed-age classes

" At our son's primary school, children aged nine, 10 and 11 are taught together in three mixed-age classes. Isn't there a danger he'll struggle to keep up at first and be bored later? "

> Yes – and no matter how skilled his teacher is, he will have to spend a lot of time working on his own, which is a pity. You should ask the governors to question the head about why the classes are organised like that. Even if it is to make best use of teachers' specialist knowledge, I doubt it is sensible.

No homework

" Our daughter's primary school doesn't set regular homework, as David Blunkett, the Education Secretary, rightly recommends. What can we do? "

> *Excellence in Schools*, the recent White Paper, said nearly 50 per cent of pupils were not set regular homework in their last year at primary school. National guidelines are to be introduced. Ask your governing body to discuss the matter at its next meeting.

Early learning goals

" What are the 'desirable learning outcomes' I keep hearing

about at my son's infant school?"

> They describe what the Government expects five-year-olds to have achieved by the end of the reception year and are to be replaced from September 2000 by "early learning goals". These cover: personal, social and emotional development (forming good relationships with adults and peers, understanding the difference between right and wrong); language and literacy (speak with confidence, write simple words); mathematical development (count up to 10, understand the meaning of adding and taking away); knowledge and understanding of the world (ask questions about why things happen and how things work); physical development (move with control and coordination); and creative development (respond to what they see, hear, smell, touch and feel). *Early Learning Goals* is published by the Qualifications and Curriculum Authority, 83 Piccadilly, London W1J 8QA; www.qca.org.uk/.

What should she be learning?

" My five-year-old is just about to finish her first year at a primary school in the Midlands. As someone who was educated in India, I don't have a feel for what is expected of her at this age. Where can I find details of what she should be learning?"

> There are two excellent official guides to the national curriculum, one covering primary schools, the other secondary schools. Unfortunately, they cost £24.95 from the Stationery Office (51 Nine Elms Lane,

London SW8 5DR). However, they can also be downloaded free on the website: www.nc.uk.net/.

National tests and league tables

Little league

" You publish a league table of independent senior schools but not of prep schools. Why not? How can one judge their academic strength? "

> With difficulty. The information on which to base a table is not available, though it easily could be. Nearly all prep school pupils take the Common Entrance exam. The papers are set centrally, but marked by the school to which the pupil is applying, according to its own criteria. These vary so much as to make comparisons impossible. All that parents can do is ask for a list of pupils' recent destinations and scholarships and plot those against the senior school league table.

Beyond the league tables

" We are about to start looking for a primary school for our three-year-old. All the local schools did well in the recent league tables. What other factors should influence our choice? "

> Primary league tables offer only the roughest guide. The most vital question is: "What proportion of the school's seven-year-olds have a reading age of seven?" Most schools set standardised reading tests, but are re-

luctant to divulge the results. If any of the schools you are considering don't set the tests or won't tell you the results, look elsewhere.

No league tables for prep schools

" Knowing of your interest in league tables, I wonder if you can tell me where can I find one for prep schools? "

I wish I could but prep schools have somehow managed to avoid them. Some heads would like the Common Entrance exam to be marked by a board (instead of, as at present, by the receiving senior school) and become a common measure of prep schools' academic achievement. The majority, though, prefer to keep that sort of information from their customers.

Past papers

" Having done more than my bit to supplement my son's primary education, I'm keen to ensure he does well in next May's national curriculum tests for 11-year-olds. Are past papers available? "

The questions and answers for this year's tests in English, maths and science are available (£4 including p&p) from SCAA Publications, PO Box 235, Hayes, Middlesex UB3 1HF. Quote reference number: KS2/97/671.

A quantum leap

" Some primary schools have reported a quantum leap in their national test results for 11-year-olds. Given the importance schools attach to their league table positions, what's to stop them cheating? "

> This year, for the first time, headteachers will have to declare that the tests were not opened more than an hour before being administered. They are marked externally.

Manipulation

" Although I'm head of a primary school, I've only just discovered that the examiners who mark the national tests for 11-year-olds are not the people who decide which marks equate to Level 4, the achievement by which the Government sets so much store. What's to stop the whole marking process being manipulated to achieve the Government's aims? "

> The Qualifications and Curriculum Authority (QCA) says it is impossible to write tests of identical difficulty year on year. So, once the papers are marked, the authority decides how many marks are required for each level to "ensure continuity of standards". The system relies on the integrity of its officials.

Does the age difference matter?

" My grand-daughter, who was born in the summer, started school just five weeks after her fourth birthday. Consequently,

some of her classmates are 10 months her senior. In May, they will all take the national curriculum tests for seven-year-olds, yet the school says no allowance will be made for the difference in their ages. Isn't that rather unfair?"

In a sense, yes, but nothing hangs on the outcome. The tests your granddaughter will take at 11 are far more significant, but then her scores in the three Rs will be "age standardised". Much more disturbing is the gap in the performance of girls and boys at 11. Last May, 79 per cent of girls reached the expected level in reading, compared with 64 per cent of boys. The gap was even wider in writing: 67 per cent of girls reached the target, compared with only 45 per cent of boys. If you also have a grandson, please read to him and encourage him to talk to you.

Previous papers

" Our daughters will take national curriculum tests in May. How can we obtain previous papers?"

Letts publishes practice papers in English, maths and science for Key Stages 1 and 2, which include not only the answers but also an explanation of what the examiners are looking for. They cost £3.99 each from good bookshops.

More informative

" Given the relationship between children's home background

and their attainment, wouldn't the league tables be more informative if they included some measure of the value primary schools add?"

The Government says it is having difficulty identifying a reliable measure. However, Wandsworth in south-west London has managed it, and this year became the first education authority to publish the outcome. It named 10 of its 58 primaries as having results "significantly lower than expected based on pupils' ability" – and nine where they were significantly higher. For a copy of the council's excellent booklet, phone 020 8871 8013.

Aren't they compulsory?

" The primary school my sister's children attend sets national tests that produce age-adjusted scores, but my children's school doesn't. Aren't the tests compulsory?"

Age-adjusted scores, which are especially useful for measuring how well a child is reading, are derived from the national tests taken by all pupils at seven and 11. Schools do not have to release them but have no good reason not to – and those that refuse should be regarded with suspicion. Most schools also use commercially available tests of literacy, numeracy and IQ for their own purposes. Although they are more accurate, the results are not usually released to parents.

The tests are too imprecise

" Among all this year's national curriculum tests for pupils aged seven, 11 and 14, only in the English test for 14-year-olds were the results worse than last year. The proportion of pupils attaining the target Level 5 (which actually represents the achievement expected of a 13-year-old) was 63 per cent, compared with 64 per cent last year. However, your readers may be interested to know that the drop occurred despite the best efforts of the Qualifications and Curriculum Authority (QCA), the body responsible for guaranteeing the reliability of the tests. As an examiner, I was originally told that the threshold for Level 5 English would be 40 marks out of a possible 100. Then, after the first batch of papers had been marked and returned, the QCA lowered the threshold to 35. Isn't that cheating? "

The QCA's response to this charge was: "Adjustments to the threshold marks are part of the process of ensuring that standards are consistent from one year to the next. The 40 marks was a suggested threshold based on a sample of pupils sitting the test last summer. It was sent to examiners for training purposes only."

My correspondent, who has been marking the tests for six years, said: "That's nonsense. The truth is that the QCA realised it wasn't going to get anywhere near the result it wanted unless it lowered the threshold."

I think the tests invite manipulation because they are too imprecise to justify the highly political conclusions drawn from them.

Earlier? No!

" I don't see the point of reports about the international performance of English nine-year-olds in maths and science. Don't many countries send their children to school earlier than we do? "

> On the contrary, the pupils in 23 of the 25 countries with which England was compared had received a year less of formal schooling. The exceptions were Norway (two years less) and Scotland (the same). Despite that handicap, in maths only six countries did worse (Greece, Thailand, Portugal, Iceland, Iran and Kuwait), while in science three did better (Korea, Japan, United States). An example of what most of the nine-year-olds in England could not do was supply the missing number in $2000 + ? + 30 + 9 = 2739$.

Grants, fundraising and scholarships

Scholarships to Harrow

" Please would you draw your readers' attention to the scholarships we offer at Harrow to able boys currently attending state primary schools whose parents would not be able to afford our fees? "

> The Peter Beckwith Harrow Trust will pay the fees for seven years – two at a prep school, five at Harrow. The tests are in English, maths and intelligence. Details: 020 8944 1288. Eton offers four scholarships on a similar basis.

The parent–school relationship

Computer-generated reporting

" My wife, an experienced primary school teacher who prides herself on knowing her pupils, is being asked to adapt to a new system of computer-generated reports for parents. She has to select appropriate comments from a database of such trite phrases as 'Charlotte shows little interest in her local area but has some awareness of the world beyond' (geography) and 'She has made good use of the documentary evidence available, which in future will enable her to build upon her understanding' (history). Is this common? "

> It is becoming increasingly so, I am afraid, not least because such bland reporting chimes with the spirit of the times. However, parents complain that the judgments are incomprehensible and seem to bear little relationship to the child. My advice is for parents to send the print-out back.

" If only a small proportion of your readers act on the advice you gave parents last week to send back computer-generated reports, you will have done a gross disservice to a profession already over-worked and demoralised at the end of another stressful year of teaching. Shame on you. "

> The argument of many similar letters was that teachers have to write trite reports, and computers do it quicker. If true, it is surely time for a change. Parents are entitled to an accurate account of their children's

progress and should therefore send back all trite reports, however generated. Please, though, send me a copy first (confidentiality guaranteed).

" Your campaign against teachers' 'bland and trite' reports to parents ignores the fact that the content is effectively dictated by law. As teachers, we're required to record pupils' progress in each subject against the relevant national curriculum attainment targets – and nothing could be more trite or bland. If the reports seem meaningless, it's the Government's fault, not ours. "

This belief is widely held among teachers, but it is nonsense. The relevant law – the Education (Individual Pupils' Achievements) Regulations – requires schools to give "brief particulars of a pupil's progress" in each subject, highlighting strengths and weaknesses and indicating "targets for development". Teachers are also required to give an overall view of the child's academic progress, behaviour and contribution to the life of the school. In the case of those who have taken national tests at seven, 11 or 14, the report should include a "brief commentary" on what the results show about the child's progress in English, maths and science and how he or she is performing in relation to others in the school of the same age. That is all the regulations require. The official commentary that accompanies them emphasises that there is no need to record pupils' attainment against every national curriculum target. It says the method of reporting should "not be unwieldy or time consuming" and concludes: "Parents should be left in no doubt as to how their children are doing in all areas of school life." As things stand, parents have the worst of all worlds: unwieldy reports that tell them little about their children's progress.

The remedy lies with teachers, and resorting to "automated reports" – banks of empty, computer-generated statements – is not the answer.

(Editor's note: see the correspondence on pp 63–65.)

Unhelpful and unaccommodating

" My children's junior school has called a meeting for new parents at 2.30pm, when those who work cannot attend. The teachers also refuse to see us before school, insisting on appointments after 3.30pm. Isn't that unreasonable? "

Yes. I would be interested to know how common it is.

" I was astonished that you agreed last week with the working mother who thought it unreasonable that her child's teacher refused to see her before school. What do you think teachers are doing at that time – knitting in the staffroom? If parents are really committed to their children's education, they should take time off work to talk to their teachers after school. Isn't that what they have to do to see doctors, dentists, lawyers and bank managers? "

Many teachers and governors wrote in similar vein. They said teachers worked a long day, were under immense strain and felt parents treated them as slaves. Before school, they had work to prepare, photocopying to do, books to get out, displays to put up and pencils to sharpen. After school, they had to prepare lessons, do their marking, attend meetings, fill in forms and find time for their own children.

On the other hand, non-teaching parents – especially working single mothers – said they were glad to learn that they were not alone in finding teachers unhelpful and unaccommodating, and that they were often made to feel unwelcome and a nuisance.

Learning and behavioural difficulties

A depressingly common experience

" We're sure our son is doing badly at primary school because he's dyslexic, but we can't persuade his teachers to do anything about it. "

A recent survey by the British Dyslexia Association shows your experience is depressingly common. Schools are reluctant to identify dyslexia and rarely address its effects until the child has fallen as much as four years behind in reading age. As the BDA says, this amounts to an unacceptable tolerance of underachievement. It is no use waiting for help: you must pay a dyslexia-trained teacher to help your son overcome his difficulties. The BDA runs a national helpline: 0118 966 8271.

Confusion

" I've seen conflicting reports about the results of the Government's summer schools for poor readers: did they raise reading levels? "

Your confusion is understandable. Stephen Byers, the minister responsible for raising school standards, claimed that "at least half" of the 1,500 11-year-olds who attended "made reading progress of six months or more" during the three weeks the scheme lasted. If true, it would fully justify his plan to extend the initiative to 15,000 children next year.

However, the National Foundation for Educational Research, which was commissioned by the Department for Education to evaluate the summer schools, found "no evidence" that they had raised pupils' scores in national curriculum reading tests.

The best that can be said of the scheme, which cost £300 a pupil, is that the children enjoyed it. The rest is hype.

Bored to distraction

" My grandson, who is just four, has been threatened with expulsion after less than two months at his primary school. He is in the reception class with more than 30 other children, and his behaviour, which none of us condones, has caused major problems. I know I sound like a doting granny but he has a vocabulary way ahead of most of his contemporaries, knows his letters and numbers and has a wonderful imagination. His

school, though, says he is clumsy and is 'perhaps at the lowest level of autism'. What will happen to him?"

> The longer he stays there, the more unhappy, frustrated and angry he will become. He is probably bored to distraction and has expectations his teacher cannot possibly meet. He needs to be in a small class with lots of stimulus and attention.

Will he grow out of it?

" We think our eight-year-old son has all the symptoms of Attention Deficit Hyperactivity Disorder (ADHD). His teacher says his attention span is virtually nil, but our doctor and the health visitor are very dismissive. They say 'boys will be boys' and that 'he'll grow out of it'. We don't believe them. Can you help?"

> This is a difficult area. Inattentiveness is certainly regarded as one symptom of ADHD, along with hyperactivity and impulsive behaviour. However, there are disagreements over the definition of the condition, its diagnosis and treatment. The best starting point is *Understanding Attention Deficit Hyperactivity Disorder*, a booklet published by Mind, the mental health charity. It costs £1, plus an A5-sized envelope with a 40p stamp, from Mind Publications, 15–19 Broadway, Stratford, London E15 4BQ (020 8519 2122; www.mind.org.uk/).

Rules and discipline

What are they thinking of?

" As a temporary teacher in primary schools, I am sometimes shocked by how the children dress. I've seen five-year-olds in 'bovver' boots with leather jackets and seven-year-old girls in high heels and denim mini-skirts. Recently, I even saw a 10-year-old wearing a tight T-shirt, leaving her midriff exposed, with a long, straight skirt slit up to her knees and backless platform shoes. What are their parents thinking of? "

> What are their schools thinking of? Children allowed to turn up in such gear are in no state to learn; heads who permit it can have no concept of discipline.

Self-righteous meddling

" The head of my daughter's primary school has banned the children from bringing juice to school. In a letter to parents, she says they're only supposed to drink water during the day and has instructed the staff to inspect their lunch boxes. She says this 'follows the recommendations of the health service, ensuring that children's teeth are not covered with sticky, sugary or acidic liquids'. Is it any of her business whether I give my daughter juice to drink? "

> No. For the record, the school in question is St Michael's Church of England Primary in Highgate, north London. Similar examples of self-righteous meddling gratefully received.

Not enough time to eat

" Do you realise that most primary school children are going hungry because they are not given enough time to eat? Most schools do not permit a mid-morning snack, allow only about 20 minutes for eating at lunchtime and offer nothing in mid-afternoon. So children who may be as young as four – and who, before they start school, are fed several times a day because their stomachs are so small – have to manage all day on what they can cram in during one brief period. This is especially bad for those who are very active, burn a lot of energy and need frequent refuelling. Adults usually have at least a coffee during the morning but children are often restricted to a few sips at a water fountain and are quite likely to become dehydrated. Many mothers at my son's school are worried about this but the head seems indifferent. Don't you think more food more frequently might improve children's exam results? "

> Is my correspondent right to be concerned? I have a set of four attractively produced *Little Grey Rabbit* books by Alison Uttley for the most interesting reply.

" I share the concerns of the mother who wrote about primary school children having to go for long periods without food or drink. At the school where I help with reading, pupils aged four to seven are given nothing until 12.30pm, four-and-a-half hours after breakfast. In the lesson after playtime, the biscuit I offer as a prize to the child who wins a reading game is hotly contested though it's no bigger than a 10p coin. At break, I have even seen parents feeding their children

through the railings. When I started teaching, every pupil received a third of a pint of milk during the morning. Then Mrs Thatcher became education secretary and put a stop to it. Most parents could afford to pay for the milk but when a local company recently offered to organise this, the school was forced to refuse. I'm convinced the answer is free school milk for infants."

This letter wins the promised set of *Little Grey Rabbit* books by Alison Uttley. Another reader wrote to say that she was one of those who, in the Thirties, had begun the campaign for free school milk, adding that its reinstatement now, when dairy farmers are daily facing ruin, would be particularly apposite. Many readers believed that reversing the fall in blood sugar levels as the day wears on would help children concentrate, make them less fractious and improve their performance. A teacher whose school does offer pupils milk, biscuits and fruit in mid-morning concluded: "If you feed them, they can do anything. If you don't, you get tears and tantrums." Others noted how crisp and biscuit manufacturers had cashed in on children's hunger, and regretted that importers of fresh and dried fruit had not risen to the challenge. Some said their children, having had nothing to eat all morning, were allowed as little as 10 minutes for lunch.

My thanks to all who wrote. There is clearly something amiss here.

Literacy

The National Literacy Project

" *My six-year-old son's primary school is participating in the National Literacy Project. What does that mean in practical terms?* "

> In theory, it means the school will try harder to ensure all its pupils learn to read and write. The teachers will be re-trained, attainment targets will be set and monitored, and every class will have a daily "literacy hour". In practice, it may not make much difference, because the project is promoting exactly the same approach to teaching reading as the national curriculum did 10 years ago without any discernible improvement in standards.

The phonic method

" *I'm teaching my five-year-old to read by the phonic method, but I can't find suitable reading books. The shelves are full of picture books designed for children taught to read by learning the shape of words, instead of sounding them out as the Government now recommends. Any ideas?* "

> I can recommend a new series of phonic readers published by Bloomsbury Children's Books. Well written and illustrated with amusing line drawings, they use a "phonetically controlled" vocabulary that enables young readers to decode unfamiliar words instead of

having to guess. There are 12 titles, each £3.99.

" *I've been studying the national literacy strategy which is to be introduced into primary schools in September. Would you agree its expectations are unreasonably low? As a hobby, I teach five-year-olds reading and spelling. I don't get them to memorise words but to work them out by sounding out the letters. Although the literacy strategy calls for a 'strong and systematic emphasis on the teaching of phonics', it also includes about 200 words that are to be learnt by sight by the age of seven. My pupils can read most of them already. Is there any evidence that it is better for children to learn words such as 'up', 'can', 'must' and 'took' by sight rather than by sounding them out?* "

No – and it is a serious issue. The national literacy strategy is one of the Government's Big Ideas, backed by big resources. By prescribing phonics, it is meant to ensure every child learns to read by seven. But the approach laid down in termly lesson plans is half-hearted and confusing. Children are instructed to guess at words instead of sounding them out. The introduction of a structured literacy hour will undoubtedly help raise reading standards. However, fudging phonics instead of putting them first is a mistake we shall come to regret.

" *Your recent condemnation of the Oxford Reading Tree, the reading scheme used by 70 per cent of primary schools, seemed rather abrupt. Would you care to expand?* "

Sorry. The scheme prides itself on not adopting a single approach to reading, but "supporting the variety of strategies that teachers want to use". That means encouraging children to learn words by their shape and guess at those they don't know. Phonics – sounding-out words – plays only a marginal role. The approach has left about a third of children unable to read properly when they leave primary school.

Phonics revisited

" Our seven-year-old is still not reading properly. His teacher says there's no need to worry but we do. Any suggestions? "

You are right to be concerned. Children should be reading by their sixth birthday – as the excellent Mona McNee points out in her new book on teaching reading by the method known as phonics. "You do not need special training," she adds, "just common sense and the will to teach reading bit by bit, and not to allow guessing to play any part." Her claim that teaching reading is "simple and does not take long" is borne out by the experience of the many parents who used her first book, *Step by Step* [see p. 124]. The new version, *C-A-T=CAT*, which I recommend, costs £5.94 (including p&p) from Elliot Right Way Books, Kingswood Buildings, Brighton Road, Lower Kingswood, Tadworth, Surrey KT20 6TD. Phone 01737 832202.

Reading Reflex

" Some time ago, you wrote about an American method for teaching children reading called Phono-Graphix. Is it avail-

able here yet?"

The British edition of *Reading Reflex* by Carmen and Geoffrey McGuinness is published by Penguin at £24.99 (01832 733497). In the hands of committed parents and good teachers, it guarantees virtually 100 per cent success. I warmly recommend it.

Phonics again

" Could you suggest an alternative to the Oxford Reading Tree that I could use at home to teach my five-year-old to read? He is not making much progress at school and his teacher says it is quite acceptable for a child not to be able to read up to the age of eight or nine."

His teacher is wrong and in urgent need of retraining. Any normal child taught properly – by the method known as phonics – will be reading fluently at seven. Even the Oxford Reading Tree has bolted on some phonics to its look-and-guess approach. I strongly recommend *Reading Reflex* by Carmen and Geoffrey McGuinness. It is published by Penguin and costs £24.99.

" Knowing of your support for Phono-Graphix, the excellent phonics system for teaching children to read, I thought you'd be interested to know that I've adapted it for blind and visually impaired pupils."

Thank you. Brian Cooney, deputy head of Dorton

House, an independent special school in Sevenoaks, Kent (tel: 01732 592565), is happy to answer inquiries.

No mystery

" I'm a governor of a primary school where about 40 per cent of the children fail to reach the expected level in reading at the age of seven. Apart from voicing my dismay, is there anything practical I can do about it? "

You could start by asking the head and your fellow governors to join you in watching "Literacy Matters", the video published by Ofsted. It shows five excellent teachers in three primary schools, using a range of highly effective techniques to teach young children to read. The video should convince parents and teachers alike that there is no mystery about literacy – and no excuse for children not mastering it. Literacy Matters (£11.75 incl p&p), Euroview Management Services, PO Box 35, Wetherby LS23 7EX (01937 541010).

Writing

Poor handwriting

" Our 10-year-old's teachers tell us he's bright, but they continually complain about his poor handwriting – which is partly the result, they say, of his 'brain racing ahead of himself'. He loses marks if he writes untidily but often fails to complete the task when he writes more slowly. "

The problem probably lies in the way he forms and joins his letters, though it could stem from how he holds a pen. A book I recommend is Rosemary Sassoon's *Practical Guide to Children's Handwriting*, (Hodder & Stoughton; out of print, so check your public library).

" Worried about my six-year-old grandson's handwriting, I bought a copy of W H Smith's Handwriting Practice. *The letter formation it teaches seems awkward and stilted. Am I out of date – or is there something better? "*

I share your distaste for the W H Smith style. Far better is *Handwriting*, published by Hodder Home Learning at £2.99 (but currently out of print, so check your public library) and endorsed by the National Confederation of Parent Teacher Associations. The book presents a simple introduction to an attractive, grown-up hand.

What about writing?

" Judgements about primary schools always seem to focus on the proportion of 11-year-olds who reach the expected level in reading. What about writing? "

The quoted figure – 71 per cent last year – is of the proportion who reach or exceed the expected level in "English". The papers are marked out of 110: 50 for reading, 35 for writing, 20 for spelling, five for handwriting. The proportion reaching the expected level in reading was 78 per cent. In writing – a 45-minute test of comprehension and composition – it was only 54 per cent.

Even-handed

" My five-year-old son has difficulty writing because he can't decide which hand to use. He frequently swaps hands and sometimes mirror writes. Should I encourage him to use one hand rather than the other? "

Even-handedness is quite common. The dilemma is that, allowed to make up his own mind, your son may have insufficient practice with the hand he finally chooses. But if you make up his mind and choose the wrong hand, it will cause him much confusion. Dr Rosemary Sassoon, the handwriting expert, says you could have his eyes tested to discover whether he has a leading eye. If he has, hand should follow eye; if he hasn't, it is probably best to await developments. The mirror writing is quite natural in the circumstances.

No statutory force

" An exasperated question: when are children going to be taught the proper use of the apostrophe? "

The answer, thanks to the Government's new, 216-page grammar guide for teachers, is Year 4, Term 2. That is to say, between January and Easter of their fifth year in primary school, 650,000 children will be taught to "distinguish between the uses of the apostrophe for contraction and possession". Good news, no doubt, but it is also an indication of how regimented teaching – particularly of the Three Rs – has become since New Labour came to power. Of course, like the rest of the national literacy strategy, the "guidance" has no statutory force. In Ofsted's hands, though, it is a stick with which to beat schools that do not conform.

Teaching aids

Does it work?

" I saw an advertisement on the DT*'s education page last week for a new edition of a book called* Step by Step *that's claimed to enable teachers and parents to teach reading with no training. Do you know whether it works? And if so, why don't teachers use it? "*

The newspaper is not, of course, responsible for what advertisers say, but in this case I know the claim to be true. I have had letters from readers who have used the book successfully to teach their children to read in about 90 days. Few teachers will use it, partly because it is based on a method called phonics – sounding out letters – that they have been told to reject, and partly because it requires a formal style of teaching that is currently out of fashion, though the climate is changing. *Step by Step* costs £5, and is privately published by Mona McNee, 2 Keats Avenue, Whiston, Merseyside

L35 2XR. *(See also p. 119.)*
   (Editor's note: this was before the introduction of the National Literacy Project.)

Spice times table

" My eight-year-old daughter can recite all 10 of the songs on the Spice Girls' CD, but doesn't seem able to learn her tables. Are there any tapes that set them to catchy tunes? "

Sounds like a good idea. Can readers help?

" The eight-year-old you wrote about who knows the Spice Girls' songs by heart but can't remember her tables will find the tape she needs at the Early Learning Centre. "

Many readers made the same suggestion, but the best of the dozen tapes I listened to (no more please!) is "Tables Disco". Produced by two brothers in 1984, and re-recorded many times since, it has sold so well that they have retired from teaching. The musical backing is a mesmerising mix of rock and rap rhythms and the words are crystal clear (though one mother recalled that her son, asked by a teacher what four times four was, replied: "Four fours are 16, yeah!"). Ladybird's *Times Table* also uses rap and a heavy beat but I found the music distracting and the words often indistinct. By contrast, the Early Learning Centre's *Musical Times Table* is sung in the style of 'The Sound of Music' and struck me as off-puttingly twee. "Tables Disco" is available as a special offer to *Daily Telegraph* readers at £4.99 (including p&p)

from Sound Ideas, 117 Athelstan Road, Bitterne, Southampton SO19 4DG; phone 02380 333405. Be warned though: the school run will never be the same.

Gifted pupils

Unable to meet his needs

" *Our nine-year-old's teachers are concerned that they may not be able to meet his needs for the next two years – he is currently working at the same level as the 11-year-olds. They suggest we consider sending him to secondary school a year early. Is that a good idea?* "

Yes. It will be a lot easier for him to cope with being younger by a year than being bored for a year.

Investigate the possibilities

" *My eight-year-old son's teacher says she has 'run out of things to teach him'. Although he has just finished Year 3, he has apparently done Year 4's work and most of Year 5's. I find this rather alarming. We can't afford independent school fees. What's your advice?* "

You are right to be alarmed. Occasional classes for "gifted" children, even if they are available, are not always good enough. However, all good prep schools offer scholarships and you should investigate the possibilities without delay. Start with the Independent Schools Information Service (020 7798 1500; www.isis.org.uk/).

Intellectually stretched

" Our seven-year-old daughter is already a year ahead in her small but excellent village school. She has a reading age of 10 and is likely to complete the primary curriculum two years early. Obviously, we don't want her to mark time, but we would also like her to remain in her age group. What's the solution? "

> There is only one answer, though I know it angers many readers. The independent sector caters better for children such as your daughter, ensuring they are intellectually stretched in the company of their peers.

You should move him

" Felix, my once happy, eager six-year-old, has turned into a nervous, tearful child who says the only thing he enjoys about school is his lunch. The problem is that he's bright and his teacher can't cope (though there are only 23 in the class). The only positive comment in his report came from another teacher, who takes him for maths. She said: 'Felix works best when challenged.' Last week, his teacher read the class a story called Fidgety Felix about a boy who had to put his hands on his head to stop himself fidgeting. She then told Felix to do the same and the whole class screamed with laughter. Now he pleads every day to be sent to another school. What should I do? "

> I don't think you have any choice: you should move him. We know from Ofsted that many schools are bad at meeting the needs of the most able, but ex-

amples of teachers bullying their pupils are thankfully less common.

Musical development

" My husband and I aren't particularly musical, but we think our six-year-old is. Could you recommend a general introduction to music education that would help us guide his development?"

BBC *Music* Magazine has just published an excellent *Guide to Music Education* (£7.95). It starts with tips on how to spot potential, moves on to choosing an instrument and finding a teacher (Kodaly or Suzuki?), explains how you can help your son practise, describes the exam system and explores the pros and cons of specialist schools.

Extra-curricular lessons

Shame on the school

" My daughter's prep school is putting on two extra lessons a week in the run-up to next month's national curriculum tests for 11-year-olds, which means her school day will last from 8.30am to 5.30 pm. Is that a good idea?"

No. It rather suggests that the school is more interested in league tables than your daughter's education. However, parents will be divided, which presents you with an uncomfortable dilemma. Shame on the school.

They need all the help they can get

" You castigated a prep school last week for offering after-hours lessons to 11-year-olds who are about to take national curriculum tests. Were you unaware that the Government is giving primary schools £18 million to do the same for 'borderline' pupils? Would you agree that it, too, is more interested in massaging the figures than doing the best for children? "

> No, I think the cases are different. Virtually all fee-paying pupils reach at least the expected levels in literacy and numeracy. Nearly 40 per cent of state school pupils do not, and need all the help they can get.

An interim incentive

" My seven-year-old has started taking piano lessons and is working eagerly towards her grade one exams. However, they are still nearly a year away and I wondered whether there might be some interim incentive? "

> For just that reason, the Associated Board of the Royal Schools of Music has introduced a "Prep Test" in most instruments designed to be taken after about six months' tuition. There is no pass or fail, "just positive and helpful comments". For details, phone 020 7636 5400 or see the board's website at: www.abrsm.ac.uk/.

Home tutoring and support

I hate to see them let down

" We moved 18 months ago from an area with reasonably successful schools to one that has worryingly poor results. Our three children, aged nine, seven and five, are not being stretched at all. In class, anyone who finishes before the rest is allowed to play computer games or asked to run errands. The staff seem to have been turned into teaching machines, overloaded by demands. How can I gain access to the national curriculum so that I can work with my children at home? I'm not a pushy parent; it's just that I hate to see them let down. "

The Department for Education and Employment has produced what amount to national textbooks for primary school English and maths. The latter, the National Numeracy Strategy, is particularly impressive: masses of lucid instruction and plenty of examples to work through. Similarly, the National Literacy Strategy comes in six hefty modules covering every detail of the syllabus. Unfortunately, neither is available to parents, so you will have to borrow them (primary schools are entitled to 23 copies of the numeracy book, which is also available free to part-time and student teachers who phone 0845 6022260) and photocopy what you need. For science and IT, a good source of materials is the DfEE's "standards" website: www.standards.dfee.gov.uk/. Beware, though: your children may end up spending all their time running errands.

Secondary education

This section discusses, amongst other topics, Ofsted reports, GCSEs and the differences in educational development and achievement between genders.

Choice of school

What's the difference?

" As the mother of two young children, I've only just begun to take an interest in secondary education and I'm confused by the differences between grant-maintained, public and private schools. Talking to my friends, I find I'm not alone in my ignorance. "

Grant-maintained – soon to be re-classified as either foundation or aided – schools are funded by the Government and are free. Confusingly, public schools are private schools, now known as independent schools: they charge fees.

Appealing

" The secondary school I chose for my son has turned him down, but tells me I can appeal. How? "

Appealing for a School, a free pamphlet published by

the Advisory Centre for Education, sets out clearly the steps you should take. Write to: ACE, 22 Highbury Grove, London N5 2DQ (020 7354 8321).

Evidence

" Is there any evidence that pupils in grammar schools and secondary moderns do better than those in a comprehensive system? "

Yes. The Centre for Policy Studies has just published a pamphlet by John Marks showing that, in Northern Ireland (which has a selective system), 52 per cent of state school pupils pass five or more GCSEs at grades A–C, compared with 42 per cent in England.

Too intense

" Our grandson's parents are planning to send the boy to a comprehensive because they think the pressure on him at the local grammar school would be too intense. What's your view? "

If it is a good grammar school and he is capable of winning a place, it is reasonable to assume that he would cope. And, in responding to the greater intellectual challenge of the grammar school, he is likely to do better than at a comprehensive.

Finding a secondary school

" *We are about to move to York and have no idea how to start looking for a secondary school for our son. Please could you help?* "

> You need this year's performance tables for York, North Yorkshire and East Riding. To order them, call the Department for Education and Employment's publication line: 0845 602 2260.

" *Last week, you rightly advised parents who were moving to York to consult the DfEE's performance tables when choosing a school. Would you not also advise them to read the reports on Ofsted's website to obtain a fuller picture?* "

> Quite so. The address is: www.ofsted.gov.uk/. Alternatively, parents may ask the schools they are interested in for a copy of their report.

A childhood prolonged

" *I have two boys at a prep school, where they can stay until they are 13. Should I send them on to their independent senior school at 11, when most of the other pupils will be starting; or keep them where they are for another two years, as their prep school, not surprisingly, is recommending?* "

> The answer really depends on the boys. Many children bloom in their last two years in the smaller, familiar environment of a prep school, gaining in self-confi-

dence as they take on the status and responsibilities of seniors. In some ways, it is a childhood prolonged. Others, though, are ready to move on at 11 and respond better to the greater challenge of being with older children in a bigger school.

A touch unconventional

" Searching for a school for our 13-year-old twins, we recently visited St Bede's, in East Sussex. We were shown round by a bright, smartly dressed boy but many other pupils paid little attention to the uniform rules, some of the boys had rather long hair and one was wearing several earrings. Should we let such things put us off an otherwise interesting school? "

Such things can indicate a sloppily run school with poor standards and low expectations of the children. However, you need to delve deeper by talking to the staff and pupils and watching what goes on in the classroom. St Bede's is a touch unconventional but it is an excellent school.

You know him best

" We have just received a legacy and can afford to send our 12-year-old son, who is very bright, to an independent school. Should we choose a top boys' school, which will stand him in good stead later, or a lesser-known co-educational one, where we feel he will grow up more normally? "

Most children at single-sex schools, some of which do

have a special cachet, grow up quite normally. In purely academic terms, your son is likely to do better surrounded by his intellectual peers. However, you know him best and must judge where he will be happier. I hope, though, you will ask his opinion.

Where should we go?

" We have just sold our house and want to live in the West Country near the sea. The education of our two daughters, aged 12 and 13, is paramount. Where should we go? "

You should start with the Government's secondary school performance tables, available from the county halls of Truro, Exeter and Taunton or on the Internet at: www.dfee.gov.uk/perform.htm/.

A closed shop

" The Roman Catholic comprehensive to which we are hoping to send our daughter is regularly oversubscribed and urges applicants to make a second choice. Ours would be a local grammar school but the comprehensive – St Thomas More in Eltham, south east London – says it will disqualify our daughter if she takes the 11-plus. Does it have the right to do that? "

Yes, but it is a curious case. Gerry Murray, the head, says St Thomas More requires parents, who must be fully practising Catholics, to prove that their "first priority" is a Catholic education for their child – which it cannot be if their second choice is a non-Catholic school, selective or otherwise. St Thomas More is effectively operating a "closed shop" on behalf of another Catholic school in the area, which I find distasteful.

Not enough good schools

" *The secondary school where our very bright 10-year-old has been allocated a place next September has a dismal reputation and a poor exam record and has even been threatened with closure. How can we find a local school that will meet her needs and is not heavily oversubscribed?* "

This is the question every parent asks. The secondary school performance tables will be released by the Government (www.dfee.gov.uk/perform.htm/) and published in *The Daily Telegraph*. They will show every school's GCSE results for the past four years and this year's A-level results. However, there are not enough good schools so the best will almost certainly be oversubscribed.

Drama school: is there such a thing?

" *Our daughter, who has just started at a comprehensive, has always been interested in drama. Although it is a good school, opportunities for acting are limited and she asks repeatedly to go to a 'drama school'. Is there such a thing?* "

Drama school comes after A-levels. In the meantime, you might like to consider Stagecoach, which runs part-time theatre arts courses (acting, dancing and singing) in about 200 locations. For details, phone 01932 254333 or consult the website www.stagecoach.co.uk/. A list of drama schools is published by the Conference of Drama Schools. Phone 01603 702021, or consult the website: www.drama.ac.uk/.

" I am 13 and determined to become a successful actress. Could you tell me which are the best drama schools? "

I admire your commitment but would urge you to concentrate first on GCSE and A-levels. Acting is an arduous and exacting profession and most drama schools do not accept students under 18. The exceptions include the Italia Conti Academy (phone 020 7608 0044), which admits pupils at 10, and the Arts Educational School (020 8987 6600), which takes them at eight. Some drama schools, such as the Guildhall School of Music and Drama (020 7628 2571), run Saturday schools for children as young as five. Further details – including information about government scholarships – are available from the Conference of Drama Schools, 1 Stanley Avenue, Thorpe, Norwich NR7 0BE (01603 702021; www.drama.ac.uk/).

How should we present our case?

" In common with many parents at this time of year, we are planning to appeal against a secondary school's decision to refuse admission to our son. Where can we find help on how to present our case in the best possible way? "

Secondary education

For advice on "how to make a well reasoned case", read *Appealing for a School*, a pamphlet published by the admirable Advisory Centre for Education. It is available from ACE, 22 Highbury Grove, London N5 2DQ, or can be ordered on the centre's website at: www.ace-ed.org.uk/.

Would Eton be a millstone?

" We are interested in sending our sons to Eton because of the excellent education and facilities on offer. However, we're worried about labelling them for the rest of their lives and concerned that universities and future employers might be prejudiced against them. Would it be a millstone around their necks? "

It is true that an Etonian is always an Etonian and that his misdemeanours in life will attract disproportionate attention. There is, though, no evidence of university prejudice, and few schools are better at inculcating the "life skills" that employers say they want. I am sure Etonians learn how to carry millstones with dignity.

This felt like blackmail to us

" In our area of Kent, the choice of secondary school is between Norton Knatchbull, a grammar school, and Homewood, a comprehensive. During a recent parents' evening at our son's primary school we understood from the head of the comprehensive that he would not offer a place to a child who applied to the grammar school but then failed the 11-plus. It felt like blackmail to us and I'd welcome your comment. "

Kent County Council says it asks parents to state a preference for both a selective and a non-selective school and regards both as "first preferences". However, some non-selective schools – Homewood among them – interpret that as a first choice for a selective school and say they will give priority only to "genuine" first choices. As long as such schools state their admissions criteria openly, they can get away with daring parents to displease them, and KCC is powerless to intervene.

" The Kent parents who complained last week that they were being 'blackmailed' into choosing a comprehensive rather than a grammar school should count themselves lucky. Most parents in the county have to choose between a grammar school and a secondary modern. The truth is that your correspondents are being invited to choose between a selective system (including its down-side) and a comprehensive one. Why should they think they can have it both ways? "

It is a fair point. Thank you.

An excellent preparation

" My husband and I have full-time jobs and are thinking of sending our 11-year-old daughter to boarding school. But her grandparents and many of our friends are quite disapproving. How can we persuade them we're not being heartless? "

The newly formed Boarding Education Alliance would say your critics owe their ideas more to Tom Brown and St Trinian's than to modern-day reality. Boarding, it insists, is no longer about isolating children from family life, and is an excellent preparation for adulthood. The alliance, which represents nearly 200 schools, runs an information line: 0020 7798 1553.

What does it mean?

" My daughter has just received a letter from the Charles Dickens School, Broadstairs, Kent, informing her that her appeal against the school's refusal to admit her 13-year-old son has failed. The school says that to offer him a place 'would prejudice the provision of efficient education and the efficient use of resources'. It adds, for good measure, that the case for admitting him 'was not sufficient to outweigh the degree of prejudice that would be caused to the school'. This sounds so offensive, but what on earth does it mean? "

Leo Rule, clerk to the appeal committee, who signed the letter, was instantly apologetic. He said the school was full. Many children had to be turned away, otherwise it would not be able to cope. That is all that "prejudicing the provision of efficient education" means – it is a phrase required by law. He promised to consider enclosing a note in future to explain this.

The future of grammar schools

Abolishing grammar schools

" How real is the Government's threat to abolish grammar schools? "

At present, not very. The decision will be left to "local parents". They have not yet been defined but will probably be those whose children attend the primary and preparatory schools from which a grammar school recruits. At least 20 per cent will have to sign a petition saying they want a ballot on its future.

Whither the grammar school?

" I am confused about the Government's plans to allow parents to vote on the future of grammar schools. Please could you elucidate? "

In nine areas covering 89 grammar schools – Bexley, Buckinghamshire, Kent, Lincolnshire, Medway Towns, Slough, Southend, Torbay and Trafford – the electorate will comprise all parents of children under 16 attending state or independent schools. For the remaining 77 grammar schools, the electorate will be limited to the parents of children at "feeder" schools. In each case, 20 per cent of the electorate signing a petition will trigger a ballot, in which respondents will have to tick one of two statements: "I am in favour of the introduction of a non-selective system of education in local schools" or "I am in favour of allowing those local schools which select their pupils by academic ability to continue to do so". The result will be determined by a simple majority.

Secondary education

Who will have a vote?

" Is it true that, in the forthcoming ballots on grammar schools, parents of children at grammar schools will be denied a vote while those whose children are not at grammar schools will have a vote? "

> Partly. The vote on the future of 69 grammar schools will be restricted to parents of children attending "feeder" primary and prep schools. However, in the 10 local education authorities where at least 25 per cent of pupils attend a total of 94 grammar schools, all parents of children under 17 will have a vote.

Ofsted reports and league tables

The wrong way to raise standards

" At a parents' evening last year, we were all delighted to be told by the new headmistress of our daughter's grammar school that it was her intention to get the school into the top 10 per cent of the league table within five years. What she didn't tell us was that she was going to raise the hurdle for entry into the sixth form. Previously, it was four grade Cs at GCSE. Now, only those likely to get As and Bs at A-level are allowed to stay on. Our daughter, who got three Bs and four Cs at GCSE and wants to be a primary school teacher, was told to enrol for GNVQs at the local college. In fact, she's gone there to do A-levels, but her confidence has been badly shaken. Do you think the school acted fairly? "

No. It is plainly unjust to change the rules in mid-stream. At the very least, parents should have been told of the new requirements before their daughters embarked on GCSE and, preferably, before they enrolled at the school.

No options

" *Ramsgate, a Kent school, came bottom of this year's league table. My 12-year-old grandson may have no option but to go there next September because Kent and the Diocese of Southwark are planning to close Holy Cross School in neighbouring Broadstairs.* "

Two non-selective schools in Broadstairs attained significantly better results than either Ramsgate or Holy Cross: St George's and Charles Dickens. There are also two reputable grammar schools in the area: Dane Court and Chatham House. Ofsted found that Holy Cross was failing to give its pupils an acceptable standard of education.

Value-added tables

" *I keep reading about 'value-added' league tables. What form are they likely to take?* "

Scotland has introduced two kinds. One, known as a "relative rating", compares the results obtained within a school for each subject at both Standard and Higher grade. Bar charts enable parents (and teachers) to identify a school's strengths and weaknesses at a glance. The other compares the progress a school's pupils make from Standard to Higher grade with the average progress made by all Scottish pupils. The tables are published in addition to the "raw" results, and deserve to be copied in England and Wales.

An immoral practice

" The school at which I teach has recently admitted a 15-year-old boy who was expelled from another independent school a term before taking his eight GCSEs. Apparently, he had not been working as hard as they wanted and they excluded him before the official census date so that his results would not harm their league table position. Re-registering him for the exams is proving very difficult. I find it exasperating that an independent school can abandon a child so cynically. Have you come across such a case before?"

Yes, and I think it is immoral. I should very much like to hear of any other examples.

Do they really understand?

" I wonder if parents really understand your A-level league table of independent schools. This year, Framlingham College, of which I am head, came 245th – half way down your third division. But had I turned away the bottom 10 per cent of this year's A-level pupils – as I could have done without staff redundancies – our results would have soared, the school would have been firmly in the second division and you would have praised me for the transformation. Yet I would have

Ofsted reports and league tables

failed eight young men and women, of whom I am exceptionally proud. What do you say to that?"

I understand the point – as, I think, parents increasingly do. However, allowing every school to discount its bottom 10 per cent would simply produce another, almost identical, table.

The downward spiral

" Do you realise how league tables are wrecking good state schools? The ones published recently showed that the comprehensive where our daughter secured a string of A grades has seen the proportion of pupils who pass five GCSEs fall from 36 per cent to 26 per cent in four years. The reason for this is that, although it is a happy place, pledged to do its best for every child, parents now shun schools near the bottom of the tables. So while their numbers have fallen, popular schools are squeezing more children into temporary classrooms. They turn away those unlikely to shine and expel disruptive pupils, all of whom are bound to be admitted by schools lower in the table. And so the downward spiral continues. What parents really need to know about a school is how pupils of a given ability improve. Surely it should be possible to demonstrate that from next year, when those who take GCSEs will have been monitored by national tests since they were seven?"

I agree, but the Government says the problem is measuring what schools have done for children who arrive with high scores. In which case, why not confine the measure to those who arrive with average or below average scores? A school that does well by them is unlikely to be neglecting the rest. Meanwhile, the damage you describe can only increase.

Flouting the law

" The Ofsted report on my grandson's comprehensive says it is not complying with the law that requires all schools to hold a daily act of collective worship. Is this unusual? "

No. Although Ofsted does not always record the fact, about 80 per cent of secondary schools flout the law, some because they do not have a hall big enough to accommodate all the pupils but most because they do not have enough teachers with the conviction to lead an act of worship. If the law cannot be enforced, it ought to be changed. But no one seems to have the courage to tackle the issue.

Can we see a copy?

" We understand our daughter's independent school has recently been inspected. Are we entitled to see a copy of the report? "

Yes. If you ask, the school cannot refuse.

" You said recently that independent schools have to show parents their inspection reports. Why, then, are we not allowed to see the report of last year's inspection by Surrey County Council's social services department of St Dominic's, an independent special school in Godalming? "

Social services departments inspect schools' boarding provision. The Government, alas, does not require councils to publish the reports. Surrey says the schools are free to do so themselves. The chairman of governors at St Dominic's has refused. Parents of potential pupils will draw their own conclusions.

Education/school policy

Mixed-ability teaching

" As the mother of a pupil at Islington Green School, north London, where the head has decided to scrap mixed-ability teaching, I have received a letter from the secretary of the local branch of the National Union of Teachers claiming there is nothing wrong with this kind of teaching and that the 'vast majority' of teachers are opposed to grouping pupils by ability. Is that true? "

No. The ineffectiveness of mixed-ability teaching at Islington Green was severely criticised recently by Ofsted inspectors. To his credit, Tony Garwood, the head, has decided to abolish it. Even by the NUT's standards, Deirdre Murphy, the branch secretary, is a radical left-winger. Pay her no attention.

Education standards

The minimum foundation

" Why is everyone so gloomy about education? As a measure of solid academic achievement, didn't 45 per cent of pupils

pass five or more GCSE grades A–C last year, and isn't that nearly twice as many as 15 years ago?"

But is it really a measure of solid academic achievement? Look more closely and you find that the proportion gaining grades A–C in English, maths, science and a modern foreign language – the minimum foundation, surely, of a sound education – was just 25.5 per cent.

No books

" At the end of her first year in secondary school, our daughter has yet to bring home a textbook. Is this a record?"

Far from it. A recent survey of secondary school pupils found that more than half had to share books in class and nearly two-thirds were unable to use them for homework. On average, textbook spending works out at £19 a year per pupil – about a third of what is required. Chris Woodhead, Her Majesty's Chief Inspector of Schools, says the shortage threatens the delivery of the national curriculum and forces teachers to waste time compiling inadequate substitutes.

Making allowances

" My grand-daughter, who is taking GCSEs next year, is worried she'll fail maths because her teacher is 'so bad'. Her mother can't afford private coaching. What would you suggest?"

Her mother should ask the head to move your granddaughter to another maths class, without making any accusations against the teacher. Pupils and teachers often don't get on and a good head will make allowances.

Not held back

" Our daughter, who has done extremely well at primary school, starts at a comprehensive this week with 180 other children. How can we help ensure she isn't held back? "

This year, every secondary school has been sent details of all new pupils' scores in reading, spelling, maths and mental arithmetic. They are derived from last May's national curriculum tests and have been "age standardised" to show every child's performance in relation to that of all others born in the same month. Teachers, therefore, will have a clearer picture of their first-year pupils' attainments. There are two things you can do: ask the school for your daughter's standardised scores (if they refuse, I would like to know) and keep a close eye on her homework.

Appalling handwriting ...

" My 10-year-old, who sits the 11-plus in October, has appalling handwriting – not much better than a six-year-old's. What can I do? "

Most of the handwriting guides on the market are aimed at teachers and are likely to tell you more about the subject than you want to know. However, I recommend *Helping with Handwriting* by Rosemary Sassoon (John Murray, £9.99; currently out of print, so check your local library).

... and spelling

" While coaching our son for his 11-plus exams, we found his spelling at a level that could only be described as remedial. Are there any books or CD-Roms to help him overcome his handicap? "

There are many. I would very much like to hear from readers about any they have found particularly effective.

Let down by his spelling

" My son, who will take his GCSEs next year, works hard and has made good progress but is let down by his spelling. We try, without much success, to encourage him to read and we doubt that he would take to learning lists of words from a dictionary. Can you suggest an alternative? "

Learning spelling lists that group similar words together makes more sense, and there are many such aids on the market. Perhaps readers who have been down this road recently could recommend the best approach.

" The answer to the reader who wrote recently about his teenage son being let down by his spelling is to go back to ba-

sics. Just like a sportsman who develops faults in his golf swing or tennis service, the boy must start again at the beginning, making sure he fully understands what he's trying to do. "

This advice coincides with the approach taken by a series of three books recommended by an astonishing number of readers. Called *English Basics*, it is a complete course in the mechanics of the language: spelling, punctuation and grammar. Each book consists of 30 units divided into questions, explanations and tests. The text is admirably clear and concise and will help anyone – child or adult – who works through it to write correct, plain English. The books, by Mark Cholij, are published by Cambridge University Press. At £3.95 each, they are excellent value. Thanks to everyone who drew my attention to them.

New status

" *My nine-year-old son is two years ahead in maths and plays chess at county level. Although the secondary school we are planning to send him to has recently been designated a technology college, its GCSE results make depressing reading. What can we expect from its new status?* "

It will mean more money for buildings, equipment and enhanced teachers' pay – which may lead to better teaching and results. As an alternative, you could enter him for a scholarship at an independent school.

Where is that sense of wonder?

" I am really interested in science, but our lessons are so boring. Our teacher says they're what we have to learn for GCSE. What do you think? "

> I am afraid your teacher is right. A report just published by King's College, London, with the backing of Sir Robert May, the Government's chief scientific adviser, says pupils are being turned off science by having to learn too many facts, which makes the subject "dull and uninspiring". They say half your science lessons ought to be devoted to explanatory stories about the "big ideas" of science to develop your "sense of wonder and curiosity about the natural world". However, the curriculum has been changed so often recently that I doubt whether their recommendations will be implemented.

Demand more

" My 14-year-old son is in the top third of his class at our local grammar school. He seems happy but, judging from his homework, I don't think he is achieving his full potential. I am sure other mothers must have similar worries. Do you have any suggestions? "

> Coasting schools and complacent teachers are a national problem. Any grammar school where all the pupils do not pass at least eight GCSEs at grades A to C is not doing its job properly, and the same is true if less than 50 per cent of its A-levels are graded A or B.

Given a similar intake, independent schools generally outperform state schools because they expect more of their pupils and make them work harder. The partnership with parents that schools like to boast about is too often left to parents to enforce. However, the best advice I can offer you is to join with others and demand more for your children.

Examinations – particularly GCSEs

Revision guides

" Exam panic is mounting in our household and the shelves of our local W H Smith are lined with a bewildering array of guides. Which do you recommend? "

I am impressed by the new Collins *Study & Revision Guides*, in English, maths and science, for Key Stage 3 tests and GCSE. I doubt many 14-year-olds will have the motivation to work through the Key Stage 3 books; however, parents (and grandparents) interested in what secondary school pupils are learning now will hardly be able to resist being drawn in. The GCSE guides, available also for French, German, history and geography, seem dauntingly detailed. But they cover every syllabus and nothing of substance has been left out.

Less ambitious is the Letts *Revise GCSE in a Week* series, available in most subjects and designed to "help you achieve a grade C pass".

A national benchmark

" *The fact that 45 per cent of pupils in state and independent schools pass at least five GCSEs with grades A–C has come to be regarded as a national benchmark. The five subjects that seem to me to matter most are English, maths, science, French and either history or geography. What proportion pass those?* "

In state schools, 13 per cent; in independent schools, 53 per cent.

What has changed?

" *When this year's GCSE results are published, we'll no doubt hear a lot more about grade inflation. Assuming O-levels were the 'gold standard', what has changed since they were abolished?* "

In 1987, the last year of O-levels, 26.4 per cent of pupils achieved five or more grades A to C; 27.2 per cent of girls and 25.6 per cent of boys – a gap in favour of girls of 1.6 per cent. Last year, the proportion achieving five or more GCSEs at grades A to C (which the Government said was equivalent to an O-level pass) was 46.3 per cent; 51.5 per cent of girls and 41.3 per cent of boys – a gap of 10.2 per cent. So the pass rate rose by 75 per cent while the gap between girls and boys increased by a factor of six.

Failures, surely?

" Why do you only count GCSE grades A to C? What about D, E, F and G? "

Grade E represents a mark of around 40 per cent; F about 35 per cent and G about 30 per cent – a failure, surely, in anyone's language?

" You claimed recently that the lower GCSE grades were a 'failure in anyone's language'. That is incorrect. The award of a grade means the necessary standard has been attained. Why do you keep writing off pupils as failures? "

Unlike the many teachers who wrote in similar vein, I do not regard pupils who fail exams as "failures". However, marks of 35 per cent (grade F) and 30 per cent (grade G) do not represent a pass anywhere outside the school gates.

What is expected of examiners

" Readers who are concerned about the mistakes exam boards make in marking GCSE and A-level papers may be interested to know what is expected of those who do the marking. This year, the Oxford and Cambridge board (OCR) gave me two weeks, from June 25 to July 9, to mark 400 scripts for GCSE combined science. Yet, like most examiners, I teach full time. Who, I wonder, would want their work marked in such circumstances, or trust the outcome? "

OCR said that it, too, was under time pressure: schools wanted the exams to be as late as possible, and science was by no means the last subject taken. Yet the results were not published until August 19, which means the board gave itself a generous six weeks for administration. My correspondent sent his scripts back unmarked.

Best "crammers"

" Our younger son has performed disastrously in his mock GCSEs and won't be admitted to his independent school's sixth form unless he achieves at least five grades A to C. Which are the best 'crammers'? "

The following tutorial colleges are all members of the Council for Independent Further Education and entered their pupils last year for at least 20 A-levels. They are ranked according to their average grade improvement, beginning with the best: Albany, London; Cambridge Centre for VIth Form Studies, Cambridge; Tuition Centre, London; Abbey, Cambridge; Rochester Tutors, Rochester; MPW, London; Cambridge Tutors, Croydon; Ashbourne VIth Form, London; Abbey, London; Modes, Oxford; Abbey, Birmingham; Bellerby's, Hove; Davies, Laing & Dick, London; Duff Mill VIth Form, London; Collingham, London; MPW, Cambridge; MPW, Birmingham; MPW, Bristol; Surrey College, Guildford; Harrogate Tutorial, Harrogate; and Exeter Tutorial, Exeter. The average improvement ranged from 2.11 grades at Albany, London to 1.10 at Exeter Tutorial.

Revision guides are not a substitute

" GCSE revision proceeds apace in our household, yet scarcely a book has been opened. My son and his friends seem to rely exclusively on CD-Roms. Am I wrong to feel nervous? "

No, I don't think so. The problem, however, is not the CD-Roms (the interactivity of which most children find stimulating) but the exclusive reliance on revision guides, which is a recent phenomenon. They ought to be regarded as a prompt, not a substitute for textbooks.

Subject choices

Keep an open mind

" I am 14 and keen to pursue a career as a scientist in the field of space exploration, possibly even going into space myself one day. My school has very little information on this topic. What subjects and courses should I take? "

Clearly, maths and physics are central, but it is too soon to close all other doors. Study what interests you most, but do keep an open mind.

Only combined science is available

" Our 14-year-old daughter is considering her GCSE options. Her eventual aim is to study medicine, dentistry or veterinary science. I would have thought she would need to take physics, chemistry and biology as separate subjects, but her school of-

fers only 'combined' science. What do you advise?"

Alas, very few state schools now offer separate sciences. To have a chance of a place on such severely oversubscribed degree courses, your daughter will need 10 excellent GCSEs including two *As for dual-award science. The step up to A-level sciences will still be a big one, but manageable for an able pupil.

" Our daughter wanted to take science as three separate subjects for GCSE but her comprehensive offers only double science, which it insists is just as good. What do you think?"

It is not just as good, but timetable pressures have persuaded most state schools to abandon separate sciences. A-levels and degree courses have been "adjusted" accordingly.

Misguided

" Having encouraged my son to take geography for GCSE, I now greatly regret it. He has spent most of his time on a 'project' about how to expand tourism in our area, which has involved studying the numbers of bus stops and burger bars there are in Canterbury. He has done almost nothing about tectonics and volcanoes, rivers, oceans, vegetation or climate. How misguided it is. He is really bored by the subject now. Please warn other parents."

Thank you. Parents tend to regard GCSE "options" evenings as rather a formality. Here is an excellent reason for asking to be taken through the syllabus before making any decisions.

Gender differences

The gender gap: a national problem?

" My 13-year-old son and his friends seem to be doing so much worse at school now than the girls of their age. If it's puberty, I guess it's a national problem? "

> I don't think puberty is a sufficient explanation but the gap between the performance of girls and boys is certainly widest at 14. In last year's national curriculum tests, the proportion of girls who reached at least Level 5 in English – the attainment expected of a 14-year-old – was 67 per cent; for boys, it was 48 per cent. But take heart. At A-level, the gap in the proportions attaining A and B grades was much narrower: 33 per cent of girls, 32 per cent of boys.

" Are there any subjects at GCSE or A-level in which boys now do better than girls? "

> Very few. At GCSE this year, the only major subject in which boys out-performed girls was geography. In the 12 biggest A-level subjects, boys did better only in history, French and general studies. Overall, 37 per cent of girls gained at least one A-level, compared with 30 per cent of boys. The gulf was even wider at GCSE, where the proportion of girls gaining at least five grades

A–C was 50 per cent, compared with 40.5 per cent of boys.

In the four subjects that really matter – English, maths, science and a modern language – 30 per cent of girls gained at least a grade C, compared with a dismal 21 per cent of boys.

Feminisation of schools

" Why do you think girls – as you reported recently – are doing so much better than boys at GCSE and A-level? It hasn't always been so, has it? "

The shift started in 1988 with the introduction of GCSE. Its emphasis on coursework and continuous assessment rewards diligence, which seems to favour girls. But I think the wider explanation is the increasing feminisation of schools. It leads to an ethos in which the aggressive instincts of adolescent boys are frowned on, and their self-esteem undermined.

Interestingly, 80 per cent of pupils categorised as having "emotional and behavioural difficulties" are boys.

The gender gap: another perspective

" I enclose a copy of a GCSE physics question. I think it is an example of the bias against boys that currently pervades the education system and that goes a long way towards explaining why they do so much worse than girls. What do you think? "

Gender differences

The question, from the Midlands Examining Group, is presented in the form of a comic strip showing "Tom and Mary watching a group of people protesting about the storage of waste plutonium near their homes". Tom says: "This plutonium stuff is not so bad. It only emits alpha particles. They are nothing like as dangerous as gamma rays, Mary." Mary replies: "But Tom, if it is buried it could eventually get into our supplies of drinking water. Then it would be dangerous." Tom says: "Don't worry. It will take years for that to happen." Mary: "Even then it will still be dangerous because" and candidates have to provide the answer. Clearly, Tom is dim or callous, or both, while Mary is well informed and caring. Do readers have other examples of such "pervasive bias"?

" I was interested in last week's item about the bias against boys in textbooks and exam papers. However, the problem goes a lot further. In most of the television that children watch, you would be hard pressed to find a man who isn't presented as useless, irrelevant or stupid. 'One Foot in the Grave', 'Men Behaving Badly' and 'Two Point Four Children' are typical examples. The women are invariably sensible, taking the lead and making decisions. Even cross-dressing men – Dame Edna Everedge, Lily Savage, Danny La Rue – portray strong, sharp-witted women who make mincemeat of dim, ineffectual males. Schools programmes, such as the BBC's 'Cats' Eyes', are cast in the same mould: the female is organised and knows all the answers, while the male is an unshaven, scruffy buffoon. Isn't this rather unhealthy? Where are the role models for boys? "

Many people – nearly all of them mothers – wrote in similar vein. Others, such as the classroom assistant below, focused on the "political correctness" of the books children are given.

" *The reading scheme we use, Fuzzbuzz, is full of positive female images, including a stunt-girl and a kindly, active grandmother. Males are represented by a hard-hearted pirate, a fey busker, an old buffer of a lollipop man and a court jester – nothing much for a boy to relate to. The result is that even the lowest achieving girls seem confident about their roles in life, whereas boys are given the idea, in many subtle ways, that they are surplus to requirements. Isn't it time educational material bolstered their self-image?* "

Are readers, I wonder, being over-sensitive? Are there really no examples of females being portrayed as irrelevant or stupid and boys as capable and commanding?

" *Further to your recent correspondence about the bias against boys, can I suggest Roald Dahl's* Charlie and the Chocolate Factory *as an antidote? I am sure my sons love it because Charlie is a hero and the girls are awful.* "

Possibly – but many girls are charmed by it, too.

Gender revisited

" *Nine photographs illustrated your recent independent schools review. Seven were of girls (showing 26 girls in all) and two were of buildings. Is there any wonder boys feel marginalised?* "

You are absolutely right. I apologise and will do what I can to prevent it happening again.

Learning to deal with girls

" Our friends tell us we should send our son to a co-educational school so that he will learn to deal with girls. What do you think of the reasoning? "

I don't think I can do better than quote Jonty Driver, head of Wellington College. In the current issue of *Conference & Common Room*, the journal of the Headmasters' and Headmistresses' Conference, he writes: "Attitudes to the opposite sex are determined infinitely more by someone's personality, family and upbringing than by anything to do with school. Some youngsters will be best off – and perhaps happier – if they stay in single sex schools until they go to university. Some should go to co-educational schools as soon as possible. Some should start in one system and change to another at 16-plus."

Sit them next to girls

" Wouldn't the best way of encouraging boys to work harder at school be to sit them next to girls? "

John Hartley, head of Notley High School in Braintree, Essex, certainly thinks so. He introduced the arrangement with two year-groups last September and the results have been so encouraging that he is planning to extend it.

"Boys," he says, "tend to be risk-takers, better at speculating and thinking obliquely. Girls stay longer at their task and are better at sorting information, analysing it and writing it down."

Both sets of skills, it seems, are catching. However, other co-educational schools have found that the performance of boys improves when they are segregated from girls.

Gender again

" The widening gap between the proportions of girls and boys who pass GCSEs at grades A to C is disturbing. Do girls do better in every subject, and is the gap as wide in every subject? "

No. This year [1998], boys did marginally better than girls in geography, PE, business studies, IT and separate sciences. Girls' superiority was greatest in English literature (by 59 per cent to 42 per cent), English (61 per cent to 45 per cent) and modern languages (47 per cent to 31 per cent). It was least marked in maths (two per cent), history (three per cent) and double-award science (four per cent). Overall, the proportions who passed English, maths, science and a modern language – the foundation of a decent education – were 34 per cent of girls and a mere 24 per cent of boys. Those are the figures that really matter, not the ever-increasing proportion (currently 47.8 per cent) who pass a disparate medley of "five or more GCSEs".

" Is the difference in the GCSE performance of girls and boys

as great in the independent sector as it is in state schools?"

No. In state schools, the gap in the proportion of girls and boys achieving at least five GCSEs at grades A to C is 11.1 percentage points (51 per cent of girls, 39.9 per cent of boys). In the independent sector it narrows to 6.8 points (84.5 per cent of girls, 77.7 per cent of boys).

Gender gap: a ceiling effect?

" Is the gap between girls' and boys' achievements at GCSE the same at all levels of ability and in all types of schools?"

No. The gap is widest among the least academically able. This year's [2000] figures for the proportions passing at least five GCSEs at grades A to C showed that the gap was 12.5 percentage points at secondary modern schools (girls, 40.5 per cent; boys, 28 per cent); 10.7 points at comprehensives (girls, 51.5 per cent; boys, 40.8 per cent); and only 1.5 points at grammar schools (girls, 97.5 per cent; boys, 96 per cent). Perhaps there is a ceiling effect? In the independent sector, the gap was 6.7 percentage points (girls, 84.6 per cent; boys, 77.9 per cent). Incidentally, the proportions who passed English, maths, dual-award science and a modern language – the true measure of five-subject GCSE achievement – were 35 per cent of girls and 25 per cent of boys, or 30 per cent overall. That is significantly lower than the 49 per cent the Government likes to trumpet, which represents a rather less testing collection of subjects.

The parent–school relationship

Independent philosophy

" The report we've just had from our daughter's independent school contains boxes for her end-of-term class positions in each subject, but they're left blank. Only percentages are given, which are rather meaningless. When I protested, the headmistress said teachers now believed that girls shouldn't be measured against the progress of others and that, while it was pleasant to come second out of 19, it was depressing to be 19th out of 19. Is this the new philosophy of the independent sector? "

> It is increasingly common. Only the most rigorously academic or determinedly traditional schools now publish form orders. Yet the pupils whose feelings are supposedly being spared still tend to know exactly where they stand.

Teaching approaches

Left to her own devices

" The Royal School, Haslemere, where my daughter is a boarder, seems to have abandoned her now that she has finished her GCSE exams. Apart from five days' work experience, she's been left to her own devices for the last two-and-a-half weeks of term – even though we've paid for tuition and boarding. I've brought her home because she was so bored. Isn't it a bit of a rip-off? "

Yes, and not uncommon in the independent sector. Jacqueline Kingsley, the acting head, explained that the period after GCSE was "not prime teaching time" because it was hard to get the girls to concentrate and, anyway, their teachers were busy marking internal exams and writing reports. In which case, why not discharge the pupils and remit the fees?

Which approach is correct?

" My daughter, who will be taking her GCSEs in the summer, has just had a change of English teacher. The previous one encouraged the class to express definite opinions in their essays and not to sit on the fence. However, the new one says they should present a balanced view and marks down those who put forward their own opinions. The pupils are now thoroughly confused. Which approach is correct? "

The examiners are interested in what candidates know. So it is the evidence they put forward in support of their opinions, balanced or otherwise, that counts.

Syllabuses

" I am not impressed with the way my grand-daughter is being taught GCSE – especially maths, physics, chemistry, English and history. Where can I get hold of the teaching syllabuses? "

It has never been easier – but you will have to go on-line. The entire national curriculum is at www.nc.uk.net/. Even more useful are the detailed "schemes of work" at www.standards.dfee.gov.uk/schemes/. Also, either site will lead you to the appropriate exam board's syllabuses (now known as "specifications"). Parents of primary school children keen to brush up on topics as diverse as electricity and the Romans will find help at www.parents.dfee.gov.uk/discover/.

Comic-strip reading

" Our 12-year-old son comes from a literate – indeed, book-lined – home but we can't get him to read a thing. Any suggestions? "

Yes: an excellent new fiction series called Graffix, which claims to be an innovation in children's publishing. The books (paperback, £3.99; hardback £7.99) combine well-written stories by established authors with a comic-strip presentation. Narrative passages link dramatically drawn illustrations, in which direct speech appears in bubbles rather than in inverted commas – ideal for older "reluctant readers", especially boys. I defy your son to pick up The *Listener* by Elizabeth Laird, for example, and not read it through to the end. Graffix: A & C Black, PO Box 19, St Neots, Cambridgeshire PE19 8FF (01480 212666).

Behavioural problems

Reinstated

" Back in the summer, I read about a girl who was expelled – quite unjustly, I thought – for criticising her school in the local paper. What happened subsequently? "

> She was reinstated. This week, the school – Queen Elizabeth's, in Mansfield, Notts – was judged by Her Majesty's Inspectors to be failing to give its pupils an acceptable standard of education. They said the head provided "poor leadership". She has resigned.

Why one group and not the other?

" Our son, who is 14 and attends a good local secondary school, has fallen in with a group of loutish boys in his year who go out drinking and causing mayhem. Would a change of school help, or is there another solution? "

> In most schools there are louts, and there are children who shun them. Although the proportion differs from school to school, the question is why your son has fallen in with one group rather than the other. Moving him, especially at this stage, is unlikely to provide the answer. He ought to talk to a professional counsellor.

Non-attendance

" It's becoming increasingly difficult to persuade my 13-year-

old son to go to school every day. He sometimes claims to be ill and often seems anxious and withdrawn. At the root of it, I'm sure, is the fact that his father and I were divorced recently. Where can I turn for advice?"

> David Philbrick and Kath Tansey, the authors of *School Refusal*, a booklet published by the National Association for Special Needs, say that at any one time the average secondary school can expect to have two or three pupils in a similar position, though the causes of anxiety vary. Others include bullying, family illness, bereavement or learning difficulties not being properly addressed. The booklet is aimed at teachers and social workers but offers parents a calm, clear introduction to the subject and advice on where to go for help. It is available from NASEN, Amber Business Village, Tamworth B77 4RP.

What help she needs

"My 12-year-old niece lives alone with her mother, who has many health problems. Recently, the child's behaviour has become quite shocking: she is defiant and abusive, has rejected school and mixes with troublemakers and truants. My husband and I feel she's an intelligent girl who needs love, understanding and firm discipline. We would welcome any suggestions you might have."

> Your niece needs, as a matter of urgency, to see a child psychologist – her GP will arrange it – to determine the type of help she requires. That could range from a small, mainstream boarding school to one

that specialises in children with emotional/behavioural difficulties. *The Gabbitas Guide to Schools for Special Needs* (Kogan Page, £15.99) is a comprehensive introduction to what is available.

Rules and discipline

Out of proportion, sport

" My 11-year-old son has been ordered by his teacher at Beverley Grammar School, East Yorkshire, to write out 'I must not make racist remarks' on two sides of a piece of paper. He was also threatened with suspension by the deputy head. His 'racist crime' was to say 'G'day sport' to an Australian classmate, who happens to be a friend. Do you think the punishment was reasonable? "

> No. Teasing – if that is what it was – can be hurtful, but the school's response does appear to be out of proportion to the offence.
>
> Anyway, the teacher should know that Australians are not a race.

Gifted pupils

A little gem

" I'm rapidly running out of problems for my maths-mad 12-year-old. Any suggestions? "

> "The result of XOXX followed by XOOX is OOXO.

Find the result of XXOX followed by OXOX." That little gem comes from *Maths Medicine*, one of the Science Museum's best-selling titles. It contains 92 such brain teasers, is linked to a website that explains the answers (www.mathsmed.co.uk/), and includes a guaranteed refund "if after three months you do not feel any better about mathematics". Both the secondary school and the junior editions can be ordered on the website or direct from Dexter Graphics, PO Box 24320, London SW17 7WQ. Warmly recommended.

" Parents of gifted children, including the father who wrote to you last week about his son being exceptionally good at maths, might like to know about the weekend courses and masterclasses we organise for the top 2 per cent of the ability range. "

The masterclasses focus on stretching the intellect, and they offer children a welcome opportunity to meet others of similar ability. The "Tomorrow's Achievers" initiative is run by Gabbitas, the educational consultants. Places are available for primary and secondary school children on weekend and Saturday courses from October onwards at venues in most parts of the country. Many are free, and means-tested grants are available for the rest. For details, call 020 7734 0161 or see the website: www.masterclasses.co.uk/.

" My 12-year-old son is exceptionally good at maths. His school is suggesting he should take GCSE two years early. Is that a good idea? "

Not according to a report to be published by the UK Mathematics Foundation. It says such acceleration can leave pupils with a fragile grasp of key ideas, as well as harming their long-term development. There is also the risk of creating a vacuum: what would your son do next? The point, the report argues, is to teach the syllabus in greater depth, not rush through it faster – a sobering message for the Government, which has made acceleration the basis of its gifted pupils' programme.

Home tutoring and extra help

Avoiding the bullies by home learning

" *A friend has decided to withdraw her 14-year-old son from school because he's being badly bullied. She plans to teach him GCSE English, maths, science and history at home. Can it be done and, if so, how should she go about it?* "

It is quite often done. GCSE exam boards will provide syllabuses and past papers, and revision guides are available. A sympathetic further education or sixth-form college will help meet the course work requirements. Phone Education Otherwise (0870 7300074) or contact the Home Education Advisory Service, PO Box 98, Welwyn Garden City, Herts AL8 6AN (www.heas.org.uk/).

(Editor's note: see the correspondence on pp 39–43.)

Vocational education and educational holidays

It's not taken seriously

" I was interested in the article last week about the need for vocational education in schools. Is its absence particularly marked in Britain and, if so, what evidence is there of the consequences? "

> Statistics published by the OECD show that the proportion of youngsters aged 16 to 19 who are not attending school and are not employed is higher in the United Kingdom than in 13 other member countries. At 19.4 per cent, it is more than three times the rate in France and four times the rate in Germany, both of which take vocational education seriously.

Exchange survival handbook

" With much trepidation, our 13-year-old is about to embark on his first foreign exchange. His French, quite frankly, isn't up to it. Can you recommend a survival pack? "

> Might he want to ask how to phone home, when to unpack and whether he could have a thinner duvet? Will he want to join in a game of Cluedo, offer to load the dishwasher, or tell his hosts he would be grateful if they talked really slowly? If so, *Your French Exchange*, a phrase book designed to take the angst out of the experience, could be the answer. Compiled by mothers who have sympathised with their own children's lin-

guistic predicament, the book is also available in German and Spanish (price, £9.99) from Yarker Publishing, 276 Banbury Road, Summertown, Oxford OX2 7ED (01993 824188).

Something useful

" Could you suggest something useful for our 11-year-old to do in the summer holidays? "

Active Training and Education (ATE) offers a selection of broadly educational and hugely enjoyable residential weeks in castles and country mansions for children who "like having fun with others and learning at the same time". Some courses specialise in maths, others in languages and singing; all offer games, acting, exploring and the experience of "learning to live together and be more tolerant". The courses, which are warmly endorsed by Estelle Morris, the schools minister, take place in August for children aged eight to 14. The cost, including full board and lodging, ranges from £165 for seven days to £270 for 10 days. Inquiries: 01684 562400.

The US–UK alliance

" Please would you remind your readers of our US–UK alliance essay competition for pupils aged 14 to 16. It offers the three winners a trip to Washington DC, including visits to the White House and Congress. The theme is the alliance between our two countries during the Second World War and its im-

pact on history. "

> The letter is from the American Embassy. For details of the competition, see: www.dfee.gov.uk/usalliance/.

Extra-curricular lessons

RSM/GCSE

" Our 13-year-old daughter has achieved Grade 6 in piano. How does that relate to GCSE or A-level? "

> The Associated Board of the Royal Schools of Music has obtained official equivalence for its qualifications in more than 30 instruments. Grades 1 to 3 are equal to GCSE grades D to G; Grades 4 and 5 correspond to GCSE grades A* to C; and Grades 6 to 8 are equivalent to A-level.

Finally ...

Sceptical

" Our son's independent school is asking us to pay £116 for a Morrisby Test to measure his aptitude for various careers. Is it worth it? "

> The test is widely used in the independent sector but I find heads increasingly sceptical of it. The test doesn't reveal much that a proper conversation would not.

Exchanging stereotypes for understanding

" Ours is a small grammar school in a charming town in the rural south of Germany anxious to set up an exchange with a British state school. Our 400 pupils aged 11 to 18 all learn English as their first foreign language and need an opportunity to go where it is spoken naturally. They also need a chance to replace mutual stereotypes (stiff upper lips, humourlessness, war reminiscences, towels on deck chairs) with understanding. The British Council hasn't been able to help us and we wondered if you could. "

The school, which is 20 miles south of Stuttgart, would prefer a partner in a small town, theirs having a population of only 20,000. It is also interested in exchanging e-mails, letters, video recordings, newspaper cuttings, school books etc. I shall be happy to put interested parties in touch with one another. It seems a particularly apt note on which to end the twentieth century.

A-level education and alternatives

This section includes how to interpret league tables, study abroad, choosing the right exam subjects for further education courses, and university entrance requirements.

Choice of learning institution

An appalling record

" Our son, who has just begun his A-levels, is in rebellion against his rather strict, academic school. He says he would work harder if he could join his friends at the City and Islington College, which is nearby. What do you think? "

> The rebellion is not unusual, but I would strongly urge you to avoid City and Islington College. Even by the standards of the further education sector, its record is appalling: last year, 75 per cent of its 13,000 students failed or dropped out, compared with a dismal 48 per cent nationally. The sector costs taxpayers more than £3 billion a year. The funding council responsible for distributing the cash (at a cost of £24 million a year) says complacently that "65 per cent of lessons are good or outstanding". You may need to consider a tutorial college.

Which college?

" As my family are moving to Suffolk, I need to find a college where I can take A-levels in physics, chemistry and maths. The two I've identified are Norwich City and Lowestoft. Which would be better? "

Last year, Lowestoft's 23 candidates had an average points score of 8.4 (where an A grade is 10 points, a B eight, a C six and so on), while Norwich City's 219 candidates had an average score of 10.7. I would recommend East Norfolk Sixth Form College in Great Yarmouth, where the average score of 208 candidates was 16.1. The average for the whole of England was 17.3.

College links

" I shall be taking GCSE next summer at a top grammar school and I hope to go to Oxford or Cambridge. My mother wants me to do my A-levels at my current school, while my father thinks I should accept a scholarship to an independent school, even though its results are not nearly as good as those of my present school. The independent school has better facilities and links with Oxbridge colleges. What do you advise? "

If you are happy where you are and doing well, you should stay there. Oxbridge entry can be a lottery, but the importance of college "links" is exaggerated. Read *How to get into Oxford and Cambridge* by Geoff Moggridge (£9.95).

Choice of learning institution

" I am the tutor for admissions at Balliol College, Oxford, and want to thank you for your answer last week in which you discouraged a student from moving from a grammar school with good results to an independent school with poorer results. You said the importance of links between schools and Oxbridge colleges was greatly exaggerated. I would say they have scarcely existed for 20 years. Please help us to kill off the idea that independent schools have some kind of back-door route into Oxbridge: they don't. Everything that applicants and their parents need to know about getting into Oxford is described in the university undergraduate prospectus. "

> The prospectus is available free from: Oxford Colleges Admissions Office, Wellington Square, Oxford OX1 2JD; phone 01865 270208.

Which FE college?

" My daughter, who takes GCSEs in May, is a keen sportswoman and would rather go to a further education college and take a vocational course in leisure and tourism than stay at school for A-levels. We have received a prospectus from the West Kent College at Tonbridge, which looks attractive, but wonder whether the colleges at Bexley or Bromley would be better? "

> The latest statistics show that the proportion of students who attained the qualifications they were working for was below the national average of 65 per cent at all three colleges you mention. I recommend Lewisham College, where the figure was 87 per cent.

A-level education and alternatives

Justly poor

" *My daughter wants to take a GNVQ in leisure and tourism at our local college, Cricklade, in Andover, Hants. However, I've heard that its reputation isn't good. Can you advise?* "

The college's reputation is justly poor. The Further Education Funding Council's inspectors recently condemned Cricklade for its weak governance and management (it is £1 million in debt) and persistently low standards (students have complained formally about the teaching).

As for leisure and tourism: "The provision lacks the vocational emphasis required for students to enter employment with confidence."

Correspondence courses

" *I am in the process of moving to France and wondered whether it would be possible to pursue my interest in art history at either A-level or degree level by correspondence?* "

I have not been able to find a correspondence degree in the subject but the National Extension College (01223 450200) offers it at A-level and the Open College of the Arts (01226 730495) has a video-based course, 'Understanding Western Art'.

No disadvantage

" *Our 15-year-old daughter is taking 10 GCSEs at a top girls' grammar school but wants to move to a co-educational sixth form college for A-levels. We would rather she stayed where she is but recognise that the college, which obtains good results, offers a half way house between school and university. We wonder, though, whether it would put her at a disadvantage when she applies to university."*

> Not at all – provided she keeps working hard. I applaud your willingness to respect her choice.

A-level by distance learning

"My son is keen to take an A-level in government and politics but his school doesn't offer it. Having achieved a master's degree by distance learning, I could help him study by that method but cannot find an organisation that offers the subject. Can you help?"

> The National Extension College offers more than 21 A-levels by distance learning, including government and political studies, which costs £295. NEC, The Michael Young Centre, Purbeck Road, Cambridge CB2 2HN (01223 450200; www.nec.ac.uk/).

Following his friends

"Instead of staying on in the school sixth form, my son says he wants to enrol at the Mid-Kent College of Higher and Further Education, where many of his friends go. Is that a good idea?"

Probably not. Last year, of the college's 4,000 full-time and 5,000 part-time students, 65 per cent of those who completed their courses failed to achieve a qualification. The average failure rate for colleges of this type is 35 per cent.

Comprehensive/Sixth-form college

" Do pupils have a better chance of gaining good A-level grades at a comprehensive or a sixth-form college? "

The proportion of A-level candidates from comprehensives who achieve at least three Bs is 20.2 per cent. At sixth-form colleges it is 23.8 per cent.

A grey area

" Is it legal for a state school to refuse a pupil permission to stay on and take A-levels? "

This is a grey area that is coming to increasing prominence as schools manoeuvre to improve their league table positions by turning away those thought unlikely to secure good grades. But if pupils want to take A-levels, what right have state-funded schools to exclude them? Schools' standard response is that the pupil is unlikely to benefit from the tuition provided. Challenging that would take an exceptionally determined parent – and I should be pleased to hear from any such.

Social and academic drawbacks

" My 15-year-old daughter is at a girls' school with a small sixth form and is keen for a change after GCSE. Are there social and academic drawbacks, as she suggests, to a small sixth form, and is there any harm in changing schools for A-levels? "

> Some see such an environment as cosy and supportive but others find it claustrophobic, and there may very well be a lack of intellectual stimulus and challenge. There is certainly no harm in a change, if that is what your daughter wants.

League tables

Nothing to prevent it

" With league tables coming round again, could you tell me what prevents an independent school keen to improve its ranking from refusing to enter pupils for A-levels in which they are not expected to gain good grades? "

> The Independent Schools Information Service requires member schools to explain any discrepancy between the census figure they declare in January and the number they enter for A-levels in May. So any school planning – dishonourably, in my view – to shed an inconvenient candidate would have to do so before the end of the first term in the upper sixth. There is nothing to prevent it, but at least it is out in the open, well ahead of the exams.

A-level education and alternatives

Shabby ...

" Our daughter, who is taking three A-levels at a partially selective state school, has failed one of her 'mock' exams. She gained an A* in the subject at GCSE, passed the internal exam last year and was predicted to achieve a B at A-level. In the mocks, she was let down by her draft coursework, which she wasn't told would account for 40 per cent of the marks. Yet the school has now refused to enter her for the A-level and told us that we may do so privately, at a cost of £32. We know of four other girls who are in the same position. Has the school the right to do this? Could it have anything to do with its league table position? "

> The school is Watford Girls', which came 11th in last year's table. Its regulations state: "A student in the upper sixth form who achieves grade U in any mock examination will not be entered at the school's expense for A-level examinations in that subject. The examination fee may, however, be paid privately." So it has the legal, if not the moral, right. The policy – a shabby one, in my view – has everything to do with its league table position: private entries do not count.

... and obnoxious

" Last week, you accused Watford Girls' – where I was head of science – of trying to protect its league table position by refusing to enter pupils for A-levels if they had done badly in their mocks. If that was the reason for the rule, it would indeed be a shabby practice. However, we introduced it be-

cause we thought public money ought not to be spent on pupils who, despite being given frequent warnings, had made little effort."

I find that reason even more obnoxious. Schools are not asked to decide which children are worth spending public money on.

Alternatives to A-levels

A-levels/Highers

"*The entry requirements of English and Welsh universities are framed in terms of A-level grades. Is there a conversion for Scottish Highers?*"

The generally accepted equivalence between Highers and A-levels is:
AAAAA=AAA;
AAAAB=AAB;
AAABB=ABB; AABB–ABBBB=BBB–BBC;
BBBBC=BCC; BBBCC–BCCC=CCC–CDD;
CCCC–CCC=DDD–DEE; CC=EEE–EE.

Aim for a distinction

"*I was sceptical when my son announced that he wanted to take an Advanced GNVQ in leisure and tourism, but I've been impressed by the work he's doing: it seems an adult and useful way of studying. How, though, does the qualification rate? Is it equivalent to two A-levels? He's also taking an A-*

level in geography. Will that be enough to secure a place at a decent university?"

> Although GNVQs had a dismal start, they are more highly regarded now. An Advanced GNVQ is equivalent to two A-levels – but your son should aim for a distinction if he wants to go to a good university.

" Our daughter is being pressed by her school to take an Advanced GNVQ in leisure and tourism, instead of A-levels. The school says universities regard the qualification as equivalent to A-levels. Do they?"

> I am afraid good universities are becoming sceptical, not least because of Ofsted's recent findings that nearly half the Advanced GNVQs awarded had been over-generously marked and graded under an assessment regime that will last at least until 2000. "The present quality assurance measures are not operating reliably," Ofsted said. None the less, an Advanced GNVQ may well suit your daughter's abilities and aptitudes better than A-levels. You should urge her to aim for a distinction.

GNVQ: no easy option

" Our son has started an Advanced GNVQ in information technology. What do universities think about GNVQs and what he can do to maximise his chances of being offered a place?"

Universities accept that Advanced General National Vocational Qualifications (absurd mouthful) are equivalent to two A-levels. However, to be sure of a place on a good course, your son needs to aim for a distinction, which is regarded as equivalent to an A and a B at A-level. A "merit" is equivalent to two Cs, and a "pass" to a D and an E. This year [1999], 5,800 pupils completed an Advanced GNVQ and just over 900 gained a distinction. However, more than half failed, so it is no easy option.

The International Baccalaureate

" The grammar school in Kent at which I am sitting my GCSEs is urging me to take the International Baccalaureate instead of A-levels. Although I do well in most subjects, I'm particularly interested in science. Does the IB cover the sciences as comprehensively as A-levels, and is it well received by universities? "

I am reluctant to discourage anyone who is academically able from doing the IB, which offers a broad and excellent sixth-form education. However, science teachers do say that the syllabus is a little long in the tooth, and some admissions tutors are depressingly ignorant of the qualification's virtues. Sevenoaks, the independent school in Kent, is a keen advocate of the IB and would be happy, I am sure, to offer you more detailed advice.

The Scholastic Aptitude Test

" I am very interested in your idea of introducing the Scholastic Aptitude Test (SAT) as a supplement to A-levels and GNVQs to give universities a more accurate understanding of applicants' abilities and help sixth-formers identify appropriate institutions. I am head of a comprehensive and would be happy to take part in any pilot study you may be planning. "

> Thank you. The campaign is beginning to win significant support. Baroness Blackstone, the Minister for Higher Education, has written to say that she regards the SAT as a simple, cost-effective way of measuring verbal and mathematical reasoning. She says she shares the aspiration of those who designed it that all students should have the opportunity to demonstrate their abilities regardless of income, class or social status, and supports the idea of a study. Peter Lampl, the millionaire philanthropist, has commissioned the National Foundation for Educational Research to design a pilot. Many schools – state and independent – have volunteered to take part, as have a number of Oxbridge colleges. Further expressions of interest would be welcome.

Is there a connection?

" I see that Sevenoaks School, which at 31st was the best performing co-educational school in your league table, offers the International Baccalaureate as an alternative to A-levels. Is there a connection, and if so, might other schools follow suit? "

Girls did better than boys in four of the six subjects that IB candidates take: English, French, economics and history. The boys did better in maths and physics. However, because pupils have to study both the arts and the sciences, the overall difference between the sexes was less marked than at A-level. On average, the 470 girls who took the IB in Britain scored 33 points out of a maximum of 45, while the 335 boys scored an average of 32.

Sevenoaks will be offering only the IB to pupils who join from now on. Other schools that had been tempted to follow suit are now less likely to do so, partly because the new A-level system that starts next week will make it easier for pupils to study complementary subjects, and partly because the "world class" tests that are to be introduced in two years' time will be based on A-level syllabuses.

Teaching standards

Breach of contract

" My daughter left grammar school a year ago to take A-levels in English, chemistry and biology at Newbury Further Education College in Berkshire. She signed a 'learning agreement' promising five hours of tuition a week in each subject for two years. Now she has been told that is being reduced to four-and-a-half hours and that first- and second-year students are to be taught together for half the time. Isn't that unacceptable and a breach of contract? "

It is – but I doubt the contract is enforceable. Gordon Bull, the principal, said Newbury, like all FE colleges, was under great financial pressure and could not afford small classes. Prospective students beware: most FE colleges have a poor A-level pass rate, and such measures can only worsen it.

Subject choices

Do they overlap?

" *My daughter has been advised not to take both English and theatre studies for A-level because universities think they overlap and regard them as one subject. Is that so?* "

A few universities do, but others see them as usefully complementary. Your daughter should do what most interests her.

A handicap later?

" *Our daughter is half way through GCSE and wants to become a solicitor or barrister. We think she should take A-level law but her school advises against it. Will this be a handicap later on?* "

No. Universities do not ask for it and some even prefer applicants not to offer it. To secure a place on a well-regarded course, your daughter will need good GCSEs and three high-grade A-levels. So she should study what she is best at and what interests her most.

No A-level course is irrelevant

" My daughter, who is taking 10 GCSEs at a top independent school, wants to go into journalism. However, her school does not offer media studies or even general studies at A-level. Apart from English, the subjects she would have to take seem quite irrelevant to her needs. Should I send her elsewhere for A-levels? "

> Certainly not. The best academic qualification for journalism is a good degree: the subject matters little. Similarly, if your daughter really wants to take media studies at university, it is her A-level grades that will matter, not the subjects. I do not believe any A-level course would be "irrelevant to her needs".

Science first, then economics or law

" Our 14-year-old son is determined to become an ornithologist. His strongest subjects are the sciences and he wants to go either to Cambridge (good birding in the Fens) or St Andrews. But what, pray, should he study? "

> If he wants to make an impact – or, indeed, a living – he should, according to our Environment Editor, take a degree in science followed by one in economics or law. Pressure groups are crying out for such expertise.

Which A-levels for med school?

" My daughter, who is taking her GCSEs in the summer,

A-level education and alternatives

is keen to study medicine but is having difficulty choosing her A-levels. She wants to take chemistry, biology and geography but we understand medical schools prefer maths and/or physics, neither of which she's particularly good at. She would be likely, though, to get an A in geography. What's your advice?"

Three A grades are pretty well essential. Chemistry is the only compulsory subject, and some medical schools are happy with an arts A-level. However, your daughter should check before applying.

Which A-levels for air traffic control?

" My son, who is taking his GCSEs this year, would like to be an air traffic controller but cannot find out which A-levels to take. Can you help?"

He will need at least five GCSEs at grade C or above – which must include English and maths – and two A-levels, subjects not specified. At the selection stage, he will have to demonstrate an ability to think logically and make decisions. A free CD-Rom offering a "dynamic" guide to being an air traffic controller is available from the recruitment services department at National Air Traffic Services, CAA House, London WC2B 6TE.

How much does it matter?

" Is it true that there has been a sharp fall recently in the

numbers of students taking French and German at A-level – and, if so, isn't it a matter of concern? "

It is true. Although total A-level entries have risen by 8 per cent since 1995, those for French have dropped by 24 per cent from 27,500 to 21,000 and for German by 10 per cent to 9,500. Spanish, however, is up by 17 per cent to 5,600.

How much it matters is harder to say. Consider, first, the subjects pupils are choosing instead. Over the same period, the most significant increases, ranked by size of take-up, have been in general studies, up 49 per cent to 85,000; maths, up 12.5 per cent to 70,000; business studies, up 41 per cent to 38,000; art and design, up 10 per cent to 37,000; and psychology, up 30 per cent to 29,000.

The proportion of university students studying languages has remained stable at around 6 per cent. In almost every survey of business opinion, the desirable skill ranked lowest by employers is proficiency in a foreign language.

Finally, the new A-level system to be introduced in September 2000, which is meant to encourage sixth-formers to take a wider range of subjects, might well lead to more studying a language for a further year. At GCSE, French has held its own, while the take-up of both German and Spanish has risen.

However, I should be interested to hear from readers who think my answer complacent.

" *We are modern language teachers at Rugby High School*

and were dismayed by your cool response to the sharp fall in the numbers taking French and German at A-level. In the appointments section of your own newspaper, you will find a range of jobs advertised requiring foreign language skills including law, engineering, sales, marketing and research. Learning a second language also introduces young people to another culture, makes travel more enjoyable, teaches them to communicate confidently and clearly and makes it easier to acquire other languages. The media should convey a more positive attitude to language learning."

This letter reflected the views of most who replied. However, a number of readers whose children had spent four years acquiring a language degree reported that employers were not interested in linguists. Michael Alpert, professor of languages at Westminster University, said he and his colleagues urgently needed to know how they could better equip their students for jobs. (Nationally, the graduate unemployment rate is highest among those with degrees in humanities, languages and biological sciences.) Some readers said their children saw no need to learn a European language ("all Europeans speak English anyway"), but would have liked to study Chinese or Japanese, which few schools offer. My thanks to all who wrote.

Choose according to your interest

" *We are GCSE students trying to choose our A-levels. Our school says those of us who are concentrating on the sciences should broaden our studies by picking a language as our fourth subject. Is it better to study an academically demanding language such as Latin, or one that is more relevant, such as French? And is it true that Oxbridge favours the former while employers prefer the latter?"*

> The answer to all your questions is no. You should study the language in which you are most interested, secure in the knowledge that that is likely to produce the best grade.

It's not true

" Our daughter, who is torn between music and medicine, is trying to make her A-level choices. She's being urged by her grammar school to include a one-year course in general studies because it 'meets new Government requirements'. Is that true?"

> No.

Maths is by far the hardest subject

" As someone who is about to take his A-level maths exams, I'd like to reinforce the views of the teachers who wrote last week about maths being too difficult. Although we have a brilliant maths teacher (thanks, Mr May), all my friends agree it is by far our hardest subject. Yet we weren't warned about that when we had to make our A-level choices at 15 and I, for one, fear I shall now lose my offer of a place to read law at King's, London, which requires two As and a B."

> Thank you. It will be no consolation, but from

September 2000, A-level pupils who choose maths (or any other subject) will have the option of giving it up after a year and receiving a credit, in the form of an AS-level, for what they have done.

A-levels for medicine

" I am planning to study medicine and trying to choose my A-levels. I understand all medical schools require chemistry, many ask for biology and some specify maths or physics. I'd like to include history but my father, who is a doctor, says that, although medical schools claim to accept an arts subject, they really favour those offering straight sciences. What would be your advice? "

Requirements do vary but you would maximise your chances in the medical lottery by concentrating on the sciences and maths. You might, though, risk an AS-level in history.

" The experiences of my daughter and her contemporaries suggest you were unnecessarily cautious in advising students intending to study medicine that they would maximise their chances of a place by confining themselves to maths and science A-levels. Third A-levels among students in her medical year include French, German, art, theatre studies, English literature and classical civilisation. Also, her (and her friends') interviews at other medical schools confirm that they are genuinely interested in breadth. "

Thank you. Many medical students wrote to say the same.

The syllabus

More challenging work, please

" The Telegraph *article by Martin Stephen, high master of Manchester Grammar, about bright first-year university students having to 'twiddle their thumbs' was absolutely right. My son, who has five grade As at A-level, is studying maths and economics at Sheffield and finds he's already covered most of the work. Is there anything he can do? "*

> Roy Wilkinson, professor of economics at Sheffield and an A-level examiner, readily acknowledged the problem. He said A-levels had become much easier. Universities were having to teach more students of a wider range of abilities with fewer resources. He saw no reason why schools should not teach first-year university modules to able pupils, who could then move on to more challenging work as long as they had taken the appropriate exams. "We admit students from Malaysia into our second year," he said. "Why not from Manchester?" Meanwhile, he will be happy to give your son something more stimulating to do.

Rewarding material

" I have just completed an A-level in French, 50 years after taking School Certificate French, and I was struck by how pervasive political correctness has become. The essays we were asked to write included: 'Explain how man is the cause of the destruction of his planet'; 'Suggest a plan of action to combat

the tobacco menace'; and 'Explain to a friend in France the objectives of the animal rights group to which you belong'. Why do contemporary issues have to be rammed down students' throats? Surely the history and culture of France would provide more rewarding material?"

They would. Thank you.

What is the point of the new A-levels?

" I do not understand the new A-levels being introduced in September. How will the system differ from the present one and what is the point of it?"

Each A-level will be split into two halves. The first (and easier) half will be taken at the end of the first year and is called an AS-level (or "Advanced Subsidiary"). Pupils will then have the option of continuing with the second half and gaining a full A-level. The Government says that the idea is to broaden A-level study. However, most pupils are expected to take just four subjects in the first year and continue with three in the second, which represents little change.

The Government, though, has a more radical agenda. It intends to introduce a new school-leaving certificate consisting of "modules" of A-levels, GNVQs (now renamed "vocational A-levels") and "key skills". This is the first, surreptitious stage in the process.

New-style A-levels: what do universities think?

" My daughter, who is in the first year of the sixth form, has just embarked on the new-style A-levels. What is universities' attitude to them likely to be? "

They all say they welcome the increased breadth of study, now that most pupils will be taking four AS subjects in their first year and three A2s thereafter. They also make polite noises about the "key skills" element – communication, teamworking, computing, etc. But don't expect that to affect the way they offer places. Although admissions tutors will take pupils' achievements at AS-level into account, offers will still be based on predicted A2 grades, most commonly in three subjects, and key skills will not be included. Spare a thought, too, for schools having to teach an extra subject in the lower sixth without any sign of the promised extra resources.

A-level syllabuses

" We would like to know more about the art and music A-levels our daughter is taking, but the national curriculum website you mentioned recently (www.nc.uk.net) doesn't seem to include A-level syllabuses. Can you help? "

The national curriculum ends at 16. You have to ask the exam boards for A-level syllabuses (now known as "specifications"), or you can download them from their websites. The three principal boards are: AQA, www.aqa.org.uk/, phone 01483 506 506; Edexcel, www.edexcel.org.uk/, phone 0870 240 9800; and OCR, www.ocr.org.uk/, phone 01223 553998.

Examinations and revision

Making the grade

" Stafford Grammar, an independent school where my son is shortly to take his A-levels, has told parents it will refuse to enter pupils who don't achieve acceptable grades in their mock exams. Isn't this another example of league-table manipulation? "

To be fair, the letter referred to "acceptable grades commensurate with ability". Michael James, the head, said that he had no intention of preventing those who were trying their best.

The limits of stress

" My friends and I have just taken A-level theatre studies and are extremely anxious about our results. Only the weekend before the first exam, we discovered that our teacher had muddled up the order in which the two papers were to be taken and the time allowed for each. As a result, we had less time to revise our set texts and only 50 minutes to write essays for which we thought we'd have an hour. Although the mistake could cost us grades and university places, our school has refused to tell the exam board what happened. Can anything be done? "

I am afraid not. Although clearly an unfortunate and unsettling experience, it is within the limits of stress with which all exam candidates are expected to cope.

Predicting the result

" Is it possible to say how well a child should do at A-levels on the basis of her GCSE score? "

Nationally, a B at GCSE produces a C at A-level.

Would it count against her?

" Our 17-year-old daughter is mildly dyslexic but refuses to apply for extra time when taking exams. She fears that if she admits to the condition it would count against her. Is she right? "

No. Please assure her that dyslexia has lost whatever stigma it had, and encourage her to apply for the relief to which she is legally entitled.

How to deal with exam stress

" Exam stress is mounting in our household. Have you any tips for dealing with it? "

I am indebted to Cambridge University's counselling service for the following advice. Beware of generating stress merely to impress others; doing the work takes less effort than thinking about doing it; be sure to keep your working and relaxation areas separate; revision plans need plenty of blank spaces to allow for the unexpected; divide the week into 21 units and aim to work for no more than 15 of them; plan rewards for yourself when you have achieved your (realistic) goals; stop working at least an hour before you intend to sleep; and arrive at the exam room comfortably in time but not too early.

For more wise advice see: www.counselling.cam.ac.uk/exams.htm/.

Home tutoring and extra study

Computer games

" Our son is struggling with A-level maths and physics and, in our view, spending far too much time playing computer games. Is there any way of combining the two? "

If readers know of any entertaining and effective revision programs on CD-Rom, I shall be happy to pass on the information.

A pleasant break

" I'm finding some of my first-year A-level work difficult to understand but my parents can't afford to send me on an Easter revision course. Is there anything on the Internet? "

Unfortunately, the BBC's Bitesize (www.bbc.co.uk/education/revision/), which is first class, goes only as far as GCSE and Standard Grade. However, you could try SAM Learning (www.samlearning.co.uk/). It offers key revision points in A-level maths, biology, chemistry and physics followed by multiple-choice questions with one-word drag-and-drop answers. The presentation is straightforward and the website, which also covers Key Stage 2 and nine GCSE subjects, makes a pleasant break from the real business of revising.

Summer courses to prepare for A-levels

" Do you know of any summer courses specifically designed to help children who have just completed their GCSEs to prepare for A-levels? "

I don't but, given the length of the holidays and the leap from GCSE to A-level, it is an excellent idea. If anyone has heard of such courses, please let me know.

Do ask for references

" My son needs help with his A-levels. How can I find a home tutor? "

The best place to look is your local paper but do ask for references. In London and the Home Counties, I can recommend Fleet Tutors (01252 812262). There is also a fledgling website: www.uktutors.com/.

" The advice you gave last week about how to find a home tutor could have been more helpful. Telling parents to look in

the local paper and ask for references is not giving them the reassurance they need. At least Yellow Pages visit the advertiser's premises and insist the address is published. Better still, the national agency I founded 10 years ago has 1,600 tutors on its books and is registered with the Department for Education and Employment. "

The letter is from Clive West, who runs Stepping Stones Tuition ("Any subject, any level, anywhere"), phone 01780 753102. The agency's extensive (and bracingly written) website is at: www.tuition.clara.co.uk/tuition/.

Improving handwriting

" *My son is expected to achieve good grades when he takes A-levels next summer, but his handwriting is terrible. His teachers constantly complain about it and we're worried the examiners will mark him down. What can we do to help him write legibly?* "

Rosemary Sassoon, the author of many sensible books on the subject, says the worst thing you can do is to nag, because it creates tension, which in turn leads to jagged and slower writing. Not getting the answers down is likely to lose your son far more marks than those the examiners are allowed to deduct for illegibility. And if they really cannot decipher a script, they will call in the candidate to read it. That said, Dr Sassoon's *Helping with Handwriting* (published by John Murray, £9.99, but currently out of print – check your local library) has an excellent section aimed at older children who want to improve their writing.

" I'm afraid the book you recommended recently to help children with handwriting difficulties is now out of print and unobtainable. Do you know of an alternative? "

Just published is *Teaching Handwriting – A Guide for Teachers and Parents* by Jean Alston and Jane Taylor. It offers 10 rules to "help to transform writing, so that it becomes something of which to be proud, rather than a subject of concern". The booklet, which is admirably lucid, costs £5 (incl p&p) from QEd Publications (to whom cheques should be made out), the ROM Building, Eastern Avenue, Lichfield WS13 6RN.

University entrance requirements

How many A-levels?

" Our son wants to study law at a good university. Would it be better for him to take three A-levels or four? "

It depends on how able and hard working he is. Three good A-levels are preferable to four mediocre ones, but four at grade A or B are best of all.

A-level education and alternatives

The next step?

Too soon to worry

" I've abandoned my plan to study medicine and decided to do A-levels in English, biology and geography. I'm interested in geology and journalism. How can I find out about what courses to do after A-level?"

> I don't think you really know yet what you want to do. Give yourself time: it is too soon to start worrying.

A choice to make

" I am half way through my A-levels and will soon have to choose which degree course to do. I'm keen to go to Lampeter, probably to study ancient history, but my real interest is in creative writing, which Lampeter doesn't offer. What should I do?"

> Few universities teach creative writing, East Anglia being a notable exception, and even there it is only a minor part of the English literature course. Lampeter has a combined degree in ancient history and English literature: why not take that?

Finally ...

A principle is at stake

" We have just had a request from Esher College, Surrey,

where our daughter has enrolled to study A-levels, for a 'voluntary' contribution of £120. We don't see why we should pay. What's your view?"

> All sixth-form colleges are under financial pressure. Most ask for money and spend it on textbooks and materials. Esher, which serves a relatively affluent area, says 90 per cent of its parents make the one-off payment. Some who refuse insist a principle is at stake. Perhaps they are campaigning for a government that makes education its priority?

Classic signs of exploitation

" As someone who will be opening his A-level results tomorrow, I am outraged that lecturers at some universities should have chosen this, of all times, to stage a two-day boycott of the admissions system. Are they completely heartless?"

> I don't think so. Their pay is relatively poor and becoming steadily poorer; they work long hours and about 40 per cent are on short-term contracts. These are all classic signs of exploitation, and the consequences are bad for students.

University and other further education

This section covers continuing education in general, and includes essential information on UCAS forms, gap years, foundation courses, gap year options, costs and funding, required A-level grades, accommodation, post-grad courses, drop-out rates and motivation problems.

Which institution and which subject?

Simply – the best

" I'm trying to help my daughter choose a university and I have a simple question: which ones are the best – and which should we avoid? "

> The list that follows is based on official reports on the quality of teaching in 1,000 departments in 79 universities in England and Northern Ireland [1998 and subsequently updated] – Scotland and Wales will be covered on another occasion. I have ranked the institutions according to the proportion of their teaching that was rated excellent or (under the new grading system) awarded at least 22 points out of 24. I have also put them into four divisions. Asterisks indicate uni-

versities in the top 20 for research.

First Division
Twenty-two universities that have had at least 40 per cent of their teaching judged excellent:
*Cambridge, York, *Imperial, *London School of Economics, *Oxford, *Warwick, *Durham, *Sheffield, *University College London, Open University, *Southampton, Lancaster, *Nottingham, *Manchester, *Birmingham, *Leeds, *King's College London, Manchester Institute of Science and Technology, East Anglia, *Bristol, *Bath, Newcastle.

Second Division
Twenty-six universities that have had at least 20 per cent – but less than 40 per cent – of their teaching judged excellent:
Exeter, Loughborough, Queen's Belfast, Oxford Brookes, *Sussex, Brunel, City, Hull, *Liverpool, Northumbria, Queen Mary and Westfield, West of England, Leicester, Reading, Plymouth, Essex, Kent, Surrey, Greenwich, Ulster, Aston, Anglia, Keele, Kingston, Coventry, Royal Holloway.

Third Division
Twenty universities that have had at least 6 per cent – but less than 20 per cent – of their teaching judged excellent:
East London, Sheffield Hallam, Nottingham Trent, Thames Valley, Huddersfield, London Guildhall, Central England, Goldsmiths', Portsmouth, South Bank, Birkbeck, Manchester Metropolitan, North

London, Teesside, Central Lancashire, De Montfort, Derby, Hertfordshire, Westminster, Wolverhampton.

Fourth Division
Eleven universities that have had none of their teaching judged excellent (number of departments inspected in brackets):
Bournemouth (7), Brighton (8), Humberside (8), Bradford (10), Leeds Metropolitan (10), Salford (10), Middlesex (12), Staffordshire (12), John Moores (14), Luton (14), Sunderland (14).

A waste of time?

" My daughter is bright, but didn't do well at A-level. She wants to do a degree in psychology with a view to going into counselling, and has taken a year out to study A-level psychology at evening classes. But the only university to offer her a place is De Montfort, which comes low down in your league table. Would anyone take seriously a qualification from such an institution, or would she have wasted her time? "

It is true that a degree from De Montfort is worth less in most employers' eyes than one from a university nearer the top of the table, but whether the three years were wasted would be largely up to your daughter. After all, there are good teachers in most subjects, and opportunities to be found in every university. As more young people have a degree, those without are increasingly finding themselves at a disadvantage.

University and other further education

Helping him choose

" My son's method of choosing which universities to apply to seems pretty haphazard. How can parents usefully involve themselves in such a decision? "

> The official guide from UCAS (the Universities and Colleges Admissions Service), which is available at libraries, lists the institutions offering each course and the A-level grades required. Having narrowed down the options, you could accompany your son to each university's open day: dates are listed in a guide published by ISCO (Independent Schools Careers Organisation), 01276 21188.

Where would *you* choose to go?

" How highly do you rate Exeter University? "

> It comes about a third of the way down my league table. As the vice-chancellor, Sir Geoffrey Holland, put it recently: "If you were an undergraduate comparing courses at different universities, and some were rated excellent for teaching quality and some were only good or average, where would you choose to go?" Of the 18 departments so far inspected at Exeter, only seven have been rated excellent. No department has been rated top for research. Curiously, from next October, the university is reducing the length of its teaching year to just 24 weeks.

No premium on language skills

"My son wants to go into business but can't decide what to study at university. I've tried to persuade him that a global economy puts a premium on foreign languages, but he isn't convinced. What do you think?"

> The Association of Graduate Recruiters recently asked more than 200 leading employers to rank the 20 graduate skills they thought most important and the 20 hardest to find. Foreign languages came last on both counts. The employers put a premium on interpersonal skills, team working, oral communication, problem-solving, motivation and enthusiasm.

Environmental issues

"My 17-year-old son, who is half way through A-levels, is interested in environmental issues. Is there a holistic degree course that combines environmental law, pollution, ecology, countryside planning and alternative energy systems?"

> There are many, some including a year's professional training or study abroad. For details, see the *Directory of Environmental Courses* (£14.99 including p&p) from the Environment Council, 212 High Holborn, London WC1V 7BF (020 7836 2626).

Best for business studies ...

" *My daughter is keen to do a degree in business studies. Which are the best universities, both for teaching and research?* "

The Higher Education Funding Councils have rated the teaching of business management as excellent at: Bath, City, Cranfield, De Montfort, Imperial, Kingston, Loughborough, LSE, Manchester, Northumbria, Nottingham, Nottingham Trent, Surrey, UMIST, Warwick, West of England, Glamorgan and Strathclyde. (*Editor's note: Lancaster should have been included in this reply.*)

Among those, research was judged to be of international excellence at: Bath, LSE, UMIST and Strathclyde.

... and best for computing

" *Which universities would you recommend for computing?* "

The following have had their teaching of computer studies rated excellent; asterisks indicate those where the research in computer science has been judged to be of international excellence: *Cambridge, Exeter, *Imperial, Kent, *Manchester, *Oxford, *Southampton, Teesside, *Warwick, *York, Swansea, *Edinburgh, *Glasgow.

Which guide to follow?

" The two universities rated highest for French teaching are Portsmouth and Westminster, both of which appear in the third division of the league table you published. What is one to make of that? "

> The table is based on the proportion of departments that have been inspected and had their teaching rated excellent or, under the new system, awarded at least 22 points out of 24. At Portsmouth, the proportion of such departments is two out of 17; at Westminster one out of 16.
>
> Students go to university to do more than simply study their chosen subject. The universities listed in the first two divisions attract a wider range of able students.

How can I judge?

" Further to your answers about which universities are best for particular subjects, I'm told that the teaching of philosophy won't be assessed until 2000, which is a bit late for my purposes. How can I judge the relative merits of different departments? "

> Philosophy has already been inspected in Scotland and Wales. It was rated excellent at Glasgow and Cardiff, and highly satisfactory at Aberdeen, Edinburgh, St Andrews and Stirling. In England, the universities judged to be doing research of international excellence are: Birkbeck, Cambridge, King's (London), LSE, Oxford and Sheffield.

Best for philosophy

" *My son wants to study philosophy. Where would be best?* "

Philosophy teaching has been inspected in Wales and Scotland – where Cardiff and Glasgow came top – but not yet in England. However, the English universities rated best for research are Cambridge, King's London, LSE, Oxford and Sheffield.

" *I've been searching the Internet for the best university at which to read philosophy, but have drawn a blank. Can you advise?* "

The Quality Assurance Agency has only just begun inspecting the subject at universities in England and Northern Ireland. Bradford, under the direction of Prof Anthony O'Hear, is the first to have been awarded the maximum 24 points. In Scotland, philosophy was rated "excellent" at Glasgow and "highly satisfactory" at Aberdeen, Edinburgh, St Andrews and Stirling.

Animal management

" *My son, who has a vast knowledge of animals, particularly reptiles, wants to study animal management but his sixth form college hasn't been able to advise him. Can you help?* "

You will find a list of the institutions offering animal science in the UCAS Guide to University and College Entrance, available at your local library or careers office. If you ask each institution for a departmental prospectus, your son will be able to identify the course he will find most interesting.

Not right

" My daughter wants to do a degree in mechanical engineering but has been told by her careers teacher that information about which universities offer the best courses cannot be given to the public. That's not right, is it? "

It is nonsense. The universities that have had their teaching of mechanical engineering officially graded as excellent are: Bath, Bristol, Cardiff, Coventry, Cranfield, Manchester, Manchester Metropolitan, Nottingham, Reading, Sheffield and Strathclyde.

Media and communications

" My 17-year-old daughter refuses to consider any degree course except media and communications. I'm concerned she may end up with a vague qualification from a poorly regarded institution. What's your advice? "

Of the 10 universities that have had their media and communications courses inspected, four have been rated excellent: East Anglia, Warwick, Central Lancashire and West of England. In each case, the graduate employment record was good.

Damaged

" My son wants to study law at Thames Valley University. Would you recommend it? "

> Absolutely not. The academic credibility of the university has been severely damaged by its recent decision to "adjust" the marks of students affected by a lecturers' work-to-rule. First-year students had their marks increased by 5 per cent, and the pass mark for those resitting their exams was lowered from 40 per cent to 30 per cent. Both moves have been condemned by the university's external examiners, who are responsible for guaranteeing its standards.

Catering at degree level

" My daughter, who is taking A-levels, would like a career as a caterer in high-class restaurants. Could you recommend a suitable degree course that includes experience in France? "

> Not, I am afraid, with much confidence. There is a plethora of degrees in catering and hospitality, but the industry is generally critical of their quality and there is little objective information to be had. However, on the basis of their A-level entry scores, I recommend that you ask for course prospectuses from Bournemouth, Manchester Metropolitan, Oxford Brookes, Strathclyde and Surrey.

Best for psychology

" Which universities would you recommend as best for psychology? They all seem to claim the highest rated research and largest library. "

> Psychology teaching has been inspected only in Wales (best departments: Cardiff and Swansea). England's best research is being done at Birkbeck, Bristol, Cambridge, Oxford, Reading, Royal Holloway, Sheffield, University College London and York; in Scotland, St Andrews.

Is Cambridge the be-all and end-all?

" I have been offered a place to read history at (in alphabetical order) Cambridge, Cardiff, Durham, Leeds, Royal Holloway and Swansea. Having visited all six, I'm still not sure which to accept and find it infuriating that I'm expected to jump at the chance of Cambridge. Is it really the be-all and end-all of a university education? "

> Of course not. Some young people find it a weird and uncongenial place. However, it has been judged excellent for teaching history (as have Durham, Royal Holloway and Swansea) and best among those you name for research.

Best for archaeology

" We are being deluged with glossy brochures from universities which all claim that their archaeology departments are

best. How do I advise my daughter which to choose?"

> The teaching of archaeology has been inspected only in Wales, where it was judged excellent at Cardiff and St David's. Research has been judged best at Bradford, Cambridge, Durham, Leicester, Oxford, Queen's Belfast, Reading, Sheffield, Southampton and UCL.

Best for BEd

" My daughter, who wants to be a primary school teacher, would rather take a four-year Bachelor of Education degree than a general degree followed by a Post-Graduate Certificate of Education. However, she would also rather go to a good university than to a teacher training institution. What is your advice?"

> The first league table of teacher training courses will be published later this summer. Meanwhile, Ofsted inspections show that the best primary courses are at Bishop Grosseteste College, Lincoln; Brunel University, west London; Ripon and York St John College, York; and Roehampton Institute, London. Universities such as Durham and Warwick scored relatively badly.

Open days

" My 17-year-old son, who is half way through his A-levels, hasn't a clue which degree to study, or where. We thought we might help by taking him to some university open days. Where can we find details?"

Taking your son to open days is an excellent idea. The information is contained in the *Sixthformer's Guide*, obtainable from ISCO Publications (to whom a cheque should be made out for £4.50), 12A Princess Way, Camberley, Surrey GU15 3SP.

First for firsts

" In which subjects is a university student most likely to gain a first? "

They are: mathematical sciences, in which 19.8 per cent of graduates are awarded a first; engineering and technology, 12.2 per cent; and physical sciences, 10.8 per cent. The subject to avoid – although it is also the most popular – is business and administrative studies, with 3.7 per cent. The average of firsts across all subjects is 7.6 per cent.

Sound advice on medical schools

" My son is half way through A-levels and thinking seriously about studying medicine. I think we both need a lot more information. Where can we find it? "

I warmly recommend *The Insiders' Guide to Medical Schools*, an "alternative prospectus" written by the BMA's medical student committee, all of whom are current students. It is full of sound advice and useful, up-to-date information. Descriptions of the 26 medical schools include the five best and worst aspects of each. The guide costs £9.99 from good bookshops or BMJ Books; phone 020 7383 6185.

Is this a good idea?

" My daughter, who is half way through A-levels, wants to take a degree in psychology and law at Keele or Swansea. A good idea? "

> Only if she knows enough about the subjects to be sure she wants to spend three years studying them – and doesn't expect her degree to lead automatically to a job.

Eclipsed

" My daughter is half way through A-levels and on course for brilliant results. She wants to study engineering, with a bias towards design, or possibly architecture. The only problem is that her boyfriend has no higher ambitions than Oxford Brookes, where she is determined to join him. How can we change her mind? "

> If she is as able as you think, Cambridge and Imperial should be high on her list. Encourage her to visit them both this term, and talk to the people who might teach her. With any luck, they will so enthuse her that the charms of Oxford Brookes will be eclipsed.

Why university?

" I am half way through A-levels in biology, chemistry and

maths, and am expected to achieve a grade B in each. Biology has always been my favourite subject and would be my natural choice for university study. However, I don't want to make a career of it – I see myself in a verbal/social job, providing a service to the public. So, should I forget about biology and take a degree in, say, events management at Leeds Metropolitan?"

> You should decide first why you want to go to university: is it to study biology, train for a job or because it is what people do? If you are truly committed to biology, put all other considerations aside. If not, are you sure that you want to commit yourself to events management? Why not work for a while until you discover what you really want to do?

An expensive option

" Is Trinity College, Dublin, a respectable option for UK students?"

> Yes, but a fairly expensive one. Although undergraduates in Ireland pay no tuition fees, there is a "student charge" of £310 a year and, more importantly, no access to cheap student loans.

Paying close attention

" My son is part way through his A-levels and is predicted to get good grades. He wants to study chemical engineering and is thinking of applying to Imperial, Newcastle and

University and other further education

Leeds. Are job prospects influenced by the university a graduate attended?"

> Employers are learning to pay close attention to where applicants studied. Imperial's reputation is outstanding; your son might also consider the Manchester Institute of Science and Technology (UMIST).

Best for geography

" Which are the best universities for geography?"

> The list of those judged excellent is too long to print, but the details are in the geography "overview report" published by the Quality Assurance Agency, Southgate House, Southgate Street, Gloucester GL1 1UB and is available for a small fee. The information is also available on the Internet at www.niss. ac.uk/education/quality.html/.

Best for media studies

" Our son is keen to take a degree in media studies. How can we find out what the course entails and the best place to study it?"

> *Media Courses 2000* (£13.99, published by the British Film Institute) offers a brief description of the 200-plus undergraduate courses that include some element of media studies – the smaller the better, in my view. Reports published by the Quality Assurance Agency show that the best courses are offered by East Anglia and

Warwick, followed by Central Lancashire, Goldsmiths', Liverpool John Moores, LSE and West of England.

" My son is interested in taking a degree in media studies. How likely is it to lead to a career, and which universities offer the best courses? "

> The competition for jobs is severe: about two-thirds of media graduates find one. Of the 18 courses inspected so far, the best are at East Anglia and Warwick. Close behind are: Central Lancashire, Goldsmiths', Liverpool John Moores and West of England.

Best Oxbridge colleges

" Which are the best colleges at Oxford and Cambridge? And which would come bottom of the league? "

> At Oxford, Merton, St John's and Jesus are usually top of the league table; at Cambridge, Trinity, Queens' and Christ's. At both, the sole women's college tends to come bottom: St Hilda's, Oxford, and New Hall, Cambridge.

Geography: quite respectable

" I read recently in The Sunday Telegraph *that those who take geography are a 'laughed-at section of student society'. Is that true? If so, why? And if my son hasn't been put off the subject, where would be the best place to study it? "*

University and other further education

There used to be some truth in this because the academic demands of the subject were not thought to be great. But now that there are so many courses with little, if any, intellectual content, geography has become quite respectable. For a list of the best places to study it, ask the Quality Assurance Agency (01242 544610) for the "overview" report. You can also find it on the Internet at: www.qaa.ac.uk/.

" You said last week that a degree in geography was 'quite respectable'. I read geography followed by law and found the geography degree more intellectually demanding. It required both a good level of literacy (essay writing is central) and a high level of mathematical competence (advanced statistical methods are part of every course). There may have been a time when geography was lightweight, but for the past 20 years all our better universities have offered courses of real rigour, attracting bright students who have gone on to good jobs. "

The letter is from Barnaby Lenon, head of Trinity School, Croydon, who writes geography textbooks. To him and all the many other geographers who were affronted by what was intended as a light-hearted remark, I apologise.

Some suggested geography was the only true training for Millennium man and woman, but I think that is going too far.

As good a degree?

" My daughter has been refused a place to read modern history

at Jesus College, Oxford, but offered one at Greyfriars, which is described as a 'permanent private hall within Oxford University'. Would a degree from there be as good as one from Jesus?"

Yes. But your daughter needs to be sure that she will be happy in a college with only 30 students, a strongly Catholic ethos and a "holistic" approach to higher education.

Where should I start?

" I feel daunted by the prospect of helping my son identify a degree course at a credible university. Where should I start?"

The best place is Brian Heap's *Degree Course Offers*, the 30th annual edition of which is published this week. Organised by subject, it groups university departments according to the A-level points they require, describes how the courses differ, gives useful tips on securing a place, and suggests where the degree might lead. It is written by the doyen of careers advisers, and offers a clear, concise and reliable guide. Published by Trotman, it costs £19.99 plus £1.50 p&p, and may be ordered by phoning 0870 900 2665.

University open days

" Could I reinforce the point Brian Wraight made on your page recently about universities' attitudes to parents who accompany their children to open days? My daughter was offered a place to study classics at Birmingham, Exeter, Leeds,

King's College London, Nottingham and UCL. We visited them all but only Nottingham made parents welcome: the department arranged a meeting for the two dozen of us who turned up. My daughter found the students particularly helpful and has made the university her first choice."

> Thank you. An increasing number of universities are paying attention. Among those that have told me recently they welcome parents are Keele, Sheffield Hallam and Central England. The 1999 edition of the *Sixthformer's Guide* to open days is available (£5.95) from ISCO Publications, phone 01276 21188.

A good general introduction

" *Could you recommend a good general introduction to the whole business of going to university?* "

> So much of what students need to know is now most readily available on the Internet that I think one of the best places to start is *Net That Course!* by Irene Krechowiecka (Kogan Page, £8.99). It is a clear, informative guide to using the web to find the right course at the right institution. As the book says: "If you're contemplating higher education, you're going to have to learn to love the computer."

Best for sport and having a good time

" *Which universities would you recommend to someone who is keen on sport and having a good time?* "

According to the *Virgin Alternative Guide to British Universities* ("written by students for students"), Sheffield, Leeds and Edinburgh are best if your A-level grades are respectable, and Manchester Metropolitan if they are not. The guide, which costs £14.99, offers racy but reliable profiles that focus as much on the way of life as on academic considerations.

No easy task

" Helping our daughter to choose a university at which to study international relations is proving no easy task. So many of our friends advise us not to pick a 'new' university, but how do we tell which they are? "

Aim to select a department that matches your daughter's abilities in a university that she will find congenial. The best starting point is *Degree Course Offers* by Brian Heap (see p. 229). It lists every subject and the A-level points each institution requires. The disclaimer that the universities insist on – "The level of an offer is not indicative of the quality of a course" – is the reverse of the truth. In most cases, those asking for the fewest points will be the "new" universities – the former polytechnics. Once you have identified the institutions that come within the range of your daughter's likely A-level performance, ask for their prospectuses and plan your visits.

More stimulating

" I have an offer of a place at Keele to study geography with philosophy, and at Portsmouth to study geography. Portsmouth requires 16 A-level points and says its geography department has been rated 'excellent'. Keele requires 20 points but makes no mention of the inspection. Which should I choose? "

Keele's approach is determinedly multi-disciplinary, so you must decide whether you want to study geography on its own or with another subject. Judged by overall teaching quality, Keele is the better university: 35th in my league table; Portsmouth is 80th. However, Portsmouth was one of 27 universities at which the teaching of geography was judged excellent; at Keele, it was merely "satisfactory". So you face a common dilemma: which is more important, department or university? If you achieve 20 points, you should choose Keele. The company is likely to be more stimulating.

" I was offended by the advice you gave last week to the geography student who couldn't decide between Keele and Portsmouth. Even though the subject has been rated as excellent at Portsmouth, you recommended Keele because the company was 'likely to be more stimulating'. What you should have done was advise the student to visit both and make up his/her own mind. Then you wouldn't have needed to cast aspersions on the university where I am very happy. "

You are right on both points. I apologise.

Take a national curriculum subject

" I am hoping to be a primary school teacher, but first I'd like to take a degree in psychology, specialising in child psychology. Would that be a suitable preparation? "

> No. If you are going to take a degree before training, it must be in a national curriculum subject.

Best for criminology with sociology

" I am looking for a good university at which to study criminology. All the prospectuses I have seen offer the subject with law or psychology, but I am interested in the sociological side. "

> Three good universities that offer criminology in combination with sociology are Essex, Keele and Lancaster.

Best for post-grad teacher training

" I am about to embark on a postgraduate teacher training course. What would top your recommended reading list? "

> I would urge you to read a report published recently by Ofsted called *Lessons Learned*. It is based on the experiences of 250 schools that were judged to be failing and have been turned round. It might seem a perverse way to approach teaching, but understanding how schools go wrong and what puts them right is genuinely illuminating. The messages are jargon-free – something you will learn to appreciate – and reassur-

ingly common-sensical: "It is important to make every lesson count; when teaching is effective, children want to behave well and to learn; progress is best when pupils see that they are making worthwhile gains; do not scatter praise indiscriminately but focus it on work of high quality; pupils should know, with certainty, what the school judges to be good behaviour, and what is unacceptable; heads cannot hide behind a closed door or seek refuge in paperwork – they need to be highly visible throughout the day; and [when all else has failed] schools should not shy away from removing staff who cannot fufil their responsibilities as teachers."

Lessons Learned is available free from Ofsted Publications Centre, PO Box 6927, London E3 3NZ; phone 020 7510 0180.

Best for film studies

" I am thinking of taking a degree in film studies. Can you tell me which universities and colleges offer it, and which are considered best? "

A search of the Universities and Colleges Admissions Service website (www.ucas.ac.uk/) shows that film studies on its own is available at five universities – East London, Kent, Middlesex, North London and Sheffield Hallam – and two colleges, Falmouth Arts and Southampton Institute. (Combine it with other "studies", though, and the list becomes endless.) As the subject has not been inspected, you will have to ask each department for its prospectus and then choose which to visit. If any readers have taken the course recently and would like to make a recommendation, I shall be happy to pass it on.

Best for graphic design

" My daughter is keen to study graphic design – as a prelude, I hope, to earning a living. Where would you recommend? "

Art and design are still being inspected by the Quality Assurance Agency but, of the 13 institutions it has reported on, only Falmouth College of Arts has been awarded the maximum 24 points. The inspectors said the quality of teaching was high and praised the college for promoting a "high level of business and professional awareness".

Best for business studies

" My grand-daughter, who is studying for a GNVQ at her local college, wishes to take a degree in business studies, but both she and her parents are bewildered about which university to choose. The college staff seem unwilling to offer advice. Can you help? "

Over the past eight years, almost every subject at every university has been meticulously inspected and graded. So it is outrageous that potential students should be denied access to information that has been gathered at such cost in time and money.

For universities in England and Northern Ireland,

subject "overview" reports, which include each university's grading, cost £2 (cheques to Quality Assurance Agency) from Distribution Department, UCAS, PO Box 130, Cheltenham, Glos GL52 3ZI; phone 01242 544610. They can also be found at: www.qaa.ac.uk/.

In Scotland, reports on each subject at each university cost £6 from the Scottish Higher Education Funding Council (to which cheques should be made out), 97 Donaldson House, Edinburgh EH12 5HD; phone 0131 313 6500. A summary of the outcomes in each subject are at: www.shefc.ac.uk/.

In Wales, subject reports are available free from the Higher Education Funding Council for Wales, Linden Court, Ty Glas Avenue, Cardiff CF4 5DZ; phone 01222 761861. A summary of the outcomes in each subject can be found at: www.niss.ac.uk/education/hefcw/.

Painting themselves into a corner

" My grand-daughter is a bright child expected to gain two As and a B at A-level. She has applied to study optometry. Is this sensible? "

Optometrists prescribe lenses. They are required to have a degree in optometry, a year's clinical experience and to pass a professional qualifying exam. Although it is probably a steady job, I doubt that it amounts to a vocation – yet such is the pressure on young people to make career decisions that it is not surprising if they paint themselves into a corner. I suggest you encourage your grand-daughter to spend a while browsing through a good careers website, such as www.bigwideworld.com/.

How does one choose?

" My son, who is taking an arts foundation course, wants to go on to study film and video. How does one choose between the many courses available? "

Nine film schools recognised by the Broadcasting, Entertainment and Cinematograph Union are regarded as offering the most professional training: Bournemouth Arts Institute; Bristol University's department of film and television; London College of Printing; London International Film School; National Film and Television School, Beaconsfield; Ravensbourne College, Chislehurst; Westminster University's media school; Newport School of Art and Design; and the Surrey Institute of Art and Design. Addresses and phone numbers are listed in *Getting Into Films and Television*, a useful introduction to the subject published, price £9.99 plus £1.50 p&p, by How To Books (01752 202301).

The important issues

" I am planning to apply to Cambridge next year but don't know which college to choose. Issues important to me include male:female ratios, the numbers of independent school students and students reading law, my intended subject. Can you help? "

The university's printed prospectus is fairly bland but you will find the information you are looking for on each college's website, a list of which is at: www.cam.ac.uk/CambUniv/colleges.html/.

Daunting

" My daughter is interested in studying architecture – a rather daunting prospect. How long is the course, and where can I find out more? "

It takes seven years to qualify, five of them at university. For a free copy of the Royal Institute of British Architects' careers leaflet, phone 020 7580 5533; or see the website: www.riba.net/.

Open days

" When do universities hold their open days and where can we find details? "

The high season is from April to June. For details on open days, see the *Sixthformer's Guide*, £5.50 from the Independent Schools Careers Organisation, 12A Princess Way, Camberley, Surrey GU15 3SP; tel: 01276 21188.

A curious kind of snobbery

" My daughter, who is predicted to achieve As or Bs in A-level chemistry, biology, English literature and psychology,

wants to take a degree in equine science. My concern is that the universities offering it are all of the 'green welly' variety and that she'll emerge a rather dull person. (The one place she won't consider is Bristol because you can graduate there without ever touching a horse.) Am I just being an educational/ cultural snob?"

> It would be a curious kind of snobbery that excluded Aberdeen, Edinburgh, Leeds, Newcastle upon Tyne, Nottingham and Reading, all of which offer equine science. Your problem, I suspect, is with the subject, but if it is what your daughter really wants to study, you will just have to get over it.

Not to everyone's taste

" My very able daughter has been offered places at Oxford and Warwick to read English literature but has chosen Warwick. She says that she prefers the atmosphere and the course, and that it's an equally good university. Surely anyone who has the opportunity to go to Oxbridge should take it? How can I persuade her to change her mind and avoid making a choice she may come to regret?"

> She is more likely to regret spending three years at a university where she does not feel at ease and which requires her to study in a manner she finds uncongenial – Oxbridge is certainly not to everyone's taste, and Warwick's reputation is first class.

Best for fine art

" *Having visited the universities to which I applied to take a BA in fine art, I'm worried that I was badly advised because the facilities I've seen do not meet the standards I was expecting. Given that I am predicted to achieve an A and three Bs at A-level, where should I be aiming for?* "

Curiously, of the 49 institutions that offer fine art, nearly all are former polytechnics or colleges of higher education not renowned for the quality of their facilities. The outstanding exception is Oxford. However, it is the quality of teaching, the nature of the curriculum and the stimulus of fellow students that matter most. I would be grateful for recommendations from recent graduates (but not, please, public relations officers).

Best for pharmacy

" *I am in the lower sixth and plan to take a degree in pharmacy (MPharm). Some of the universities I am considering ask for A-level grades as low as three Cs. Will employers think less of my degree if it comes from such a university? Also, please could you say which courses are most highly regarded?* "

In general it is true that the most academically selective universities are the most highly regarded. However, employers know that some less selective institutions have specialised successfully in particular vocational areas. Pharmacy courses in England are still being inspected by the Quality Assurance Agency but Aston, Manchester and Portsmouth have been awarded 24 points out of 24; Bath, Brighton and Nottingham, 23; and King's, London, and Sunderland, 22. The courses at Cardiff and Strathclyde were earlier judged excellent.

It matters very little

" Having no particular vocation, I'd like to know how much it matters in relation to my career prospects which subject I study at university. "

It matters very little. About 45 per cent of graduate vacancies are advertised without a discipline being specified. Employers say they are principally interested in A-level point scores, class of degree, work experience and evidence of all-round competence.

Both are first rate

" I am currently in the upper sixth preparing for A-levels and planning to read maths at university. Cambridge has turned me down but I hold offers from Warwick and Nottingham. Should I take a gap year and reapply to Cambridge – perhaps to a different college – or settle for one of the other two? "

The chances of being accepted second time around are slim (what, after all, will have changed?), and it is a poor reason for taking a gap year. Both the other universities are first rate.

Stick to your guns

" I am studying English, French and economics at A-level and have a strong desire to read theology at university. However, my father forbids it because he thinks it would make it difficult for me to enter the City – which I would like to do – and insists that economics or business studies, which I do not enjoy, would be a wiser choice. Is he right? If not, how might I argue my point? "

> He is wrong. The City – like most employers – looks for intelligence, aptitude and personal skills. You should stick to your guns: having to spend three years studying for a degree in the wrong subject would be deeply dispiriting.

Choose modern languages

" My daughter can't decide whether to study English or modern languages at university. Any advice? "

> A degree in modern languages, particularly if it included a year abroad, would widen your daughter's horizons and improve her chances of finding a job.

Foolish

" My daughter, who is predicted to achieve A grades in A-level French, Spanish, business studies and art, is being urged by her teachers to apply to Oxford to read modern languages. However, she would prefer to take a business degree, which

Oxford doesn't offer. Would it be foolish of her, as her school suggests, to turn down the chance of going to Oxford?"

> It would be more foolish of her to enrol on a course she did not want to do.

Best for sports science

" My twin sons would both like to take a degree in sports science but not at the same university. Could you recommend a choice of courses?"

> The good news is that more than 40 universities offer the subject. The bad news is that sports science has not yet been inspected, so there is no objective information about where the teaching is best. However, entry requirements – for details see the website www.ucas.com/ – range from two Ds at A-level to three Bs. Your sons should aim as high as they can.

Best for interior design

" My daughter is interested in taking a degree in interior design. How do we find out which universities offer it, which courses are most highly rated and what the employment prospects are after graduation?"

> The answers, which apply to all subjects, are most readily found on two websites: www.ucas.ac.uk/ for a list of the courses on offer (136 in interior design); and www.qaa.ac.uk/ for reports on the quality of the rele-

vant department (in this case, art and design). The reports – each, incidentally, costs an average of £75,000 to produce – include a reference to graduates' employment records. Check first to see if all the departments offering the subject have been inspected. If they have, there will be an "overview" report listing the marks out of 24 awarded to each. If the inspections are continuing – as they are in art and design – you will have to open each published report to discover the mark. If the subject has not yet been inspected, you should be guided by the university's overall position in the *Daily Telegraph* league table, which can be found at www.telegraph.co.uk/.

Degree subject guides

" *My son wants to take a degree in sports science. Where can we find out what it entails and where it might lead?* "

This being the term when second-year A-level pupils have to fill in their university application forms, I have had a stream of similar questions in relation to law, media studies, business and management, art and design, and psychology. All, I am happy to say, are covered in a series of booklets called *Q&A Degree Subject Guides*, published by Trotman (0870 900 2665) with the official blessing of UCAS. Costing £4.99 each, they are written by recent graduates who set out to answer the same basic questions about the nature of the course, where best to study it and what the career prospects are. The booklets do vary in quality but the one on sports science is particularly well written and informative.

Its academic standing is unclear

" I am considering studying at Buckingham, Britain's only private university. Could you tell me how it stands academically – it doesn't appear in the league tables – and how employers regard it? "

Being privately funded, the university, which opened in 1976, is not subject to official inspection so its academic standing is unclear. Its most distinguishing features are that it teaches honours degrees in two years rather than three and charges tuition fees totalling £21,000 – reduced to £8,000 for those who live or went to school in Buckinghamshire or surrounding counties and for those who achieve an average of three Bs at A-level. Robert Pearce, the acting vice-chancellor, points to the willingness of good universities to accept Buckingham's graduates as post-graduate students; a staff–student ratio of 1:10, compared with 1:17 nationally; and a sound employment record. For a prospectus, call 01280 814080, or visit the website www.buckingham.ac.uk/.

Best for film

" My 16-year-old son, who is taking A-levels in English literature, media studies and computing, is interested in a career in the film industry. What would you recommend him to do? "

It is difficult to give specific advice because there are so many possible pathways – including, for example, a choice of no fewer than 1,000 university courses (for details, see: www.ucas.ac.uk/). The best starting point is either *Media Courses UK*, a guide published by the British Film Institute (020 7255 1444), costing £13.99, or the institute's extensive website: www.bfi.org.uk/.

Best for boat design

" Our 15-year-old son has had a long-standing ambition to design ships and yachts. Which A-levels should he take, and which are the university centres of excellence? "

Five good universities offer degree courses in either naval architecture or ship science: Glasgow, Newcastle-upon-Tyne, Southampton, Strathclyde and University College, London. Maths and physics are an essential foundation; design, technology and computing are all relevant.

University and FE college performance

Official judgements

" You sometimes cite official judgements of the quality of teaching in university departments. Where are they obtainable? "

Reports on about 1,500 departments are obtainable (£2 each) from the Higher Education Funding Councils for England and Northern Ireland (0117 931

7493), Scotland (0131 313 6500) and Wales (01222 761861).

Another poor performer

" Last week, you gave details of the poor exam performance of a further education college in Kent. Where can one look up the results of colleges in other areas? The one I'm particularly interested in is Swindon. "

The "performance indicators" of more than 400 colleges are published by the Further Education Funding Council (02476 863000) but unfortunately the booklet costs £16.95. Swindon comes near the bottom of the table. Last year, 52 per cent of its 36,000 students who completed their courses failed to achieve a qualification. The average is 35 per cent.

Dumbing down

" Is there anything employers can do to prevent universities 'dumbing down' their courses? "

Yes: they can follow the example of the Engineering Council, the profession's regulatory body. It has just decided not to recognise the degrees of institutions that admit large numbers of students with low-grade A-levels.

For example, it will require 80 per cent of those enrolling on a four-year MEng course to have at least 24 A-level points, equivalent to three grade Bs. For a three-year BEng, the requirement will be that 80 per cent of students should have at least 18 points, equivalent to three grade Cs.

The council's laudable intention is to ensure that those studying engineering do so in the company of others "of sufficient intellectual capability". The new rules will be phased in from October 1999.

Which would come top?

" In all this talk of league tables, why have we lost sight of the only one that should matter to an academic school: the number of pupils who win a place at Oxford or Cambridge? Do you know which would come top? "

Eton wins about 60 places a year, closely followed by Manchester Grammar (58 this year); Westminster, 55; Winchester, 50; and St Paul's and King Edward's Birmingham, both about 45. Such a table would discriminate against girls' schools, which are usualy smaller.

Indistinguishable

" My son has been advised to apply to colleges such as King Alfred's and Canterbury Christ Church, which are affiliated to universities – Southampton and Kent respectively – but which have much lower entry requirements. Are the degrees conferred true university degrees? "

The degrees are those of the university to which the college is affiliated and are indistinguishable from those awarded to the universities' own students.

Performance profiles

" My daughter is thinking of training to be a teacher. Where can we find out about the quality of the courses available? "

> The Teacher Training Agency has just published a detailed but curiously uninformative booklet containing "performance profiles" of 100 universities and colleges. For each, it shows the percentage of trainees who entered with above-average qualifications, the proportion who passed the course and found a job, and a summary of Ofsted's inspection judgements, which are particularly unenlightening. You can obtain a free copy by phoning 0845 6060323.

Last bastions of high standards

" The university where I teach Building Surveying has just had its accreditation withdrawn by the Royal Institute of Chartered Surveyors (RICS) because the students we recruit don't have high A-level grades. The Government, though, is determined to widen access and pressures us to admit such students. Hasn't the RICS heard? "

> It may seem old-fashioned, but the Institute is trying to protect academic standards – which universities might be expected to have an interest in too.

Follow the official procedure

" *My daughter, who is in her first year at Nottingham Trent, studying hospitality management, is critical of the way the course is organised. I agree with her. Is it my place to complain, or should I leave it to her and her fellow students?* "

> You should encourage her to follow the official complaints procedure. If she does not receive a satisfactory response from her course leader, year tutor or head of department, she can register a formal complaint on a form available from the student advice centre.

Grading the teacher trainers

" *You sometimes advise for or against particular teacher training institutions: is there an official league table?* "

> The Teacher Training Agency has graded the 100 institutions into five categories – A to E – on the basis of their Ofsted inspection reports, and funds them accordingly. Those that train primary teachers are allocated a single grade; those that train secondary teachers have a grade for each subject. For a copy of the relevant list, write to the TTA at Portland House, Stag Place, London SW1E 5TT. Stress that you do not want the agency's 'Performance Profiles', a 101-page tome of baffling statistics. Warwick University points out that, although it was awarded the lowest grade, E, for training primary teachers, its provision has been reinspected and judged good.

Which have been judged excellent?

" How can I find out which universities have been judged excellent in the subject that interests me? "

> The easiest way is via the Internet; the Quality Assurance Agency's address is www.qaa.ac.uk/. Alternatively, phone the agency on 01242 544610 or write to PO Box 130, Cheltenham, Glos GL52 3ZF.

Encourage them

" I have two daughters who worked hard to secure places at what we thought was a top university but which turns out from your table to be half way down the second division. What should we say to them? "

> No matter how far down the table it comes, no university has been judged bad, and many at the lower end have a respectable employment record. You should encourage your daughters to work for the best degree possible.

Not subject to state inspection

" Why doesn't Buckingham, Britain's only independent university, appear in the league table that you published last week? "

> Because it is independent, Buckingham does not receive state funding. It is not therefore subject to state inspection, on the results of which the table is based. If you are

seeking information about admissions to Buckingham, you should telephone 01280 814080.

Performance profiles

" You reported recently on a league table of teacher training institutions. How can I obtain a copy? "

"Performance profiles" of the 104 universities and colleges that train primary and secondary teachers are available, free, from the Teacher Training Agency, phone 0845 606 0323. They are also on the Internet at: www.teach-tta.gov.uk/.

"Substantial independent study"

" Our daughter, who has just gone to Leicester University to read history, has only seven hours of lectures and tutorials a week. She has been told that students are expected to work on their own for 75 per cent of the time. Is that right? "

It is one of the consequences of the largely unfunded move to mass higher education. Some universities make a virtue of how little teaching they do by boasting they have switched to a "learning culture". Leicester's response was: "Students must expect to commit themselves to substantial independent study in order to develop the powers of analysis and expression that are crucial for their future contribution to society."

" My son, who is supposedly studying full-time at Hertford-

shire University, has four hours of lectures a week plus three hours of tutorials/seminars. Some of the lectures are so overcrowded that students have to sit on the floor or stand. Has this become the norm?"

> To judge from my postbag, it is certainly not unusual. Indeed, MPs are so worried about the situation that the Commons Select Committee on Education has decided to hold an inquiry into the "quality of the student experience". For details of how to submit evidence, phone Robert Rees on 020 7219 1361.

Degree course is "below GCSE level"

"The first year of my nephew's three-year degree course in English and history at Plymouth University is being taught under a 'franchise' arrangement at a further education college. He did not study either subject at A-level and his knowledge of them seems negligible. What particularly concerns me, a former teacher, is the low standard of work he is doing at the college. It would be more appropriate for a pupil aged 12 or 13 and is certainly below GCSE level. Is this what studying for a degree means nowadays?"

> It is not yet the norm. However, the Government, in its drive to increase the proportion of young people in higher education from 30 per cent to 50 per cent, is committed to funding many more such courses.

Impossible to justify

" *My daughter is still recovering from the exhaustion and stress of her first year at Cambridge reading natural sciences. The volume and difficulty of the work was a shock to her but what made it worse was that the academic 'year' is squeezed into three eight-week terms. It's the same at Oxford, yet other universities manage to teach 12-week terms. What's the justification for putting high-achievers under such pressure? My daughter, incidentally, achieved a first in her end-of-year exams.* "

We need good universities to do research as well as teach, and the best of them derive a substantial proportion of their income from the former. Students benefit, too, from contact – however limited – with lecturers working at the frontiers of their subjects. The system does, though, demand a lot of those who were accustomed to being intensively taught at school, and perhaps they are not as well prepared as they ought to be for the change in learning style.

What I find impossible to justify is the 30-week teaching year that has now become customary at dozens of universities that do little or no research of any use to anyone. By lengthening their terms to 15 weeks, they could teach a three-year degree in two years – to the benefit of, among others, vocationally minded students who want to get on with earning a living.

" *Contrary to the impression given last week, Oxford and Cambridge are not the only universities that force students to cram a year's work into three eight-week terms. As at all London University colleges, the academic year at Royal Holloway, where I am studying, is officially 30 weeks, but we're taught for only 22 of them. Two weeks are set aside for exams and the rest is dead time, when nothing is timetabled. So we waste more than half the year and then work ourselves into the ground for what's left. Something is wrong, surely?"*

> Universities are clearly not doing enough to explain to students that they are expected to learn more than they are taught.

Gap years

The last chance

" I have obtained a grant for a teachers' training course starting in the autumn, but I also have the opportunity of a round-the-world trip. Would I be foolish to miss the last chance of a grant?"

> Don't be silly: you will be a much better teacher after going round the world.

Voluntary work abroad

" My son has a deferred place at Manchester next year. During his gap year, he'd like to do voluntary work in India or Africa. Any ideas?"

> The best-known organisations have filled most of their

places, but one that has not is Teaching Abroad. It arranges conversational English teaching to secondary pupils in South India and Ghana. Teaching Abroad, 46 Beech View, Angmering, Sussex BN16 4DE; 01903 859911.

" Further to your reply last week to a reader seeking gap-year voluntary work, we at Youth for Britain run a computerised inquiry service that matches volunteers' wishes with the requirements of over 700 organisations involved in 250,000 volunteer projects, here and abroad. Please pass the information on. "

Gladly. Youth for Britain, a registered charity, asks volunteers to fill in a questionnaire and then for a small fee sends details of the 10 most suitable organisations. Youth for Britain, Higher Orchard, Sandford Orcas, Sherborne, Dorset DT9 4RP (tel/fax 01963 220036).

Unusual – and far away

" I graduated this summer but, before buckling down to the daily grind, I'd like to do something really unusual, preferably far away. Any ideas? "

Are you "physically and mentally healthy, open-minded, flexible and able to cope in living conditions significantly different from those of the UK"? If so, why not spend 10 months teaching English at a university or college in China? The Council on International Educational Exchange is looking for graduates (no teaching experience necessary). Apply to the Council at 52 Poland Street, London W1F 7AB (020 7478 2000).

Gap year before, or after?

" When I've finished my A-levels, I want to read history. Should I take a gap year before or after university? I'm planning to go to Africa to spend six months travelling and six months teaching. "

Before. You will learn a lot, not least about yourself, and gain more from your university years as a result.

Misunderstanding

" Didn't the Government agree last year that gap year students should be exempted from the new tuition fees? Why, then, has our local education authority turned down our application to have our son's fees waived? "

I am afraid you have misunderstood the concession. It applied only to those who had been offered a deferred place (firm or conditional) before last year's A-level results were announced.

Postpone the decision

" Our daughter is taking A-levels this summer in geography, economics and biology and has been offered places by several

universities. However, she has no real idea of what she wants to do and isn't sure she wants to go to university. What would you suggest? "

I applaud her willingness to stand against the tide that sweeps every school-leaver with A-levels straight into full-time higher education. She will lose nothing by postponing a decision. Far better to try a variety of jobs until she finds one that interests her and then decide how she wants to carry on her education.

What are the pros and cons?

" *The youngest of our three daughters is 15, extremely clever and currently torn between choosing a career as a forensic pathologist and 'bumming around America in a rock band'. We know better than to venture an opinion at this stage but she is interested in studying at a prestigious American university. What are the pros and cons, and how should she apply?* "

The only drawback is the cost: the more prestigious, the greater the expense. Tuition and board at Harvard, for example, come to nearly £20,000 a year. However, many excellent public universities charge little more than half that. US News World Report (2400 N Street, Washington DC) publishes annual rankings of all 228 public and private institutions and explains how to apply. The information is available on the Internet: www.usnews.com/.

"A gap year will change your life"

" Is taking a gap year between school and university a good idea? Where can we find out more? "

> At least one in five students now does it and the proportion is increasing rapidly. I am strongly in favour, as long as the year has some sort of structure. As Richard Branson says in his foreword to The *Virgin Student Travellers' Handbook*: "A gap year will change your life." Among the many guides on the market, the Virgin book, by Tom Griffiths (£12.99), is best on how to plan the year – emphasising that "it's not some sort of fixed thing that you can go into the shops and buy". For those who want to do more than keep moving, *Opportunities in the Gap Year* (£4.95 from ISCO, 12A Princess Way, Camberley, Surrey GU15 3SP; phone: 01276 21188) offers a wealth of information about paid and voluntary work abroad and at home, as does *The Gap Year Guidebook* (Peridot Press, £9.95).

Professional culinary ambitions

" During her gap year, my daughter would like to learn how to cook well enough to pay her way. Any suggestions? "

> Cookery at the Grange, which is based near Frome, Somerset, offers a range of expensive but classy residential courses, including a five-day "chalet" course (£490) for those who want to work in a ski resort, and a four-week "essentially cookery" course (£2,000) for

those with "professional culinary ambitions". For a brochure, phone 01373 836579. *(See also p. 262.)*

Is this really a good thing?

" My daughter, who is in the lower sixth at an independent school, is asking for £3,000 to join her friends on a month's trip to Borneo organised by one of the gap-year bodies. Is this really a good thing? "

Such expeditions have become very common in the independent sector. The gap-year organisations may be educational charities but they are not averse to the hard sell and know how peer pressure works. I think independent schools should stop acting as their recruiting agents.

" Further to last week's question from the mother whose daughter wanted £3,000 for a trip to Borneo, my son is debating whether to spend his gap year travelling abroad or to volunteer for a charity called CSV, which offers free board and lodging in the UK. I want him to get the most out of the year. Which would you recommend? "

It partly depends on the nature of the gap year: although some ventures are designed to help others – building a school in the African bush, for example – most benefit no one but the traveller. So if your son's purpose is charitable, he will need to bear that in mind. If he decides that charity begins at home, he could hardly do better than CSV – Community Service

Volunteers, phone 0800 374991. He will be making his choice at a time when all who rely on student helpers are noticing a sharp decline in applications as young people come under pressure to earn and save for university. As for Borneo, the organisation responsible, World Challenge, took umbrage at the description of it as a "trip". They said it was a "genuinely educational" expedition involving "seriously demanding phases of jungle and mountain survival".

More sensible choices

" Does taking a gap year after A-levels make it harder to obtain a university place? "

Not at all. Universities welcome students who are more mature and clearer about what they want to study and why. Also, gap year applicants, knowing their A-level grades, can make more sensible choices.

Not challenging

" My daughter has been offered a university place to study Spanish and marketing but now thinks that she'd like to work for a year first, preferably at something challenging. The trouble is that only clerical jobs seem to be available. Can you help? "

A clerical job in an organisation that might be interested in her when she graduates is the best that she, and thousands of other school-leavers, can expect.

More employable

" Having just graduated, our 21-year-old son is working to pay for a nine-month, round-the-world trip beginning in November. He still doesn't know what he wants to do, beyond 'something in the City', and we worry that, when he returns, all the best jobs will have been taken by next year's graduates. "

It does not work that way. His adventure will make him more employable – provided he has decided what he wants to do by the end of it.

Gap year cookery course

" My son is thinking of taking a short cookery course during his gap year, and I am keen to encourage him. Any suggestions? "

There are courses to suit every taste and pocket. At the top end there is Leith's School of Food and Wine (020 7229 0177; www.leiths.co.uk/). At a more modest cost is a two-week course at the British Institute in Florence (0039 055 2677 8270; website www.britishinstitute.it/). Courses specifically for the gap year are offered by the Edinburgh School of Food and Wine (0131 333 5001; www.cookerycompany.com/). Or you could approach your local further education college. The one in Middlesbrough advertises a course in "cookery for men".

Application and entrance requirements

Rejected

" *My son, who is taking his A-levels in June, has applied to five universities to study medicine and been rejected by them all, despite being predicted to get at least three grade As in maths, physics, biology and chemistry. What are his options?* "

> The Government controls the number of places medical schools offer and they are heavily over-subscribed. At Edinburgh, for example, 2,500 apply for 200 vacancies. Your son has three options: phone every medical school during "clearing" in August, after A-level results have been announced (slim chance); take a medically related "gap" year and try again (better chance); apply to study biological sciences (the competition is less severe) and hope subsequently to arrange a transfer.

Entrance lottery

" *Can you explain the selection procedures of certain universities? My daughter, who obtained 11 grade As (seven of them starred) at GCSE, is predicted by her sixth-form college in Wigan to achieve four grade As at A-level. She has also passed high-grade exams in cello and piano – she is a member of the Wigan Youth Orchestra – and has gained a gold medal in the Duke of Edinburgh's award scheme. Yet Durham University refused her a place to read law. Is it because she didn't go to an independent school? Or is university entry just a lottery?* "

It is increasingly a lottery. This year, Durham University's law faculty received 1,800 applications for 98 places. Without conducting interviews, the university made conditional offers to 260 of these applicants (guessing that 162 would fail to achieve the requisite two As and a B, or decide to go elsewhere). Even allowing for an abundance of talent, it is astonishing that your daughter was not among them. I doubt, though, that discrimination against applicants from the state sector plays a part – if only because I receive so many similar letters from parents of children who attend independent schools. A more likely explanation is that an overloaded system produces random results.

Which grades?

" I understand some university courses require much higher A-level entry grades than others. What is the range? "

At the top are medicine and veterinary science, both requiring three grade As; at the bottom are teacher training, social work and librarianship, for which three grade Ds will suffice. In between, English, history and psychology need, on average, grades BBC; computer science and sociology, grades CCD. The average grades obtained by last year's successful applicants were three Cs, the requirement for most courses in engineering and science.

What's the score?

" My daughter has had to drop one of her A-levels, which leaves her with only two and a half. Will that be enough to secure her a place on a degree course of repute? "

Depending on the course, she will need at least 18 points, an A grade being worth 10, a B eight and so on (AS-level grades count half). So two full Bs and a half C should do it.

The Oxbridge lottery

" I wonder whether your readers realise how much of a lottery gaining entry to Oxford and Cambridge has become. Last term, Oxford awarded a former pupil of mine – I'm the head of a prominent independent school – a brilliant First in English. Yet he'd previously been rejected by admissions tutors at Cambridge, who ignored my assurance that he was an outstanding scholar and a star by any standards. Why don't university dons accept the judgements of heads, who know their pupils so much better than the dons can after a brief interview? "

As you acknowledge in your letter, headmasters' swans can sometimes turn out to be geese, but I sympathise with your frustration: such decisions should not turn on the hasty opinions of hard-pressed dons. It underlines the case for a post-qualification admissions system that would allow students to delay applying to university until after they had their A-level results. For

Oxbridge, that would have the additional benefit of encouraging more state school applicants.

Is PE an acceptable A-level?

" Our daughter, who wants to study law, is planning to take A-levels in English, geography and physical education. We are concerned that PE may not be acceptable to universities, though her school insists it is. What is your view? "

Places to study law at good universities are among the most heavily over-subscribed. Your daughter should substitute a more academic subject – and aim for three grade Bs, at least.

Fulfilling their contract

" Our daughter has been offered a place to study business at Bath University, on condition she achieves an A and two Bs at A-level. It looks likely that she will get two As – for business studies and psychology – and a C for maths. Will they still take her? "

Probably not. The department is heavily oversubscribed and has made 130 offers but has only 80 places. Priority will go to those who fulfil the terms of their contract.

Check the procedures

" As you pointed out recently, applicants who have been rejected by medical schools can start a science degree and switch to

medicine later. However, our experience shows how important it is to check on the local education authority's procedures. Staffordshire has refused to pay our daughter's tuition fees for three years of clinical studies because she didn't tell them she was switching to medicine until the end of her second science year – but they would have funded the change at the end of the first year. On the other hand, a friend who lives in Leicestershire made the decision at the same time and will have her fees paid."

A cautionary tale: thank you.

A refusal to consider?

" *People tell us that some universities – notably Bristol, Durham and Nottingham – refuse to consider an applicant who is also trying for a place at Oxbridge. Is there any firm evidence of that? My son would prefer to go to Oxford and doesn't want to waste his other choices.* "

The allegation is often made, as frequently denied and, to my knowledge, never proved. Any evidence to the contrary will be gratefully received.

" *You asked last week if there was any evidence that universities such as Bristol, Durham and Nottingham discriminated against candidates who were also applying to Oxbridge. This year, our daughter was offered a place by all three, though she eventually chose Cambridge.* "

Thank you. I have had so many letters to the same effect that I am convinced the suggestion is untrue.

Vigorous pursuit

" Our son is preparing for an interview at Cambridge. Any tips? "

> The dons will want to be sure that he is suited to the course and will be rewarding to teach. They will look for evidence of his enthusiasm for (and wide reading in) the subject. They will probe his ability to argue logically and lucidly, and seek to discover how receptive he is to new ideas. They will probably ask about what he likes doing – interests vigorously pursued go down well – and will try to make judgements about his self-discipline, motivation and maturity.

No fall-back

" My daughter has had a provisional offer of a place to study management with French from three universities, all requiring an A and two Bs at A-level. Her two other choices turned her down, so she has no fall-back position. What should she do? "

> I am afraid she will have to wait and see what happens. The worst case would be to end up in the August "clearing" system, when universities that have been unable to fill their courses offer places to students who have failed to achieve their grades. A logical solution would be for students to apply only when they know their results. However, the vice-chancellors think that presents insuperable difficulties.

Oversubscribed

" I have been rejected by the five veterinary schools I applied to, despite being predicted to achieve three As in the appropriate A-levels. I have 10 A grades at GCSE (five of them starred), some farm experience and a good spread of other interests, including playing the violin and taking part in the Duke of Edinburgh's award scheme. I despair. What advice can you offer? "

> Veterinary science is the most heavily oversubscribed subject. If you are committed to it, you will try again next year and spend the intervening period working for a vet. There will still, though, be a significant element of chance.

She's changed her mind

" Our daughter, who is taking A-levels this month, has changed her mind about studying the subject for which she has been provisionally accepted at university. She wants to read psychology and is planning to apply during the clearing period after A-level results have been announced. Is that a good idea? "

> Psychology is heavily oversubscribed, so the chances of a place becoming available on a good course during clearing would seem to be even more remote than usual. However, the Quality Assurance Agency, which is inspecting the subject, has already judged psychology excellent (at least 23 points out of 24) at Lancaster,

Sheffield Hallam, Hertfordshire, Portsmouth and Staffordshire. All except Lancaster recruit a significant proportion of their students during clearing.

Disappointing results

" My A-levels have been very disappointing: just two grade Es. Can I train to be a primary school teacher? "

Why not? Four points are all that Central England University, Swansea Institute of Higher Education and University College Scarborough require.

Is that wise?

" My son, who wants to study biology, achieved two As and two Bs at A-level but failed to fulfil the conditions of his offer at Oxford, which was three As. Rashly, he turned down his insurance offer from Bristol and is now insisting on applying again to Oxford next year. Is that wise? "

No: it is likely only to prolong his disappointment. Alternative universities could be Birmingham, Imperial, Southampton, UCL and Warwick, all of which have had their teaching in the biosciences judged excellent.

The Abitur exams

" I am a British citizen working in Germany for a German company. My two children will take the Abitur examinations when

they are 19. Is that an acceptable qualification for entering a British university, and will they be entitled to a student loan?"

> The qualification is acceptable. Coming from the European Union, they would pay the same (heavily subsidised) tuition fees at English and Welsh universities as British students. At a Scottish university, they would have to repay a smaller proportion of the fees once they graduated. They would not be entitled to a student loan.

It matters not one whit

" I'm planning to apply to Oxford or Cambridge but don't know which colleges to choose. Would I be disadvantaged by making an open application? Could I specify that I didn't want an all-female college?"

> Both universities say there is no disadvantage in making an open application. At Oxford, the colleges do not know which route their applicants took, while at Cambridge the admissions tutors know but interviewers do not. However, only a small minority of candidates make an open application, not least because open days tend to be organised on a college basis. In fact, it matters not one whit which college you choose. If, though, you have set your face against a women's college, you cannot take the open route.

A-levels not necessary for the OU

" Does one need A-levels to enrol at the Open University? "

No. You must, though, "have the basic skills needed for study at university level" and the commitment and money to undertake it. A first degree requires students to accrue 360 points. A 60-point course assumes 16 hours of study a week and costs about £650. The Open University, Walton Hall, Milton Keynes MK7 6AA; www.open.ac.uk/.

Ten is the norm

" We read recently that Oxbridge entrants have invariably passed at least 10 (presumably A grade) GCSEs in addition to their A-levels. Our son, however, is taking only nine. Will that disadvantage him if he were to apply to Oxbridge? "

No, but 10 GCSEs have become the academic norm and eight are an absolute minimum. Most, if not all, will need to be A*.

" May I, on behalf of Oxford University, correct the impression you gave last week that applicants need straight As at GCSE? We do not prescribe such grades, and GCSE results are only a small part of the information tutors use when making offers. "

Thank you. I meant only to suggest that straight As would help an applicant's case.

Alternatives within her reach

" My daughter, who wants to take a degree in English literature, has been predicted to achieve an A and two Bs at A-level next year. However, Warwick and Leeds, her preferred universities, require two As and a B. Could you suggest similarly high status alternatives within her predicted reach, and also tell us what we should do if her actual grades are higher? "

> I suggest you ask the following for their English department prospectuses: Birmingham, Cardiff, East Anglia, Lancaster, Manchester, Newcastle upon Tyne, Nottingham, Southampton and York. If your daughter's grades exceed predictions, she should take a gap year and apply again.

Selection procedure

It resembles a lottery

" Our son is predicted by his independent school to achieve three As at A-level this summer, and yet he has been turned down by both Oxford and Bristol. Is this a record? "

> Probably not, I am afraid. In 1994, when your son began his secondary schooling, about 10,000 pupils gained three As. This year, the number is expected to be 20,000. Entry to over-subscribed courses at top universities increasingly resembles a lottery because, as the Qualifications and Curriculum Authority admits, A-levels no longer distinguish between the bright and the

very bright. However, no one in authority seems unduly concerned.

" The reader who wrote last week about his son having been turned down by Oxford and Bristol despite being predicted to achieve three As at A-level might draw comfort from the experience of my son, who is also at an independent school. A prefect, house captain and sportsman – glowing reports, exemplary record and so on – he has been rejected by both universities (to read modern history) despite being predicted to achieve four As. Can you explain that?"

No.

" Your readers whose highly qualified children are being rejected by top universities should be advised that it is Section 10 on the UCAS form – the 'personal statement' – that counts most. When nearly all the other applicants have glowing reports, exemplary records and are predicted straight As, candidates must use Section 10 to convince admissions tutors that they really want – to the point of obsession – to study their chosen subject."

Thank you. The letter is from Brian Heap, author of *Degree Course Offers*, published by Trotman, which is the most comprehensive guide to university entry. I have received up-to-date advice, too, from Nick Redman, a sixth-former at an independent school, who has just been offered a place to read modern history at Oxford. He concluded that tutors were looking for potential, measured by candidates' ability to adapt their

A-level knowledge to topics and ideas they had not previously considered. If true, it could help explain why James Morgan, another sixth-former predicted to achieve four As, was turned down by the same university. "What is the point," he demanded, "of a group of stuffy old men sitting in antique armchairs asking you questions that (a) you could never prepare for and (b) have absolutely nothing to do with your A-levels?" However, James, one of five pupils in his year rejected by Oxford or Cambridge, did raise a question that has not been answered: why, after being called for interview, was none of them given a reason for being rejected? Surely common courtesy would require no less?

Many parents wrote to say that their children, despite being turned down by Oxbridge, had gone on to enjoy glittering careers. Reassurance came, too, from an Oxford reject who phoned the graduate recruitment departments of companies he would like to work for, including Arthur Andersen and McKinsey, the management consultants. Did it matter, he asked them, which of the top 50 universities he chose? All said no.

Are student numbers still rising?

" Is the headlong expansion of universities over, or are student numbers still rising? "

Ten thousand full-time degree places were created this year and another 6,000 will be added in October. That is equivalent to a new university the size of Birmingham.

Reluctant to make wasted offers

" Our daughter, who is at an independent school, wants to go to Oxford or Durham university. However, we've heard that Durham isn't keen on offering places to pupils who also apply to Oxford. Is that true? "

> Durham tends to assume that applicants who are made an attainable offer by Oxford are likely to take it and, like all oversubscribed universities, it is reluctant to make wasted offers. However, like other good universities against which the same charge is made, it does admit candidates that Oxford has rejected. All suspicions about this issue will be dispelled in three years' time, when the admissions system is changed to prevent universities knowing where else candidates have applied.

Much depends upon interview performance

" Like Laura Spence – whose rejection by Oxford caused such a stir – our daughter attends a northern comprehensive and is planning to apply to Magdalen College. What advice would you give her? "

> As Miss Spence discovered, much depends on how applicants perform at the interview. In an attempt to demystify the process – and make some money – a group of recent graduates has assembled an elaborate package that claims to offer the inside track. Tailored to each applicant's course and college, it includes a detailed account of how the interview is structured, what the interviewers

are looking for – intelligence, enthusiasm, intellectual curiosity, teachability and love of the subject – and the questions they are likely to ask. The advice on how to prepare for the ordeal includes: read round your subject, practise thinking ("it's surprising how few people do"), don't forget to take an alarm clock, and "wear the smartest, best quality clothes and shoes you can afford". The reports cost £40 each from Application Research; phone 01789 552962 or look up www.applicationresearch.com/.

Foundation courses

Cost of a foundation course

" Our son wants to take a one-year, full-time foundation course in graphic design. How much would it cost? Would he get a local authority grant? Does it matter that he goes to an independent school?"

Students are entitled to free tuition, means-tested mandatory grants and subsidised loans only if they are studying full-time for a degree or vocational equivalent. Your son could apply to your local authority for a discretionary grant, but few are given. His school is irrelevant. If he is under 19 when he starts the course, the year's tuition will be free; if he is not, it will cost about £600 – but some colleges offer cut-rate deals.

Follow her talent

" My 19-year-old daughter is taking an art foundation course,

having obtained grade As at A-level in art, history of art and French. She also won the art prize at St Mary's, Ascot and is evidently gifted. The question is whether she should take a degree in art alone, which would restrict her career choice, or – as I believe – combine art with another subject, such as French or business studies?"

I don't know of a good fine art course that can be taken in conjunction with another subject. Art and design, on the other hand, can be combined with almost anything. While I understand your anxiety about where fine art might lead, I think you should encourage her to follow her talent and inclinations.

Compromise

" My son, who is half way through A-levels in art, economics and maths, wants to take an art foundation course and a degree in design. I am concerned that he's limiting his options and I think a broader-based degree would be a better qualification. Is there a course that would enable him to combine his interest in art with, say, business management?"

I sympathise with your concern but wonder whether your son will find the compromise appealing. London Guildhall, whose art and design provision is rated excellent, is one of a few institutions that offer a combined course in business and design studies. Another is Worcester University College.

Best art foundation course

" My son is thinking of taking a one-year art foundation course after A-levels. Is that a good idea – and how do we find a good course? "

> The aim of the course is to help school-leavers with a strong interest in art and design to identify the specialist area that best suits their skills, temperament and hopes for employment. So it is a good idea. Most further education colleges offer the course and so do many universities and art schools. You will find a comprehensive list in *Art & Design Courses*, which is published by Trotman (0870 900 2665) at £12.99. It also describes the huge variety – "the most extensive choice in Europe" – of undergraduate courses available. Quality is harder to identify and the best advice is to ask your shortlisted institutions to put you in touch with students who have recently completed the foundation year.

"Foundation" degrees

" Some months ago, David Blunkett, the Education and Employment Secretary, announced plans to introduce two-year 'foundation' degrees. What happened? "

> The idea is coming along nicely. Nottingham Trent has just announced two-year degrees in flower arranging and horse-riding, though it prefers to call them "floristry design" and "equitation".

Which way forward?

" My daughter is interested in a career as a graphic designer but her teachers can't agree on the best way forward. Some say she should take a one-year art foundation course, while others say she should start on a degree. "

> A good foundation course introduces students to the whole spectrum of arts. However, if your daughter is really committed to graphic design there is no reason to spend a year exploring the options.

Costs and funding

(Editor's note: quoted costs vary slightly from letter to letter; readers should assume the highest figures to be the most up-to-date.)

Means-tested access

" When subsidised loans replace student grants, will all students have equal access to them, as they do to the current loan? "

> No. Access will be means-tested, as it is to the current student grant.

Will fees be waived?

" My daughter, who received her A-level results last week, has arranged to spend six months of her gap year working as a volunteer at a Red Cross hospital in Japan. She did not apply

for a deferred place at university because there seemed no need and she wanted to see if her grades would be good enough to study medicine. Now that the Government has changed the rules, will her tuition fees be waived?"

> No. Quite unjustly, the "concession" announced by Baroness Blackstone applies only to those who have a deferred place. Going to university will cost her at least an extra £1,000 a year.

" My son did not apply for a deferred place next year because he wanted to do a one-year arts foundation course at a further education college before deciding which degree to take. Surely his tuition fees should be waived?"

> I am afraid they won't be – see above.

Cost per week

" Could you give me an idea of how much a student reasonably needs to live on per week?"

> Depending on the location of the college, private rented accommodation costs about £35–£45 (for a minimum of 30 weeks); self-catering in university accommodation, £40–£50; catered university accommodation, £60–£75. In all cases, add about 15 per cent for London.
>
> For food, entertainment and buying the odd book, allow about £50; for utilities, another £10. In other words, expect maintenance to cost not less than £3,500 a year – the value of the current grant plus student loan.

Phasing out the grant

" I understand student grants are being 'phased out'. How? "

Full-time students who started their courses this year are entitled to a means-tested grant equivalent to 50 per cent of what the Government assumes the cost of maintenance to be; that varies between about £2,800 and £4,200 a year, according to where they will be living while studying. The balance is made up by the student loan. Such students will retain their entitlement for the duration of their course. For those starting next year, the grant will be reduced to 25 per cent and the loan entitlement increased accordingly. However, they will lose their grant in their second year (1999), from which point no new grants will be made. Students will then be dependent on the Government's new loans scheme, access to which will be means-tested, though details are not yet available. Parents should start saving.

Industrial sponsorship

" My daughter is considering a career in civil engineering. Is there any prospect of industrial sponsorship while she's studying? "

The Institution of Civil Engineers (020 7222 7722) awards 25 scholarships each year, worth £1,250 a year, to students with a good academic record who are likely to be a credit to the profession and genuinely need financial support. In addition, many large firms of consultants and contractors run their own schemes. The Smallpiece Trust (01926 33200) offers a 28-week engineering foundation course – including European work placement – to 25 gap-year students with good A-levels and a university engineering place. Tuition and accommodation are free.

Scholarships

" Now that universities are going to charge fees, will they also offer scholarships? "

It is not clear to what extent universities will benefit from the fees the Government is imposing. However, one of the first to announce a scheme to help needy British students is the London School of Economics. It is offering 10 scholarships worth £7,500 over three years to those applying for a place next October, who will be under 21 and can prove significant financial need. Further details from the Admissions Office, Houghton Street, London WC2A 2AE (020 7955 7124).

Not our responsibility

" My wife and I want our daughter to go to university next year, but don't understand why her fees and entitlement to a government loan should be means-tested on our income. By then, she'll be over 18 and we won't have any legal responsibility for her. Why should our income be relevant to her circumstances? "

The Department for Education says: "Providing loans to cover the whole of living costs, without taking family income into account, would disproportionately benefit the better off. It would also be expensive."

An interesting investment

" *I am entitled to an interest-free student loan of £1,685, which I don't need. Is there any reason why I shouldn't put it in a high-interest building society account?* "

None at all. Your profit will be the difference between the rate of interest and the rate of inflation.

No tuition fees

" *What is the parental income level below which university students will not have to pay annual tuition fees of £1,000?* "

According to the Government, it is £23,000 before tax. However, local education authorities say it will be nearer £18,000. Students from such backgrounds studying away from home will be entitled to borrow £3,440 a year to cover their living costs, which suggests they will finish a three-year course with debts of more than £10,000.

A bizarre coincidence

" *My son and his French girlfriend both want to study English at a Scottish university, where the degree course lasts four years rather than three. My son, who lives in England, will have to pay tuition fees for all four years while his girlfriend will have to pay for only three. Some mistake, surely?"*

No, I'm afraid not: it is one of the more bizarre consequences of the Government's decision to charge students £1,000 a year. The fourth-year fee will be waived for Scottish students (to discourage them from decamping south of the border) but not for students from elsewhere in the United Kingdom who choose to study in Scotland. Under EU law, however, EU students must not be treated less favourably than local ones.

Debt, or business sponsorship?

" My daughter has always wanted to be a vet. But now that the Government is abolishing grants and introducing tuition fees, she's daunted by the prospect of the debts she would accumulate over five years of studying. Wouldn't she do better taking the sort of degree that's likely to attract business sponsorship? I understand Manchester University's Institute of Science and Technology offers a BSc in paper science subsidised by the paper industry."

Your daughter's apprehension is understandable: she is likely to have to borrow at least £15,000. But if she truly wants to be a vet and is able enough to secure a place, it is surely preferable to incur a debt than a lifetime's regret. Paper science seems a very poor substitute.

Scholarships and bursaries

" Do universities offer scholarships and bursaries? If so, where can I find details? "

Quite a few institutions do and, with the advent of tuition fees, the number is growing. Scholarships and bursaries are offered in most subjects as well as for music and sport. They are listed in *Awards*, which is published by the Independent Schools Careers Organisation, 12A Princess Way, Camberley, Surrey GU15 3SP. The booklet costs £4.50 (including p&p). Be warned, though: it is a slim volume, and the competition for the relatively few awards available is likely to be severe. *(Also see p. 287.)*

We're confused

" Our daughter, assuming she achieves the necessary A-level grades, will go to Birmingham University in the autumn. On our income, we expect to have to contribute to her £1,000-a-year tuition fee but we're confused about the arrangements for her maintenance. (She'll be living away from home.) "

The tuition fee first: if the family income is below £23,000 a year, you will not pay anything; if it is more than £35,000, you will have to pay the full £1,000; if it is between the two, you will pay a proportion.

Regarding maintenance: in her first year, your daughter will have a means-tested entitlement to a grant of £810, and an absolute entitlement to a loan of £3,545. From her second year onwards, she will have no access to a grant but an absolute entitlement to 75 per cent of a loan of about £4,000 a year, and a means-tested entitlement to the rest.

No better off

" My grandson, who lives in England, wants to study engineering with architecture at Edinburgh. However, under the Government's bizarre new rules, he would be charged tuition fees for four years, whereas Scottish students would pay for only three. Could you suggest alternative universities south of the border? "

I could: Bath, Cardiff, Leeds, Manchester and Sheffield. But their equivalent courses all last four years, so your grandson would be no better off.

Scholarships and awards

" With tuition fees looming and student grants being phased out, where can I find out about university scholarships and bursaries? "

Many universities offer help in specific subjects: engineering at Liverpool, law at UCL, physics at Surrey, geography at Oxford Brookes, textiles at Leeds, linguistics at Bangor, music at Warwick, economics at Hull – and so on. Others assist particular categories of students: the children of Devonshire Freemasons at Exeter, the sons of Nonconformist ministers at Aberystwyth, students of Asian or West Indian origin at South Bank, the physically disabled at Sussex and (unusually) the children of parents named Stewart at St Andrews. Full details in *A Guide to University Scholarships and Awards* by Brian Heap, published by Trotman.

Anomaly

" Trainee teachers who take a Post-Graduate Certificate of Education won't have to pay tuition fees for their fourth year in higher education, while those who take a four-year BEd or a BA/BSc with qualified teacher status will. Isn't that unfair? "

It is certainly an anomaly. Intending teachers, please note.

A red herring

" I am troubled by the implications of the recent case in which the High Court upheld Portsmouth City Council's refusal to pay for Alexander Faludy, a gifted and dyslexic 15-year-old, to go to Cambridge. I know the council later changed its mind, but will disabled students elsewhere still have to fight the same battle? "

No. The case was a red herring. There are more than 50,000 disabled students in higher education. They are eligible for support from the disabled students' allowance. This is funded not by the local education authorities but by the Government. "Alexander need only have applied", says the National Bureau for Students with Disabilities, which can be reached on

0800 328 5050. I can also recommend *Applying to Higher Education for Dyslexic Students* by Dorothy Gilroy. It costs £4 (including p&p) from the Dyslexia Unit, Bangor University, LL57 2DG (cheques should be made payable to Dyslexia Unit).

What would it cost?

" *A friend in India would like his daughter to take a degree in Britain. What would it cost?* "

For arts courses, £6,000–£7,000 a year, for science and engineering £2,000 more. Living expenses are about £5,000 for nine months.

Funding to be withdrawn

" *My daughter, who wants to be a primary school teacher, is thinking of taking a Post-Graduate Certificate of Education at Kingston University. Would you recommend it?* "

No. A recent Ofsted inspection found that Kingston does not teach trainees how to teach reading, and the course is in danger of having its funding withdrawn. Your daughter would do far better at Brunel or Roehampton.

Confused

" *I am confused about the new rules on university fees, grants, loans and means-testing. Where can I find help?* "

Financial Support for Students, which is published by the Department for Education and Employment, is available free by calling 0800 731 9133.

A 33 per cent rise

" *Last year, when my elder daughter started a Higher National Diploma (HND) in business studies at Farnborough College, the annual course fee was £750 and it was paid by the local education authority. This year, my younger daughter started the same course at the same college but the fee had gone up to £1,000 a year – which, under the new legislation, I have to pay. Why the 33 per cent rise?* "

The Government imposed the rate – which is the same for all diploma and degree courses – when it introduced means-tested tuition fees.

Can she avoid paying for her studies?

" *My 14-year-old grand-daughter is an Italian national attending an English school in Indonesia. In time, she will want to come to university in England. Is it true that if she establishes residence here for three years prior to that she won't have to pay for her studies?* "

Not entirely. First, she will have to have been "ordinarily" resident here for three years, which means not for the purpose of receiving full-time education. Second, depending on her parents' income, she may have to pay tuition fees of up to £1,000 a year.

Qualifying for the subsidy

" Although I am English and was educated in England, I have been denied a student loan because my parents moved to Germany three years ago. I remained at boarding school to take my A-levels. Why should I be penalised just because my parents live elsewhere in the EU? "

> To qualify for a loan at a subsidised rate of interest, a student must have been "ordinarily resident" here for three years. Your time at school does not count because the test is about whether you or your parents have been paying British taxes. Your tuition fees, however, are being paid.

How much is it all going to cost?

" Now that our elder child is busy completing her university application form, could you give us a rough idea of what it's all going to cost? "

> According to a survey by the National Union of Students, £5,881 for a 38-week year, including tuition fees, rent, food, books, clothing, travel and leisure. The maximum student loan (for those living away from home and studying outside London) is £3,635 – an annual deficit of £2,246.

Scholarships and bursaries

" I understand some universities offer students scholarships

and bursaries. Where can I find out more?"

Among others, Aberdeen gives them to engineers, Hull to economists, Lampeter to geographers, Nottingham to organists, and Staffordshire – where they are worth up to £3,000 a year – to "gifted athletes". All are listed in *Awards*, a directory that costs £5.95 from ISCO, tel: 01276 21188.

What should we expect?

" I am becoming concerned about the rising cost of putting young people through university. Our 16-year-old daughter is hoping to go in two years' time and her younger brother will almost certainly want to follow. Please could you tell us what to expect?"

You are right to be concerned. The expansion of higher education, the introduction of tuition fees and the abolition of the student grant amount to a profound but little-remarked change for middle-class parents and their children. In broad terms, a student's tuition, board and lodging is likely to cost around £5,000 a year. The Government thinks most of that should be borne by the student. So, for example, one living away from home and studying at a university outside London has an absolute entitlement to a loan of £2,726 a year, and a means-tested entitlement – based on parental income – to up to another £909. The liability to pay tuition fees of up to £1,025 a year is similarly means-tested. Parents are expected to help meet the combined cost on a sliding scale once the household income exceeds about £25,000. In theory, students from low-income homes should be able to borrow their way through university (and start work with a substantial debt). For better-off parents, though, the higher their income the tougher the decisions they face about how much to sacrifice to keep their children out of the red.

A more attractive proposition

" Don't the introduction of tuition fees and the abolition of the student grant make Buckingham, our only independent university, a more attractive proposition, given that degree courses there last two years rather than three? "

They do. The fees are £9,996 a year, but all UK and EU students are entitled to a government award of £2,340. Those who achieve three Bs at A-level (three Cs if they live in Bucks, Beds, Berks, Herts, Northants or Oxfordshire) are also entitled to a scholarship worth £3,656. That brings the fees down to £4,000. The saving is on one year's board and lodging – a year that could be spent earning.

Dance and drama

" I understand there's a new scholarship scheme for dance and drama students. Where can I find out more? "

The 820 scholarships, each worth about £6,000 a

year, have been allocated to 29 private institutions, which have all been judged to provide an excellent training. They are listed in the news section of the Department for Education and Employment's website: www.dfee.gov.uk/.

What will it cost?

" *Our daughter is about to start a one-year art foundation course, after which she hopes to embark on a degree. Apart from the annual tuition fee of £1,025, what is it all going to cost?* "

If she studies away from home, not less than £4,500 a year, which she will have to borrow or earn, unless you can help her out. With the abolition of grants, I predict a sharp fall in the proportion of students going away to university.

Debts are mounting

" *Less than six months into my university career, I find my debts mounting alarmingly and the need to find work in the summer – here or abroad – correspondingly pressing. Where do I start?* "

There are plenty of jobs in Europe and beyond for waiters, chambermaids, receptionists, campsite couriers, expedition leaders, nature guides, sailing instructors, au pairs and so on. In Britain, most of the work on offer is in shops, hotels, restaurants and telesales. You will find details of these opportunities and many more in

Summer Jobs Abroad and *Summer Jobs in Britain*, both published by Vacation Work, 9 Park End Street, Oxford. The guides cost £9.99 each but are £2 cheaper if bought through the website: www.vacationwork.co.uk/.

By implication, we'll be responsible

" *When our son goes to university he will be 18 and legally an adult. Yet the level of his tuition fees and his entitlement to a student loan are decided by reference to our income, which implies we'll still be responsible for him. How can that be?* "

The Government assumes that if you can afford to contribute to the cost of your adult son's education and upkeep, you will. If you choose not to, he will have to fend for himself.

A rip-off

" *Portsmouth University, where I am on a four-year 'sandwich' course, is insisting that I pay nearly £600 in tuition fees next year, when I shall be away on my industrial placement. The university did not help me find the placement and I won't be receiving any tuition. Isn't the charge a rip-off?* "

Yes – and as far as I know, every university imposes it.

We don't know what to expect

" *In September, our daughter will be the first member of our family to go to university. My wife and I are not well off but, naturally, will do all that we can to help her. The problem is that we don't know what to expect over the next three years or what sort of support – material and otherwise – to offer. We would very much appreciate any advice from readers who have recent experience of this."*

So, I think, would many others. Replies from parents and students will be gratefully received.

" To the parents who asked for advice about what support to offer their daughter when she goes to university, I would say first, keep in weekly contact and, second, teach her how to feed herself well on a budget."

Readers' other dos and don'ts included: do let go the apron strings – but let them know you're there for them; don't give advice unless asked; do ask what they're doing but don't fret if it sounds as if they're not working – they probably are but it's not much fun to talk about; do visit when invited (and take food); do ensure that they know they can call or come home at any time; don't pester them every week about what they're eating or whether their socks match; do be proud of them; and do be flexible, because if you are, you'll learn a lot about each other over the next few years.

Most estimates of the cost ranged between £5,500 and £6,000 a year. My thanks to all who wrote.

Costs and funding

Bench fees

" Our son, who is studying chemistry, has been asked by his university to pay a non-refundable £100 to cover 'equipment breakages'. Is that legal? "

> Yes. Tuition fees apart, universities are forbidden to charge students for goods or services that constitute "core provision", but the exceptions include art materials, field trips and "bench fees".

Changing a will

" I am considering changing my will so that my grandchildren, aged seven, six and four, benefit directly, reducing the proportion of my estate that will go to my daughter, their mother, accordingly. In relation to fees and grants, would that be advantageous or disadvantageous when they reach university? "

> It is difficult to predict what higher education policy will be in 10 or 15 years' time but the trend suggests that students will be expected to bear an ever-increasing proportion of the rising cost of a university education. Although governments will strive to ensure that cost is not a disincentive to the less well off, those who are better provided for will undoubtedly have an easier time.

Is there a catch?

" I've heard there's a website that gives details of university

scholarships and bursaries. Do you know the address? And is there a catch?"

> Thousands of scholarships and funding sources are described at the website www.freefund.com/. Freefund is a marketing operation and, although membership is free, you will find yourself on a lot of mailing lists and will have to give a month's notice to terminate the relationship.

Student life

Accommodation swap

" The arrival this week of our son's A-level results prompts the thought that, come October, thousands of students will be criss-crossing the country, leaving their parents' home in one place to seek expensive rented accommodation in another. Is there not some way of putting them in touch with one another so they could arrange a swap and save each other money?"

> Precisely the thought that occurred to Celia Dempsey, a college lecturer with five children, three of whom are hoping to go to university next year. She has set up the University Student Exchange Partnership, a non-profit-making scheme. Parents of students who are going away to study and can offer a minimum of a single, heated room with access to bathroom, kitchen and washing and drying facilities are invited to register with USEP for a small fee. Once a suitable swap has been found, another fee is payable to cover administration.

Mrs Dempsey acknowledges that most students would rather not live in someone else's home. However, with rents currently averaging £60 a week, the financial incentive is strong. For details, send an s.a.e. to: USEP, 35 Quarry Bank, Keele, Staffs ST5 5AC.

Breach of regulations

" Since my son was awarded a place at Leeds, we've been looking at student accommodation in the area. I'm in the furniture trade and have a working knowledge of the fire regulations for foam-filled products. In several of the houses we visited, I was appalled to see how flagrantly the rules are breached, even though landlords and agents can be imprisoned for failing to comply with them. Parents should be aware of the danger and students should not sign an inventory that includes furniture without the appropriate labelling. "

A timely warning – thank you. Copies of the regulations are available from the Furniture Industry Research Association, phone 01438 313433.

Cost of living

" I am hoping to go to university in the autumn, but have no idea what it will cost, particularly in terms of rent and food. Could you help? "

Costs vary around the country, but expect to pay £40–£45 a week (£55 in London) for a room in a flat or student residence, probably for 40 weeks of the year. For full board, which is at least two meals a day in single or shared accommodation, the range is £65–£70 a week (£82 in London).

Own TV: own licence

" *My son has his own television set which he wants to take to university. Will it still be covered by our household licence?* "

No – and TV Licensing would like you to know that the penalty for not having a valid licence is a fine of up to £1,000.

A poor deal

" *My daughter starts at West of England University on September 20, when freshers' week begins, but has been told she must pay rent for her university accommodation – at £49 a week – from September 6. Why?* "

It is worse than that: she will have to pay rent for 46 weeks, even though the teaching year lasts only 30 weeks. The university says the amount would be higher if the rental period were shorter and that it makes no profit on the deal.

A balanced diet on £19 a week

" *My son has just departed for university incapable, I'm ashamed to say, of boiling an egg. Could you suggest a user-*

friendly guide to preparing a modest range of appetising and, if possible, healthy dishes that won't cost him more than, say, a pint of beer?"

I have just the thing: tuna Napolitana, goulash, pea and ham risotto, herb tortilla and chicken and courgette sauté are among the 21 lip-smacking, easy-to-prepare recipes clearly set out in *Eating for Students*. It is published by Sutcliffe Collegiate Services, which says the meals have been designed to help maintain a balanced diet on £19 a week. For a free copy, phone 0117 900 3200.

New territory

" Our student son is thinking of moving out of his hall of residence to rent a house with friends. This is new territory for us and the law appears to be complex. Could you recommend a guide?"

The Which? Guide to Renting and Letting seems to have all the answers to the questions tenants (and landlords) might ask. It is available from bookshops, or can be ordered by phoning 0800 252100.

" The reader who asked recently about the law affecting students who rent property will find the answers in Assured Tenancies, *a free government guide."*

The booklet is available from: DETR Free Literature, PO Box 236, Wetherby LS23 7NB; phone 0870 1226 236.

Students are always short of money

" *We are worried that our son, who is in his first year at York University, is spending too much time delivering pizzas instead of studying. We know students are always short of money, and we help as much as we can, but how much time do they normally devote to part-time jobs?* "

A recent survey by the TUC found that, on average, students are working 14 hours a week and earning £4.37 an hour – £61 a week. More than half reported that their studies had been affected and a quarter said they had missed lectures and seminars.

They like British students over there

" *I am a first-year university student anxious to find a summer job in the United States. Any suggestions?* "

The Council on International Educational Exchanges says American employment agencies like British students for their "competency, computer literacy and exotic foreign accents". There are thousands of jobs available in offices, shops, restaurants (with 15 per cent tips) and the tourist industry. For details, contact the Council at: 52 Poland Street, London W1F 7AB (020 7478 2000; www.councilexchanges.org/).

Cost and standards of accommodation vary

" *I think you're right that Oxbridge students tend to be happy with whichever college they find themselves in, but it doesn't follow that the colleges are all equal. In cost and accommodation standards, they vary remarkably – a fact not advertised in their prospectuses. At St Anne's, Oxford, my college fee is £666 for an eight-week term, much more than at St John's, for example. Poorer students should be warned.* "

> Thank you. College fees are quoted in the Oxford "alternative" prospectus (www.ousu.org/pubs/ap/), which is written by students [2000]. The cheapest (without meals) appear to be Worcester, "average £387 but highly variable – consult bursary"; Jesus, £431; Queen's, £440; and Merton, £450. St John's is "£420 plus a fixed charge of £72.60". By contrast, St Edmund Hall costs £586 without meals, more than New College charges with dinner (£565). The most expensive appears to be Oriel: £770 "including 58 dinners, 50 lunches". Cambridge's alternative prospectus (www.cusu.cam.ac.uk/publications/altpro/) does not, alas, give college fees.

Halls are not covered for fire

" *Your readers who have children living in student halls of residence may be interested in my disturbing discovery that these are not covered by the 1971 Fire Protection Act. Instead, they are treated as 'houses in multi-occupancy', which means that they're not required to have any kind of smoke detection system. Given the unhappy connection between students, alcohol and fires, this is most worrying.* "

Thank you. Parents please note.

I wish I had been better prepared

" *Having survived – just – my first year at university, I know I'm not alone in wishing I had been better prepared for the shock of living away from home among thousands of strangers and being expected to make my own way in an unfamiliar environment. Please would you pass on this warning to the class of 2000?* "

Thank you. Research just published by Dr Meg Barker of Cheltenham and Gloucester College of Higher Education found that one university student in six suffers from chronic loneliness during his or her first year. The worst times were: during the first week; in the middle of the first term (when the excitement has died down); just after Christmas (when homesickness is common); and at the start of exams. The most vulnerable included those with low confidence in their social skills, students living off campus or in single-sex halls of residence, and those taking joint honours degrees (because they did not feel they "belonged" in either of their fields of study). Disturbingly, a quarter of the 500 students Dr Barker questioned – at a "traditional" university – had considered leaving, and half had considered changing course.

As I have argued here before, such findings emphasise that schools and colleges are not doing enough to counter the rosy view of themselves that universities project. Young people need more realistic information about what to expect before embarking on the "best days of their lives" – and far more advice and support when they get there.

Dropping out and other problems

Time to consider

" I have just heard that I failed the first year of my maritime studies degree. I don't feel motivated to re-take it and would like to take a year out while I consider what to do next. Would that affect my entitlement to a further grant? "

Grants are being phased out from next year. A further grant this year would be at the discretion of your local education authority (you have lost your entitlement). You may be eligible for a future student loan but that won't become clear until the Government publishes a White Paper in the autumn. From next year, you will also be liable for a means-tested tuition fee – if not, in your case, the full fee. To be thinking of a "year out" in such circumstances seems a luxury, if not an avoidance. You should look on it as the first stage in a "portfolio" career.

The wrong choice

" My 18-year-old daughter, who is artistically talented and gained three grade As at A-level, is in her first term at Bath University doing business administration. She realises now that she made the wrong choice and would be much happier

with a career in something more creative, such as design, advertising or fashion. Bath doesn't offer a suitable alternative. What can she do?"

She should immediately tell the university and her local education authority that she has changed her mind. There is no shame in that and as long as she leaves the course within 20 weeks of starting, she will not lose her right to a further grant. Then she should consider the range of art and design courses in the UCAS (Universities and Colleges Admissions Service) guide. She might find a suitable place in January as other students discover that they, too, made the wrong choice. Alternatively, she could apply for entry next year and spend the interim gaining work experience in the area that interests her.

No motivation

" Having obtained decent A-level grades last summer, I embarked on a university degree course. However, I realise now that I have no motivation for the course and I am on the verge of leaving. I'd be grateful for your opinion on my predicament. "

Congratulations on having the courage to acknowledge that you have made a mistake. I think the pressure on young people to continue seamlessly on to university is quite unreasonable. Clearly, you need time to find what interests you. Your tutor will tell you how to ensure that the way is clear for you to return to higher education later, should you wish to do so.

Let him take a break

" Our son, a scholar at his independent school, has decided to drop out of university after two terms, even though he loves the life. He says he is not motivated – he had already changed courses – and doesn't know what to do. We're devastated. Have you any suggestions? "

> Perhaps he needs a break. If he did not take a gap year after school, encourage him to take one now. If he did, suggest he find a job, any job, while he sorts things out. "Devastated", though, makes me uneasy. Have you been pressing too hard?

No magical properties

" My daughter, who is half way through a four-year degree course, is unhappy and disillusioned with the subject she chose. She has warned her brother, who is mid-way through A-levels and very unsure of what to do, not to make the same mistake and to take a psychometric test. Is that a good idea? "

> The tests, which are conducted by careers analysts, can be useful in helping to identify aptitudes and interests. However, they have no magical properties and cannot be relied on to ward off unhappiness and disillusionment.

She'd like to transfer

" My daughter has just started a degree in sports studies but

finds the teaching poor and the timetable rather empty. She'd like to transfer to another university. Where would be best?"

> The subject has not been inspected yet, so she should choose a university with an academic reputation to maintain.

Make the best of her chosen university

" My daughter is disappointed in the university at which she has started reading English, but doesn't have good enough A-level grades to go to a better one. What should she do?"

> She could either switch to a further education college or independent tutorial college and try to improve her grades, or buckle down and make the best of her university (which, incidentally, has had its English teaching judged excellent). The important point is that students who drop out must tell their local education authority or risk losing their entitlement to subsidised fees in the future, a penalty they will almost certainly suffer if they hang on and then fail their first-year assessment. For further details, see *Financial Support for Students*, available free by calling 0800 731 9133.

No one will offer me a place

" Help, please. I'm 21 and waiting to start my second year at Bangor, where I'm reading criminology. But I haven't settled in and dislike the course and the university. If I struggle on, I'll probably end up with a poor degree and a £10,000 debt.

I really want to take film studies but no one will offer me a place. What's your advice?"

> You should give criminology your best shot because you will feel better about yourself if you do and the degree will be useful in ways you cannot foresee. In your spare time, develop your interest in film so that when you next apply, you will be taken seriously.

She would like to switch

" My daughter has just started a degree in Spanish at Southampton but is not enjoying the course and would like to switch to geography. What should she do?"

> She will have to act quickly if she is to move this year because universities impose a deadline. She should talk first to her personal tutor about her reasons for wanting to change and then to the geography admissions tutor. Southampton's student advice centre publishes a useful booklet, *Changing or Leaving Your Course*. If your daughter does switch, she needs to tell her local education authority.

Drop-out rate

" While I'm digesting the news that the Government is allowing universities to recruit another 80,000 students, could you remind me what the current drop-out rate is?"

> One in five – about 75,000 students.

Appalling

" The appalling failure and drop-out rates that you reported recently suggest far too many young people are being encouraged to go to university. Are there any plans to reduce the proportion? "

> On the contrary. David Blunkett, the Education and Employment Secretary, told the CBI last month that he wanted one school leaver in two to "take advantage of the academic challenge of higher education". At present, the proportion is one in three.

Degree results

Hidden failure

" My son, who is in the final year of his honours degree, has been told he may have to content himself with an 'ordinary' degree. What does that mean? "

> Ordinary or pass degrees are awarded to students who score between 35 per cent and 39 per cent. It means they have failed – but no one need know.

Appeals

" My son has just been awarded an upper second-class degree in business studies at Canterbury Christ Church university college and is very disappointed. He achieved first class marks throughout the course and was led to believe he would gain a first. Is there an appeals system? "

Every university has one. The general principle – as Manchester, for example, makes clear – is that "there shall be no provision for appeal against the academic judgement of the examiners". A "review" of their decision may be granted if there were "circumstances affecting the student's performance", procedural irregularities in the examination process, or evidence of prejudice or bias on the part of one or more of the examiners. Bristol, where an appeal can be taken all the way up to the Queen (in practice, the Law Lords), says that it receives a steady trickle now that students pay fees and increasingly see themselves as consumers. At Canterbury Christ Church, the only grounds for appeal are "illness or other grave and exceptional misfortune", and "material administrative error".

Recognising experience in the measurable world

" Is it true that engineers and scientists are more likely to be awarded a first-class degree than arts graduates? If so, why? "

It is true. Last year, 7.4 per cent of the 35,000 students who graduated in engineering and technology were awarded a first, compared with 3.1 per cent of the same number who took social, economic and political studies. Similarly, 8.2 per cent of the 19,000 who took physical sciences were awarded a first, compared with 5.4 per cent of the 14,000 who graduated in the humanities. The lowest proportion of firsts was in law (2.1 per cent), business and administrative studies (1.9 per cent) and education (1.6 per cent). It is unlikely that the ablest students shun the arts, so the answer must be that universities are more confident of recognising excellence in the measurable worlds of engineering and science.

She shouldn't brood

" My daughter graduated from Cambridge in the summer with a lower second in social and political sciences, a class of degree she seems to regard as a 'fail'. Her disappointment saddens me and I'd welcome your comments. "

There is no denying that a lower second is a failure of a kind when a "good" degree is defined as a first or upper second and – thanks to academic inflation – 70 per cent of those who graduate from the most selective universities are now awarded one or the other. However, your daughter has had a fine education at one of the best universities in the world, so I don't think she should brood.

" I am in a similar position to the mother who wrote to you recently about her daughter's disappointment at gaining a lower second from Cambridge. What especially disturbs me is that friends of my daughter who did half as well at A-level were awarded upper seconds by far less academically selective institutions than the one she chose. Could her friends really have overtaken her from a much lower base? "

It is not impossible but I take your point, as do most employers. Hardly any now believe that a degree from, say, Derby or Teesside is worth the same as one from, say, York or Nottingham. However, degree classes do confuse the issue (is a first from Derby worth more than a lower second from York?), and perhaps the time has come to abolish them.

" Your claim last week that degrees from top universities are more highly regarded takes no account of the many departments at more lowly ranked institutions that have been judged excellent by the Quality Assurance Agency. Examples from the paramedical sciences include speech therapy at Manchester Metropolitan (61st in your league table) and physiotherapy at Bradford (86th). "

It is a fair point, which underlines the importance for applicants of considering both the quality of the course (for details, see www.qaa.ac.uk/) and of the institution.

Studying abroad

Is this feasible?

" Our son wants to go to an American university after A-levels. Is this feasible, and how do we start looking? "

There are more than 4,000 British undergraduates studying at American universities. College league tables are on the Internet at: www.usnews.com/.

University in the US

" Our son and some of his grammar school friends are interested in exploring the possibility of going to university in America. How much would it cost, and where could they find out more? "

> The all-in cost ranges from about £10,000 a year at the least expensive state university to three times that at the most expensive Ivy League institutions. The best guide is *Undergraduate Study in the United States*, published by the Fulbright Commission. It can be ordered on the website, www.fulbright.co.uk/, or by phoning 020 7404 6994.

Study in Europe

" What opportunities are there for students to spend part of their time studying at universities in Europe? "

> Extensive. Options under Erasmus – the European Communities Action Scheme for the Mobility of University Students – include studying accounting in Austria, business in Belgium, drama in Denmark, geology in Germany, nursing in the Netherlands and physiotherapy in Finland. Although most courses require students to have at least a GCSE in the relevant language, some include language teaching from scratch. The period abroad lasts a minimum of three months and a maximum of 12. Those who spend a full academic year away have their tuition fees paid by the

Government. Although every university offers Erasmus opportunities in a range of subjects, only five per cent of UK students take advantage of them. A detailed guide, costing £13, is published by ISCO, the Independent Schools Careers Organisation, phone 01276 21188; www.isco.org.uk/. Or see the website: http://europa.eu.int/comm/education/socrates/erasmus/home.html./

Post-graduate study

Post-grad funding

" My daughter, who is in the final year of a degree course in microbiology, is expected to gain an Upper Second and wants to take a post-graduate degree. But I am loth to commit myself to funding it. What help is available to me? "

The main sources are the research councils – in her case, medical or biotechnology and biological – which offer a limited number of studentships covering tuition fees and living costs. For job-related postgraduate study, a government-sponsored Career Development Loan may be available (for details, phone 0800 585505). General information about grants and awards can be found in *The Grants Register*, published by Macmillan but available in most large libraries. Universities reckon that a postgraduate student needs £5,000 a year to live; on top are tuition fees, which average about £2,500 a year.

University and other further education

MBA: not a passport to a job

" After gaining a good degree in Arabic from Edinburgh, my son worked for three years as a reasearcher for an Arabic TV station in London and then, because he seemed unlikely to be promoted, as a tour leader in Arab countries for an adventure travel company. Two years later, he is back in England, unemployed and has found careers consultants and employment agencies no help. What should he do? Would an MBA lead to a more stable and rewarding career? "

> Being able to speak Arabic, unless your son wants to be a translator, does not amount to much of a career qualification – though if he wants to go into business, choosing a company that has Arab customers would be sensible. An MBA is an expensive introduction to management (fees top £10,000), not a passport to a job. Five years after graduating, your son needs to decide what he wants to do. Simply wanting a job is not enough.

In the university's interest

" My son is in the final year of a degree course in music and music technology and has been told that he is likely to achieve an upper second or first and should consider taking a master's degree. Is that a good idea? "

> Not necessarily. More than half of students are now awarded at least an upper second, so it is not a mark of particular distinction. Also, remember that it is in the

university's interest to encourage graduates to stay on.

Find a job before further study

" My son is taking a degree in history and European studies and hopes to make a career in finance. What sort of course should he take after he graduates? "

Enough courses for the time being. When he has found a job he will have a better idea of what to study next.

Better to work her way up

" My daughter, who is not expected to gain very good A-levels, wants to take a degree in media studies but has had offers only from rather second-rate universities. Wouldn't she be better off taking a computing or secretarial course and working her way up in a publishing firm? "

The media courses at some universities low down the league table – Bournemouth, Central Lancashire, Liverpool John Moores, Luton and Sunderland among them – have been judged excellent and boast respectable employment records. Highest rated of all – better than 31 universities – is the Chichester Institute of Higher Education, now redesignated a university college. I do not think you should consign your daughter to a secretarial course if she really wants to study for a degree.

Will it pay off?

" Our daughter, who is just starting the final year of a joint honours degree in French and history, wants to follow her course with a PhD. After so many years of school fees and university upkeep, we had been hoping not to have to pay out any longer. Could you tell us what funding might be available, how long the course will last, and whether it will pay off? "

> You should assume little or no funding, a minimum of three years' study and little financial advantage. In short, your daughter needs to be very clear about why she wants a PhD and what she proposes to do with it. If the answer is university teaching, I am afraid you will all have to pull in your belts.

They can't write English

" I was appalled by your recent story about the inability of foreign post-graduate students at Kent University to write English. It was followed by a letter from the vice-chancellor, who said such students were required to pass the British Council's International English Language Test. How hard is that? "

> There are two tests: academic reading and academic writing. A sample passage from the first, which tests comprehension, includes the sentence: "Out of the numerous wind turbine designs proposed or built by inventors or developers, the propeller-blade type, which is based on detailed analytical models as well as exten-

sive experimental data, has emerged as predominant among the more than 20,000 machines now in commercial operation world-wide."

Then there are 10 questions with multiple-choice answers. A sample of the academic writing test includes a 40-minute essay on: "It is inevitable that as technology develops so traditional cultures may be lost. Technology and tradition are incompatible – you cannot have both together." Both tests are taken under exam conditions and marked by British Council examiners. Sue Holness, the source of my story, who is employed by master's and PhD students at Kent to turn their essays and theses into English, says she finds it hard to believe that any of her customers could have understood the questions, let alone pass the tests.

Overseas students make up a quarter of the postgraduates at British universities. They pay fees of up to £10,000 a year.

" I rent rooms to postgraduate students at Nottingham University. One of them is Japanese and I know from the notes she writes me that her command of English is rudimentary. Yet she's doing a PhD in English literature. She has her work re-written by one of a growing band of people on the campus who do it for a living. Can her department be ignorant of what's going on? More fundamentally, what effect is it having on the standing of British degrees? "

Clearly, the assumption that students awarded a British degree can read and write English at graduate level no longer holds true. Yet the line between correcting their English and writing their dissertations for them is a fine one. Further examples, please, of what is beginning to look like an academic scandal.

" As a footnote to your disturbing reports about universities recruiting overseas students who can't write English, you might like to know that the International English Language Test, which some but not all universities require, is not a pass/fail exam. Students are awarded marks out of nine for each of four skills – reading, writing, listening, speaking – which are then averaged to a single mark. Nine is said to be equivalent to the English level of an educated native speaker. Departments set their own pass mark, and I know of many that accept a score of six, which is below GCSE level, or even less. That – no matter what vice-chancellors say – is how the dumbing down occurs. "

Thank you.

The next step

Topics in this final section include work experience, graduate employment prospects and expectations, career changes and lifelong learning.

The only route to a career?

On probation

" My daughter has just graduated with a 2:1 in criminology. She wants to join the probation service, but has been told that they're not recruiting at present and that her degree is irrelevant because they do their own training. Is this true? "

> It is worse than that: there is no system of training or recruiting probation officers and no requirement for a specific qualification. However, the Home Secretary has announced that a Diploma in Probation Studies is to be introduced. It will take account of trainees' work experience and academic record.

Best for hotel management

" My son is considering a career in hotel management. Among the many courses on offer, are any highly regarded by employers? "

The short answer is no: indeed, the industry recently complained to the Higher Education Funding Council that universities and colleges were failing to meet its needs. However, universities you might consider include Manchester Metropolitan, Oxford Brookes, Surrey and Strathclyde.

A positive choice

" The assumption now is that any half-intelligent child should go to university and that a degree will lead to a job. But is it true? Our elder daughter did well at A-levels and graduated in geography from Birmingham last year. After a fruitless and discouraging search for worthwhile employment, she is working as a receptionist for £6,000 a year without any prospects. With hindsight, we think she would have done better to have started work at 18 in a bank or an insurance company. By now she would have had four years' experience and earnings behind her, and we would have saved £10,000. If the principal purpose of education is to fit people for a role in society, it has failed in her case. It is also sad to see a girl who, until a year ago, was happy and positive become cynical and disillusioned. Now our younger daughter is half way through A-levels and hoping to go to university. Should we discourage her? "

I would like to answer this question together with the one that follows.

" My 23-year-old grandson graduated from Liverpool last summer with an upper-second in politics. He likes sport but

little else seems to interest him. Had he qualified in accountancy, banking, law, engineering or the sciences, I'd have known how to advise him. But politics? He doesn't want to teach or be a researcher at Westminster, and the career opportunities seem limited. In my day, people found a job after going to university. I wonder if your readers share my puzzlement?"

It is true that a degree no longer guarantees a worthwhile job (something the graduate unemployment statistics disguise), but then 30 per cent of the age group now goes to university compared with five per cent a generation ago. For the substantial minority who enrol without having identified a career, the principal purpose of higher education is personal development. So I don't think young people who really want to go to university should be discouraged – but nor do I think they should be shielded from the financial consequences, which are greater now than ever.

However, I do deplore the cultural pressure on school leavers to go directly to university. For those not strongly committed to a course by interest or vocation, there is no advantage in terms of job prospects or personal development. Far better to try a variety of jobs until light dawns; then going to university, full-time or part-time, becomes a positive choice.

Back off

" Our son achieved 10 good GCSEs and then dropped out of school for a year. Now 18, he has just finished his first year at a tutorial college, where he is taking business studies and

history of art. He dropped history, refused to take up a third subject and is adamant that he doesn't want to go to university. He also has no idea what career he wishes to pursue. What can we do? Will companies consider management trainees with two A-levels?"

> I am afraid you are going to have to get used to the idea that your son, like many others of his age, does not yet know what to do with his life and does not want you trying to decide for him. Offer him encouragement, sympathy and judicious support – but otherwise back off. (PS: I have just such a one of my own.)

A better preparation

" Could I enlist your support in my campaign to persuade young people who want to be hairdressers that the best way to learn is not to go to a further education college for two years but to be apprenticed to a reputable salon? Not only is there a severe national shortage of apprentices but the failings of the college route have led to a dearth of talented hair stylists. "

> The letter is from Trevor Mitchell, current world hairdressing champion and owner of a chain of salons. He complains that aspirant hairdressers are being pressured by careers advisers and colleges that are funded on the basis of the number of students they can attract to take a two-year, full-time National Vocational Qualification (NVQ), which is not necessarily the best preparation for the job. "An apprentice with two years' experience will have far more advanced hairdressing skills than his

or her college counterpart", he says. Apprentices start at £63 a week, receive tips and are encouraged to study part-time for their NVQ. Details from the National Hairdressers' Federation, phone 01234 360332.

Culinary arts

" I am 17 and determined to be a chef. What's the best way of going about it? "

Most further education colleges offer a range of catering qualifications but none as intriguing as the "academy of culinary arts" at Bournemouth and Poole, which is striving to "change the workhouse image" of the British catering industry. During the three-year course, students aged 16 to 18 receive a salary, free accommodation and work experience at such venues as the Savoy and the Connaught. Graduates include Gary Robinson, chef to the Prince of Wales. Phone 01202 205836.

Motoring ahead

" The summit of my 17-year-old son's ambition is to be a car salesman. I think he should at least go to university first. What would you advise? "

Don't despair: at Loughborough he could do a BSc in "retail automotive management", a part-time degree run in conjunction with Ford. Loughborough says it represents a "quantum leap forward in increasing the professionalism of the sector". Then he could do an MSc in the same subject.

The Montessori method

" Please could you tell me where I could find out more about the Montessori method? I am interested in training as a nursery nurse."

Contact the Montessori Centre, 18 Balderton Street, London W1. Or see the website: www.montessori.ac.uk/.

Graduate job prospects

Not a clue!

" My grand-daughter, a shy, sensitive girl, has just gained a BSc degree from Cardiff, but doesn't have a clue what to do next. What would you advise?"

I receive an astonishing number of similar letters, and yet there is a wealth of advice to be had – from university careers offices, the Government careers service and libraries and bookshops. Also, for those who need help in focusing their interests, vocational guidance and psychometric testing are widely available. The problem is that, after 16 years of education, many young people have no idea how to shift for themselves.

Graduate jobs

" Now that we have a 'mass' higher education system, aren't there more graduates than graduate jobs? "

It depends what you mean by graduate jobs. A survey by the Institute of Personnel and Development found that many employers were astonished by the number of graduates applying for low-level jobs. As one – a recruiter for a Yorkshire-based retailer – put it: "I've had graduates with history and physics degrees in here virtually begging me for a job that, in my opinion, could be done by a monkey and pays absolute peanuts." However, another considered that routine clerical work was "very suitable for someone with a Lower Second from a new university who has only ever worked part-time in Sainsbury's". With the advent of mass higher education, graduates are no longer necessarily high fliers with high-flying expectations, and most would rather get a toe in the door than sit at home doing nothing.

There is also evidence that graduates can turn mundane jobs into challenging ones. As the Institute of Personnel and Development survey concluded: "A graduate job now is any job a graduate can get."

Where are they now?

" What happens to sociology graduates? "

Six months after graduating, 33 per cent of the class of

1996 were working as clerks, cashiers, sales assistants or waiters/waitresses; 10 per cent were unemployed. Media studies graduates fared even worse: 45 per cent were working in "unrelated" areas; 12 per cent did not have a job.

In no hurry

" My daughter did well at school: 10 A grades at GCSE followed by an A and two Bs at A-level. She spent a gap year teaching English to Arabs in Israel. Now she's in her final year at university reading government and law. She spends her weekends at Officer Training Corps camps and plans to go to Belize in the summer with Raleigh International. What she lacks, though, is any interest in finding a job. Do you think all these extra-curricular activities really help? Or do they merely distract her? "

Many would say your daughter is acquiring a model CV. But I understand your unease and urge you to be patient. The culture has changed: many young people today are in no hurry to commit themselves and the progress from education to employment has become much more erratic.

What future?

" My son wants to take a course in hospitality and catering. What sort of future is there in such a subject? "

Rosy, according to the Hotel and Catering Management Association. It says the "leisure industry" employs one in 10 of all employees, creates one new job in five and will require 30,000 trained people at management and supervisory level every year until 2010. It has just introduced a professional certificate to be taken part-time over two years at further education colleges.

Biology degree: what next?

" My daughter is in the final year of a biology degree and is beginning to wonder where it might lead. Any suggestions? "

Almost anywhere, according to the Association of Graduate Careers Advisory Services. Last year, about 25 per cent of biology graduates found related jobs – as laboratory technicians, for example; another 25 per cent were employed as managers, administrators or trainees in other professions; and 30 per cent became clerks, secretaries, sales assistants, check-out operators and waiters or waitresses. The last category accounted for 40 per cent of graduates in English.

English: an alternative?

" You reported recently that 40 per cent of English graduates become clerks, secretaries, sales assistants and so on. As my son plans to read English and has no specific career in mind – he doesn't want to teach – I wondered whether you could suggest an alternative course that might lead to a fulfilling job. "

I am afraid I can't, but I am convinced that students

can no longer afford to put off choosing a career until they are half way through their final year. I do not want to detract from the value of study for its own sake, but, like it or not, going to university is a preparation for earning a living and the sooner students make – and develop – the connection, the better.

A good reputation

" My son is hoping to obtain a degree in underwater studies from Plymouth: a new course at a new university. How is the employment market likely to view it? "

The title sounds slightly risible: it is actually underwater science. Those who employ such graduates will know that Plymouth's reputation is good.

He's disillusioned

" My son, a mature student, graduated recently from Edinburgh with an MA in Scottish history and philosophy. He can't find a job and is very disillusioned. Have you any suggestions? "

Why, I wonder, is he disillusioned? It is hardly a vocational degree. On second thoughts, perhaps the Scottish Parliament will offer him a berth.

What should they do?

" My elder daughter graduated in psychology at

Manchester last year and, like many graduates, is still undecided about a career. She is torn between taking a job in personnel and studying for a further qualification in psychology. My younger daughter is half way through a degree in microbiology at Newcastle but doesn't enjoy the laboratory work and would rather be in publishing. I would welcome your advice. "

> Your elder daughter ought to find a job and study part-time. Your younger daughter should finish her degree: publishers value scientific literacy.

What went wrong?

" *After passing 11 GCSEs and three A-levels at an independent school, my son went to Lampeter University where he studied archaeology and, to our dismay, was awarded a third. Now, nearly five years later, he has had a series of low-paid, temporary jobs and his self-confidence has drained away. What went wrong?* "

> Perhaps you and he thought a degree would automatically lead to a graduate-level job. As a growing number of graduates and their parents are discovering, it does not – and assuming it does can be a real handicap. It discourages job-seekers from understanding that, whatever the class of their degree, they may have to start at the bottom and that progress will depend entirely on their own efforts.

A warning to others

" Eighteen months ago, my son, who is now 28, completed a PhD in soil science at London University. Since then, despite several hundred job applications across a wide range of occupations, the only work he has been able to find is as a stable boy and a gardener. Usually, he's told he is too old, overqualified or that his degree subject is not relevant. I would appreciate your advice. "

I publish this more as a warning to others than because I think I can help.

Before embarking on his PhD, your son must have known that the demand for soil scientists was limited. Why, then, did he persist? Was it because his lecturers – whose jobs depend in part on recruiting graduate students – persuaded him that it was a sensible way to spend his time? Did they neglect to warn him that, outside their narrow areas of expertise, most PhDs are beached whales?

The best advice I can give your son is to abandon his scatter-gun approach to job hunting, pick something he really wants to do and set about gaining the appropriate qualifications.

Increasingly common

" Since my grandson gained a first in modern history at Oxford last year, he has toured Australia and languished in a series of odd jobs. What is to be done? "

Nothing, I am afraid. He will find a career if he wants one. The phenomenon is not confined to Oxford graduates and is becoming increasingly common.

An awfully risky step

" My daughter, who has just graduated in art and design, has decided to set up in business on her own. It seems an awfully risky step. What are her chances? "

The graduate market is changing and your daughter is part of a growing trend. The Institute of Employment Studies estimates that one in three graduates would like to be self-employed but only about half of them make it, chiefly because they tend not to have the necessary entrepreneurial and business skills. Universities should wake up to the problem.

A cultural phenomenon

" I have two sons at different stages of education but with the same problem: neither knows what to do about a career nor where to turn for advice. The elder is in the final year of a master's degree in chemistry at Oxford. He doesn't want to be a chemist and, after visiting several graduate fairs, has decided he isn't interested in finance, the City, teaching, the police or management. My younger son obtained 10 good GCSEs without much effort but dropped out of A-levels after a year and is now completing an NVQ in catering. He doesn't want to take that any further and refuses to return to academic study. All he can say is that he'd like to 'work with people'. Any

advice would be gratefully received as I have two unhappy and despondent young men on my hands."

I receive so many letters in similar vein that I am convinced we are witnessing a cultural phenomenon. It stems, I think, from our liberal insistence on divorcing education from employment (in sharp contrast to Germany and Japan, for example). The consequence is that many young people see no connection between the two, so the need to find a job, when it is at last grudgingly acknowledged, comes as a surprise. Aptitude testing by a reputable vocational guidance body – such as Career Psychology, phone 020 7976 1010 – may help, but the most powerful stimulus is likely to be the discovery that having no money or a boring job is no fun.

Is it true?

" Is it true that those who study modern languages at university have a good employment record?"

On the face of it, yes, but six months after graduating, 31 per cent are working as clerks or secretaries, compared with 23 per cent of all new graduates.

" As an employer and member of the council of Bristol University, I was surprised by your apparently disparaging reference recently to clerks and secretaries – which is what, you said, 31 per cent of language graduates become. In my experience, the secretarial route is one of the best ways for arts grad-

uates to get a foot on the ladder of many careers."

Thank you.

They're all in New York

" My daughter has recently graduated in fashion design but can't find a job. She has approached agencies, answered advertisements, networked, taken work experience placements, combed the Internet, cold-called, etc. Have you any suggestions? "

> The best my own search produced was the website www.fashion.net/ – "the world's leading fashion site" – but the advertised jobs all seemed to be in New York.

Expected salaries

Graduate salaries

" My daughter, who graduated this summer, is still looking for a job. What salary do you think she should reasonably expect? "

> According to the latest figures [2000], the median (middle point of the range) starting salary for graduates this year is £17,000.

Myths

" My daughter is thinking of taking engineering at university but is put off by stories that it is underpaid, leads nowhere and is unsuitable for girls. What do you think? "

> These are all myths, according to the Engineering Council. It says chartered engineers earn more than £40,000 on average; that 17 of the top executives of the FTSE 100 companies are engineers (14 are accountants); and that 15 per cent of engineering undergraduates are female. In the words of Women into Science and Engineering (Wise): Go for it.

" Recently, in response to a reader whose daughter was thinking of taking engineering, you quoted the Engineering Council's assertion that chartered engineers earn more than £40,000 on average. As a 28-year-old, female, chartered civil engineer working for one of the largest civil engineering consultancies in the UK, I earn half that. I simply do not believe the quoted figure. Although I enjoy my job, it was the supposedly excellent pay that initially attracted me, and discovering the truth has come as a great disappointment. "

> The Engineering Council stands by its figure, which came from a survey last year of 10,000 chartered engineers at all stages of their careers in a range of disciplines.

" Forgive me for pursuing the matter, but as a chartered engineer I simply cannot accept the Engineering Council's claim

that we earn £40,000 a year on average. I have strongly advised my daughters not to take up engineering as a career because it does not lead to a good living."

I have had so many similar letters that I can only conclude the Council's figure is based on an unrepresentative sample. The universities' inability to recruit enough able students also lends weight to the view that job prospects are unattractive.

Does it pay?

"*Does it pay to have a degree?*"

Handsomely. On average, male graduates earn 60 per cent more than non-graduates of the same sex, and women earn 90 per cent more (though taking all levels of education together, women still earn only half what men do).

Which pay best?

"*Can you tell me which degrees lead to the highest salaries?*"

Those who are best paid 10 years after graduating studied dentistry, law, economics, maths, physics, accountancy, engineering, geology and medicine.

Careers advice

Animated

" My 17-year-old grand-daughter, who has passed 10 GCSEs and is taking three A-levels, is keen to pursue a career in animation. How should she go about it? "

> Two colleges – Newport, Wales (01633 432432) and the Surrey Institute of Art and Design (01372 728811) – run BA (Hons) courses in animation, while the Glamorgan Centre for Art and Design (01443 663309) offers an HND (Higher National Diploma), which can be converted to a degree in the third year. All three attach great value to candidates' portfolios and emphasise the importance of life drawing skills.

Best for PR

" Our daughter, who is due to graduate next summer with a degree in modern languages, wishes to pursue a career in corporate hospitality or public relations. She's personable and gregarious, but we feel she'll need more vocational skills. What would be the most appropriate post-graduate course? "

> Some universities, including Stirling and Manchester Metropolitan, offer one-year, full-time courses leading to a Master's degree in public relations. More convincingly, Cardiff runs a two-term diploma course plus 200 hours' work placement. Details are available from the Institute of Public

Relations, 15 Northburgh Street, London EC1V 0PR (020 7253 5151).

How to become a journalist

" My son, who has been told he has a gift for writing, wants to become a journalist. How should he go about it? "

Journalism is a broad church with many doors and lengthy queues at most of them. Academically able youngsters seeking a career in the national media should take a degree in whatever most interests them and then consider a one-year post-grad course at a well-regarded journalism school, such as those at Cardiff and City universities.

Candidates with more modest ambitions, or those who are less academically inclined, should consider the vocationally oriented courses in journalism and media studies now offered by more than a score of universities – many have first-rate employment records. Among the departments officially graded excellent are those at East Anglia, Warwick, Central Lancashire, Goldsmiths', Liverpool John Moores and West of England. School-leavers who have completed their A-levels and are keen to go straight to work should consult the National Council for the Training of Journalists: 01279 430009. *Media Courses UK*, which is published by the British Film Institute (020 7957 8920), costs £13.99 and offers a detailed guide to available courses; it is stocked by most large bookshops. But it is worth bearing in mind that opportunities for exercising a gift for writing are generally limited.

The next step

" My son, who is half way through A-levels and expected to gain reasonably good grades, wants to become a journalist. However, he's an exceptionally shy, sensitive lad and is insisting on applying to the same universities as his friends, even though they don't offer exactly the course he wants. Surely it's the course that matters – or should I leave him to make his own decisions? "

> I think it is more important that he should be where he wants to be. Besides, modularity makes almost any course possible. Shyness in journalists, incidentally, is rare: it could be a handicap.

" My son, who is studying economics at university, has decided he wants to be a journalist. I'd like to encourage him but don't know where to start. "

> Write to the National Council for the Training of Journalists at Latton Bush Centre, Southern Way, Harlow, Essex CM18 7BL or, better still, see the website: www.itecharlow.co.uk/nctj/.

A career in the Stock Exchange

" My son is interested in a career in the Stock Exchange. Could you advise? "

> The Exchange does not employ stockbrokers but represents about 400 firms that do. For a list of the companies and a booklet about the Exchange, write to the London Stock Exchange, London EC2N 1HP. For de-

tails of qualifications required for the securities industry, write to: The Securities Institute, 24 Monument Street, London EC3R 8AJ.

An unusual gift

" My 15-year-old son shows no inclination for any particular career but has an unusual gift: a very highly developed sense of smell. Wine and tea tasting seem to be possibilities. Do you have any other suggestions? "

Career opportunities in tasting are limited, but your son might consider perfumery. A degree in chemistry would be the first step.

A career at the Bar

" Our daughter, who is in the first year of the sixth form, seems to have set her heart on becoming a barrister. We would like to know more about what it might entail. Could you advise? "

The Bar Council publishes an excellent guide, *Steps to the Bar*, which is both informative and realistic. It points out that only about 50 per cent of those who start the post-graduate Bar Vocational Course secure a pupillage, and only 60 per cent of those secure a tenancy. "You will need a great deal of dedication", the guide explains. "The chances are that you will also need to face up to several years of financial hardship." The booklet is free from The Bar Council, 2–3 Cursitor

Street, London EC4A 1NE; tel 020 7440 4000.

Career options in nursing

" My academically able daughter wants to be a nurse. Should she take a degree course and start her career with a student loan to pay off, or do the diploma course, for which she would receive a bursary? Also, is there a league table of university nursing departments? "

Her career options and earning potential would be greater if she took a degree, which 10 per cent of student nurses now do. And, as Christine Hancock, general secretary of the Royal College of Nursing, puts it: "Where nurses have stronger theoretical skills, they provide higher quality care." The Quality Assurance Agency has only just started inspecting nursing at English universities; in Scotland, it was rated "highly satisfactory" at Edinburgh, Glasgow and Glasgow Caledonian.

Best for speech therapy

" My daughter is interested in becoming a speech therapist. What A-levels should she have, and which universities are best? "

One of her subjects should be biology, and she will probably need at least a B and two Cs at A level. However, Newcastle and Sheffield require an A and two Bs, while Leeds Metropolitan is satisfied with three

Cs. For further information, send an sae to the Royal College of Speech and Language Therapists, 7 Bath Place, Rivington Street, London EC2A 3SU.

Working with animals

" My grandson has set his heart on becoming a vet but, unfortunately, his grades will not be good enough to get him into a veterinary college. He very much wants to work with animals. Can you suggest an alternative? "

I found one answer on a new website which I recommend – www.bigwideworld.com/. It aims to guide those aged 15 to 24 through the education and careers maze, and includes a factual introduction to more than 600 jobs. Under "nature & animals", for example, I found veterinary nurses, who assist vets with their duties ("manual dexterity is needed, as is a willingness to undertake messy jobs"). I also learnt that the Royal College of Veterinary Surgeons (020 7222 2001) runs a two-year nursing scheme, entry to which requires five GCSEs.

" You recently recommended veterinary nursing to someone unlikely to gain the grades necessary for veterinary school. You should have pointed out that veterinary nursing is poorly paid and no substitute for practising veterinary medicine. Far better to gain a good science degree and then apply to one of the vet schools. The Cambridge school, where I work, accepts students by that route. "

Thank you. Writtle College, Chelmsford, says most of the students on its animal science course are in a similar position and that career opportunities for those who graduate are becoming increasingly attractive.

Not sure about the commitment

" Our daughter, who is studying A-levels, is thinking of becoming either a barrister or a solicitor, but is still not sure that she wants to commit herself to taking a law degree. Does that matter – and how long is it all likely to take? "

In principle, a non-law degree is no bar to the profession. However, non-law graduates must take a one-year full-time (or two-year part-time) conversion course, known as the Common Professional Examination, to put them on the same footing as law graduates. Thereafter, those hoping to be barristers take the Bar Vocational Course (one year full-time or two years part-time) followed by a one-year pupillage. Intending solicitors take the Legal Practice Course (one year full-time or two years part-time) followed by a two-year training contract while working with a firm of solicitors. For further information, contact the Bar Council (barristers) on 020 7440 4000, website www.barcouncil.org.uk/, or the Law Society (solicitors) on 020 7320 5600, website www.lawsociety.org.uk/.

Art therapy

" My nephew, who has a degree in art, is working as a hos-

pital orderly and is interested in becoming an art therapist. What other qualifications are required?"

After gaining a year's clinical experience, he will need to take a two-year full-time (or three-year part-time) post-graduate diploma in art therapy or psychotherapy. The tuition fees are about £2,700 a year. Further details, including a list of institutions offering accredited training, are available from the British Association of Art Therapists, 5 Tavistock Place, London WC1H 9SN. Phone 020 7383 3774; or visit its website, www.baat.co.uk/.

He wants to be a physiotherapist

" My grandson's ambition is to be a physiotherapist. What advice can you give him?"

Apart from commitment, he will probably need three Bs at A-level. The degree courses offered by nearly 30 universities (for details, see the UCAS website: www.ucas.ac.uk/) tend to be heavily oversubscribed. Further information from the Chartered Society of Physiotherapy, 14 Bedford Row, London WC1R 4ED; phone 020 7306 6666; www.csphysio.org.uk/.

Psychometric testing

" My son, who is shortly to return home after teaching English in Brazil, doesn't know what to do next. Where could he find good careers advice?"

The university from which he graduated would be a good place to start but until he has some notion of how he wants to earn his living it is hard for anyone to help. Psychometric testing as performed by an organisation such as Career Psychology (020 7976 1010; website www.career-psychology.co.uk/) might help him to focus.

No way to choose a career

" Our daughter is taking A-levels in art – which is her best subject – English and geography but has no idea what career to pursue. Is there a database listing the universities that offer degree courses for which those subjects are a suitable preparation? "

I can see the logic of the question because everyone who takes A-levels is encouraged to regard university as the automatic next step. However, it is no way to choose a career. Your daughter should not go to university until she knows how she wants to earn her living or unless there is something she particularly wants to study.

Combining study with work

" My son, who is half way through A-levels, is interested in accountancy as a career. Would he need to go to university? "

No. Accountancy is one profession that encourages students to combine their studies with full or part-time work. Details from the Association of Chartered

Certificate Accountants, 29 Lincoln's Inn Fields, London WC2A 3EE (020 7396 5800).

Teaching as a career

Best for teacher training

" I have a good degree in English and am planning a new career in teaching. How can I find out which universities offer the best training courses? "

The Teacher Training Agency is planning to publish its first league table next July [now available at www.canteach.gov.uk/]. Meanwhile, the advice of Anthea Millett, the agency's chief executive, is to avoid institutions that admit students with low A-level scores (which is most of them). The best on that basis include: Cambridge, which requires 20 A-level points, though it will accept 16 (where an A is worth 10, a B eight, a C six, and so on); Warwick, 18, though it will accept 14; Durham, 16; Brunel, 14–16; Reading, 14, though it will accept eight; Stirling, 14; Exeter, 12, though it will accept eight. On the other hand, Plymouth, among others, is happy with two points (one grade E).

Para to PE teacher

" My son left school with an A-level grade E in English and an N in economics. His heart wasn't in the academic side and he joined the Army. Now 23, he's in the Parachute Regiment, doing well and has two more years to serve. After that, he des-

perately wants to be a PE teacher. What should he do? "

> Trainee teachers embarking on a BEd course need two A-levels, but your son may be able to convert his Army qualifications into the one he lacks. Be warned, though: PE courses are heavily over-subscribed.

High levels of dissatisfaction

" *I want to be a primary school teacher and I'm thinking of taking a Post-Graduate Certificate of Education at Liverpool University. Is it on your recommended list?* "

> No. Ofsted found recently that the course had "serious weaknesses" and that newly qualified teachers reported "high levels of dissatisfaction with many aspects of their training". If you are committed to the city, you would do much better at Liverpool Hope.

No bar to training

" *Our daughter, who has a degree in silversmithing and jewellery design, cannot teach in the state sector because she hasn't passed GCSE maths. Short of going back to school, what can she do to qualify?* "

> The lack of maths is a bar to teaching but not to training to be a teacher. The institution where she chooses to take her Post-Graduate Certificate in Education will be able to help.

Training to teach special needs

" Our daughter, who gained good GCSE results and is in the middle of A-levels, has decided she wants to teach at a special needs school. To advance her career, should she take a degree in a subject she enjoys and then undertake the training, or go straight to a specialist course? "

> Either route will advance her career. Taking a general degree first – if that is what she wants – would broaden her education and enable her to keep her options open longer.

Marks for teaching the Three Rs

" My daughter, who is due to graduate this year, wants to train as a primary school teacher and is thinking of applying to Reading. How is it rated by Ofsted? "

> Of the 55 institutions inspected recently, only five have been judged worse at preparing trainees to teach the Three Rs (Edge Hill, Kingston, Liverpool, Warwick and Westminster College, Oxford). The two best are Canterbury Christ Church ("the provision was judged to be very good with several outstanding features") and Homerton College, Cambridge. Of the latter, Ofsted said: "The course is intellectually challenging and the tutors provide excellent role models."

A career in music teaching

" *My daughter-in-law is an accomplished pianist. What qualifications would she need to teach and how could she, as a full-time mother, obtain them?* "

> Music teaching is not a regulated profession but having a qualification would help her to find pupils. The Associated Board of the Royal Schools of Music (020 7636 5400) offers a licentiate, which is an exam without tuition, and a teaching certificate, which requires attendance at a five-day residential course followed by four weekends spread over a year. The Incorporated Society of Musicians (020 7629 4413) publishes a leaflet on careers in teaching.

Giving preference to sports science graduates

" *My son has a degree in geography and plays rugby professionally. He wants to be a teacher but cannot find a place to study for a PGCE in physical education because he did not read sports science. Does he have to take another degree?* "

> Teacher training institutions tend to give preference to sports science graduates because they have covered the academic part of the PE curriculum. However, a geography teacher who offers PE as a subsidiary subject will always be in demand.

Becoming a maths teacher

" I have been working for an investment bank and now wish to become a teacher. I have A-levels in double maths, English and French and a degree in economics. I would like to teach maths to children aged eight to 11. Is there a need for such teachers? Does one have to teach more than one subject? Does it matter where I study for a PGCE? "

> There is an urgent need for maths teachers; in a primary school you would have to teach other subjects (with luck, you might find one that offers French); and it matters very much where you study for a post-graduate certificate. Given your background, I would recommend Homerton, Cambridge.

Reports not encouraging

" I am 25, have a good degree in biochemistry and would like to train to be a primary school teacher. Which, in your opinion, is the better route: school-centred initial teacher training (SCITT) or a Post-Graduate Certificate of Education (PGCE)? If the latter, where in London would be best? "

> The attraction of the on-the-job training offered by SCITT is that it cuts out a lot of dubious academic theorising. However, Ofsted's early reports have not been encouraging. I recommend a PGCE at, in descending order: St Mary's Twickenham, Brunel and Roehampton.

Best for post-grad teacher training

" I am about to embark on a postgraduate teacher training course. What would top your recommended reading list? "

I would urge you to read a report published recently by Ofsted called *Lessons Learned*. It is based on the experiences of 250 schools that were judged to be failing and have been turned round. It might seem a perverse way to approach teaching, but understanding how schools go wrong and what puts them right is genuinely illuminating. The messages are jargon-free – something you will learn to appreciate – and reassuringly common-sensical: "It is important to make every lesson count; when teaching is effective, children want to behave well and to learn; progress is best when pupils see that they are making worthwhile gains; do not scatter praise indiscriminately but focus it on work of high quality; pupils should know, with certainty, what the school judges to be good behaviour, and what is unacceptable; heads cannot hide behind a closed door or seek refuge in paperwork – they need to be highly visible throughout the day; and [when all else has failed] schools should not shy away from removing staff who cannot fufil their responsibilities as teachers."

Lessons Learned is available free from Ofsted Publications Centre, PO Box 6927, London E3 3NZ; phone 020 7510 0180.

The better route

" Our daughter is taking A-levels in biology, geography and art, and wants to become a primary school teacher. Which would be the better route: a BEd or a degree in another subject followed by a Post-Graduate Certificate in Education? "

> It is more a question of which would better suit your daughter. The BEd focuses on preparing students to teach across the curriculum, while a first degree (in a relevant subject) represents a more academic approach. Your daughter's spread of A-levels points to the former. Both routes take four years but PGCE students do not pay tuition fees.

A three-year alternative

" You recently described the two main routes into teacher training, which both take four years, but neglected to mention that many universities offer a three-year alternative: a first degree with qualified teacher status. "

> Quite right. Details from the Teacher Training Agency, Portland House, London SW1 5TT, or the website, www.teach-tta.gov.uk/.

What's the difference?

" My daughter wishes to be a primary school teacher and has been offered places at five universities. Three are for four-year BEd courses, one is for a four-year BA with qualified teacher

status (QTS), and one for a three-year BA with QTS. Could you explain the difference and say which would be most acceptable to an employer?"

> The most important considerations are the status of the institution and the quality of the course. As a rough guide to the former, the higher the A-level grades required the better; for an account of the latter, see the "performance profiles" published by the Teacher Training Agency (phone, 01245 454 454 or see the website, www.teach-tta.gov.uk/). BEd courses tend to emphasise how to teach, BAs what to teach. Since the best way to learn is to do, the shorter the course the better, especially as the cost of the fourth year in tuition fees, living costs and lost earnings is more than £20,000.

A "golden hello" worth £4,000

"Is it true that trainee teachers who enrol in September for a Post Graduate Certificate of Education will get £10,000? If so, is there any guarantee that they will become teachers? What is to stop them taking a paid year off while they look for something more congenial?"

> All PGCE students at universities in England and Wales will be paid a £6,000 "training salary". Those who train to teach maths, science, technology or modern foreign languages will qualify for a £4,000 "golden hello" at the start of their second year in teaching. Every year, a significant number of trainees apparently change their minds.

" You were wrong to say last week that trainee teachers taking a Post Graduate Certificate of Education in England and Wales will qualify for a £6,000 grant. It is available only in England."

My apologies. The restriction is a cause of concern to Welsh universities.

" Partly on your advice, my daughter, who wants to be a primary school teacher, is planning to apply to Homerton College, Cambridge, to take a four-year BEd degree. But now that the Government is introducing £6,000 'training salaries', wouldn't she be better off taking a three-year degree followed by a Post Graduate Certificate in Education?"

She would – which is why Cambridge is hastily devising a new three-year degree followed by a PGCE.

TEFL (Teaching English as a foreign language)

Teaching English abroad

" Our daughter, a graduate frustrated at her inability to find a worthwhile job, is thinking of going abroad to teach English. Would she need a special qualification, and how should she set about looking for a post?"

Most employers require a qualification in TEFL – teaching English as a foreign language. You will find much information about that and job opportunities in the *English Language Teaching Guide*, the ninth edition of which has just been published by EFL. It costs

£12.95 plus £2 p&p at good bookshops or from Books System Plus, phone 01223 894870.

What, where, how long and how much?

" I'm considering going abroad to teach English as a foreign language. Could you tell me what qualification I'll need, where I can study for it, how long it will take and what it will cost? "

Two qualifications are recognised internationally: the Trinity College London Certificate in Teaching English to Speakers of Other Languages (TESOL), tel: 020 7820 6100, www.trinitycollege.co.uk/; and the Cambridge Certificate in English Language Teaching to Adults (CELTA), tel: 01223 553789, www.cam.ac.uk/. Both courses take four weeks and cost about £1,000. A good general website is: www.prospects.csu.ac.uk/.

Career changes

A second career

" I am 46 and have been made redundant by the engineering company I was employed by for 20 years. I'd like to explore teaching as a second career. "

There is a severe shortage of secondary school teachers of maths, science, design and technology, modern languages (especially French and German) and religious education. A series of three-day taster courses offering "suitably qualified professionals" an opportunity to explore teaching the above five subjects is run by the Institute of Education at London University (20 Bedford Way, WC1H 0AL). One day will be spent in classroom observation. The course currently costs £30. Call 020 7612 6591 for further details.

She lacks confidence

" My daughter, who is 28, has an MA in illustration from St Martin's School of Art. She's creative and intelligent and has worked as a freelance, but has never been able to earn sufficient to support herself financially. Although she lacks confidence, I think she'd be good at teaching art to children, or working, perhaps, as an art therapist. Any suggestions? "

To work in a state school, she would need Qualified Teacher Status, which would mean taking a one-year Post Graduate Certificate in Education. However, independent schools are not bound by the regulation and she might be able to find one that would enable her to teach part-time. Art therapists are required to have a year's work experience (generally unpaid) with patients or children with special needs.

Worried sick

" My 36-year-old son has decided to give up a successful career in banking to take a PhD in environmental studies at Plymouth. I know there's nothing I can do about it but I'm worried sick. What do you think? "

Plymouth has a good research record in environmental sciences. If you are asking about your son's abrupt career change, I think you should give him all possible support and encouragement.

She feels out of touch

" As a 'post-motherhood' graduate, I am anxious to pick up the reins of my career but feel very out of touch with the business world. Any suggestions? "

Westminster University's business school runs a three-month course designed to turn older women graduates into "newly marketable products". Benefits include unlimited computer access and a two-week work placement. Thanks to the European Social Fund, it is free. Details from Jill Jones, the course leader, on 020 7911 5180.

Proofreading courses

" Do publishers recognise the proofreading courses that are regularly advertised on the education page? Do many people find gainful employment after taking one? "

Chapterhouse ("Spot our errors"), which has been in business for eight years, says publishers recognise its "certificate of competence", but that – a familiar Catch 22 – finding a job before you are experienced is not easy in a competitive market. Its home-study course, which costs £82, includes marketing advice from successful freelancers.

Train on the job

" After graduating 10 years ago in statistics and computing, I worked in computer training and then left to start a family. Now I'd like to become a teacher. Presumably I should brush up my study skills by taking an A-level, but what would be the best course after that? "

> Please do not waste time on A-levels: schools are crying out for people with your qualifications and experience. By joining the Graduate Teacher Programme, you could train on the job and qualify for financial assistance. For details, write to the Teacher Training Agency, Portland House, London SW1E 5TT or consult its website: www.teach-tta.gov.uk/.

Teacher training on the job

" I am a graduate in my early 30s. I am thinking of switching to teaching as a career but am not keen on going back to university. Can one train on the job? "

> Yes, but the hitch is that you have to find a school prepared to train you. The Teacher Training Agency (phone 020 7925 3700; www.teach-tta.gov.uk/) may be able to advise, though readers frequently complain about how unhelpful and inefficient it is. As you live in Kent, I can recommend South London Teacher Training, a consortium that includes some first-rate schools. Contact: Simon Linsley, Haberdashers' Aske's Hatcham College, Pepys Road, London SE14 5SF; phone 020 7652 9500.

Work experience

Work experience in marine biology

" *My 14-year-old grandson is fascinated by the sea and is set on becoming a marine biologist. This time next year, he has to do two weeks' work experience. Could you help us find a suitable placement?* "

Do readers have any suggestions? I shall be happy to pass them on.

" *One of your correspondents asked where a 15-year-old set on a career as a marine biologist could do two weeks' work experience. We offer a degree in the subject at Portsmouth and may be able to help, or at least direct him to one of the marine aquaria around the country.* "

The letter is from Dr William Farnham of the university's Institute of Marine Sciences. He adds that "larval" marine biologists should join the Marine Conservation Society (01989 566017; www.mcsuk.org/) and learn to dive through the British Sub-Aqua Club. "Such activities," he says, "will enhance their appreciation of marine biology and may impress admissions tutors. Marine courses are now very popular."

Work experience in a good hotel

" *My daughter is looking for work experience in a good hotel in the hope of furthering her career in the hospitality and tourism industry. How should she go about it?"*

The British Hospitality Association publishes details of 800 hotels, restaurants and caterers where employment practices are considered to "match the best in the industry". For a copy of the directory – *Your First Choice* – phone 020 8977 4419.

Lifelong learning

Learning to repair quartz watches

" I have just started my own business as a market trader and would like to offer a repair and battery replacement service for quartz watches. Unfortunately, I have been unable to find a course in the subject. Do you know of one?"

I am stumped. Can readers help?

" Please would you tell the reader who asked about courses in repairing quartz watches and replacing batteries that we provide them?"

I'm happy to do so. The letter is from the British Horological Institute; telephone 01636 813795.

Time to repair the damage

" Having missed out on a good deal of formal education, I feel it's time now to repair the damage. How can I do that while looking after two small children?"

I recommend the Cambridge-based National Extension College. It offers tuition in a wide range of GCSEs and A-levels (at, respectively, £245 and £285 a course) as well as tutorial support for those studying at home for London University degrees and many professional qualifications. For a course guide, phone: 01223 450200.

European Computer Driving Licence

" I have become fascinated by computers and, I think, quite knowledgeable about information technology. Is there any way of having that formally acknowledged and accredited? "

I am very taken by the ECDL – the European Computer Driving Licence – a Europe-wide qualification designed to enable people to demonstrate their competence in information technology. It is divided into seven modules, each of which must be passed (over any period of time) before the "driving licence" is awarded. Testing is carried out at audited centres. The syllabus costs £5 (including p&p) from the British Computer Society, Freepost, 1 Sandford Street, Swindon SN1 1BR (cheques should be made payable to British Computer Society).

Wiping out the shame

" Having failed O-level maths in 1941 – I'm 74 – I'd dearly like to wipe out the shame by taking a correspondence course in GCSE maths. Could you recommend one? "

Maths is among the 20 GCSEs – and A-levels – offered by Oxford Open Learning (01865 798022). It belongs to the Association of British Correspondence Colleges, which is some guarantee of quality. Other members offer courses in everything from Arabic and astrology to veterinary nursing and writing for radio programmes. For a leaflet, phone 020 8544 9559.

Individual Learning Account

" I'd like to take an Italian language course but can't afford it. The Government says it's keen to encourage 'lifelong learning'. Does that mean I can get government help? "

Surprisingly, yes. As a demonstration of its commitment, the Government is offering everyone over the age of 18 an Individual Learning Account, which includes a discount of up to 80 per cent on many courses provided by colleges and training companies. The first million learners to sign up will receive a minimum discount of £150. As the scheme was launched on June 12 [2000] without, oddly, any publicity, you are bound to qualify. Further details can be obtained from the Individual Learning Account Centre on 0800 072 5678, or see the website: www.dfee.gov.uk/ila/.

" Now that I've firmly decided to become computer literate, what should I do next? "

Obtain a European Computer Driving Licence. It certifies that the holder has the knowledge and skill needed

The next step

to use the most common computer applications efficiently and productively. More than 100,000 people in Europe have passed the test. For information about course providers in your area, contact the British Computer Society on 01793 417424 or, if you are already semi-computer-literate, see the website: www.bcs.org.uk/ecdl/. For help in paying for the course, sign on for an Individual Learning Account (see my reply to the previous letter).

Local courses in computing

" How can I find somewhere local that offers courses in computing? "

Typing "computing" into the search box of www.hotcourses.com/ ("the UK's largest adult education website") brings up 747 results. You can also search by postcode.

Useful contacts

Active Training and Education (ATE: 01684 562400).

Advisory Centre for Education, 22 Highbury Grove, London N5 2DQ (advice line: 020 7354 8321); (www.ace-ed.org.uk/).

Bar Council (020 7440 4000; www.barcouncil.org.uk/).

Boarding Education Aliance (information line: 0020 7798 1553).

Boarding Schools Association (020 7798 1580; www.boarding-association.org.uk/).

British Computer Society, Freepost, 1 Sandford Street, Swindon SN1 1BR.

British Dyslexia Association, 98 London Road, Reading RG1 5AU (0118 966 8271; www.bda-dyslexia.org.uk/).

British Film Institute (020 7255 1444; www.bfi.org.uk/).

Choir Schools Association, The Minster School, Deangate, York YO1 2JA (01904 557230).

Conference of Drama Schools, 1 Stanley Avenue, Thorpe, Norwich NR7 0BE (01603 702021; www.drama.ac.uk/).

Useful contacts

Council on International Educational Exchange, 52 Poland Street, London W1F 7AB (020 7478 2000).

Countering Bullying Unit, University of Wales Institute, Cyncoed Road, Cardiff CF23 6XD.

DfEE Publications Centre, Sherwood Park, Annesley, Nottinghamshire NG15 0DJ (0845 6022260).

Directory of Social Change, 24 Stephenson Way, London NW1 2DP (020 7209 5151).

Directory of Social Change, 24 Stephenson Way, London NW1 2DP (020 7209 5151; www.dsc.org.uk/).

Eating Disorders Association (helpline 01603 621414); (www.edauk.com/).

Education Otherwise (emergency helpline 0870 7300074); (www.education-otherwise.org/).

Electronic Telegraph provides a free site to help teachers and students get more from the Internet (www.telegraph.co.uk/).

Environment Council, 212 High Holborn, London WC1V 7BF (020 7836 2626).

Higher Education Funding Council for Wales, Linden Court, Ty Glas Avenue, Cardiff CF4 5DZ (01222 761861; www.niss.ac.uk/education/hefcw/).

Useful contacts

Home Education Advisory Service, PO Box 98, Welwyn Garden City, Herts AL8 6AN (www.heas.org.uk/).

Independent Panel for Special Education Advice (IPSEA), 6 Carlow Mews, Woodbridge, Suffolk IP12 1DH (0800 0184016 or 01394 380518).

Independent Schools Information Service (020 7798 1500; www.isis.org.uk/).

Kidscape, 2 Grosvenor Gardens, London SW1W 0DH (020 7730 3300).

Law Society (020 7320 5600; www.lawsociety.org.uk/).

Marine Conservation Society (01989 566017; www.mcsuk.org/).

Mind Publications, 15–19 Broadway, Stratford, London E15 4BQ (020 8519 2122; www.mind.org.uk/).

National Association for Gifted Children (01908 673677; www.nagcbritain.org.uk/).

National Association for Special Needs (NASEN), Amber Business Village, Tamworth B77 4RP.

National Bursars' Association (01460 65628).

Oxford Colleges Admissions Office, Wellington Square, Oxford OX1 2JD (01865 270208).

Useful contacts

PIN (Parents' Information Network), PO Box 1577, London W7 3ZT (www.pin.org.uk/).

Qualifications and Curriculum Authority, 83 Piccadilly, London W1J 8QA (www.qca.org.uk/).

Quality Assurance Agency, Southgate House, Southgate Street, Gloucester GL1 1UB (01452 557000).

Royal British Legion, 48 Pall Mall, London SW1Y 5JY (020 7973 7200).

Scottish Higher Education Funding Council, 97 Donaldson House, Edinburgh EH12 5HD (0131 313 6500; www. shefc.ac.uk/).

State Boarding Information Service (020 7798 1580).

Teaching Abroad, 46 Beech View, Angmering, Sussex BN16 4DE (01903 859911).

Technology Colleges Trust, 37 Queen's Gate, London SW7 5HR.

University Student Exchange Partnership (USEP), 35 Quarry Bank, Keele, Staffs ST5 5AG.

Young Writer, Glebe House, Weobley, Herefordshire HR4 8SD (01544 318901).

Youth for Britain, Higher Orchard, Sandford Orcas, Sherborne, Dorset DT9 4RP (tel/fax 01963 220036).

Index

A
A-levels 179–209
  distance learning 183
  mocks 186, 202
  new-style A-levels 200–1
  refusing to enter pupils for 184, 185–7, 202
  syllabuses 199, 201–2
abroad, studying 258, 313–15
accountancy 346–7
admissions policies
  schools 8, 11, 94–5, 138–9, 140
  universities 263–4
advertising in schools 81–2
air traffic control 194
animal science 218–19, 238–9, 343, 344
animation courses 338
anorexia 82–4
appeals system
  schools 9–10, 97, 131–2, 137–8, 140
  universities 310–11
archaeology 221–2
architecture 238
armed services personnel 5–6
art and design 182, 235, 277–9, 280, 333, 335, 344–5
art therapy 345, 357
Assisted Places Scheme 18–19
Attention Deficit Disorder 40, 113
awards, grants and scholarships 19, 23, 28, 107, 282–3, 286, 287–8, 291–2, 293–4, 297–8

B
back-to-basics education 17
behaviour, loutish 61–3, 169
bilingualism 67–70
biology 225, 329
biosciences 270
Boarding Education Alliance 3, 139, 140
boarding schools 3, 5–6, 59–60, 139–40
  state boarding schools 4, 6–7, 21
Buckingham 245, 251–2, 293
bullying 53–5, 56, 127–8
bursars 33
business studies 216, 235–6, 266
business/industrial sponsorship 282–3, 285

C
career decisions 258, 278, 316, 322–4, 326, 328–35, 345–6
catering 220, 259–60, 262, 325, 328–9
Catholic schools 135–6
CD-Roms 39, 157
choir schools 2
class sizes 97
clockwork radio appeal 24–8
collective worship 146
Common Entrance 102

Index

complaints procedures 66, 250
comprehensive schools 132, 184
computer studies 216, 362, 363–4
computers 49, 73–6, 204–5
cookery courses 259–60, 262
crammers 156
creative writing 208
criminology 233, 308–9, 321

D
dance 88, 293–4
deaf children 46
disabled students 288–9
distance learning 182, 183, 362–3
drama schools 136–7
drugs 56–7
dyscalculia 50–1
dyslexia 44–6, 47, 49, 50, 52, 111, 203, 288–9

E
early learning goals 100
Edspeak (jargon and acronyms) 34
Education Action Zones 16, 23–4
education guides 86–8, 100–1, 229, 230, 231
educational psychologists 47
emotional and behavioural difficulties 40–1, 46, 47, 60, 112–13, 170–1
engineering 219, 224, 225–6, 282–3, 336–7
English as a foreign language 71–2, 256–7, 355–6

English literature 208, 239, 308, 329–30
environmental studies 215, 357–8
essay competition 175–6
Eton 98, 138, 248
EU pupils at British schools 21
EU university students 270–1, 284–5, 291
European citizenship 17–18
exam stress 202–4
expulsion 56–8, 112, 144, 169

F
failing schools and colleges 2–3, 8–9, 179
failing teachers 30
film studies 234, 237, 245–6
fine arts 240
food and drink in school 114–16
foreign exchange visits 174–5, 177
foreign students 289, 290, 318–20
form orders 166
foundation courses 277–80
foundation degrees 279
free school meals 31–2
fundraising 19–23, 24–8, 28–9
further education colleges 181, 183–4, 191–2, 247

G
gap years 241, 255–62, 280, 307
GCSEs 159–60, 164–5, 167
    grades 132, 148, 152, 154–5
    marking 155–6
    syllabuses 167–8
gender differences 104, 159–65

general studies 197
geography 158–9, 226, 227–8, 232
GNVQs 182, 187–9
Government education policies 14–15
Government spending on education 10, 15–16
graduate employment 322–4, 326–8, 328, 329–35
graduate salaries 335, 336–7
grammar schools 132, 140–2, 152
grant-maintained schools 131
graphic design 235, 277, 280
guardianship 91–2

H
hairdressing 324–5
high-ability pupils 66–7, 126–7, 171–3
history 221
home education 40–1, 43, 173
homework 99
honours 86
hospitality/hotel management 250, 321–2, 338

I
Individual Learning Accounts 363
interior design courses 243–4
International Baccalaureate 189, 190–1
international relations courses 231
Internet 42–3, 73, 204–5
Irish universities 225

J
journalism 193, 339–40

L
language schools 72
Latin 42
law 192, 207, 224, 263–4, 266, 341–2, 344
league tables
  schools 2, 7, 9, 96, 101, 102, 104–5, 133, 135, 136, 143, 144–5
  teacher training 250, 252
  universities 211–13, 217, 251
  value-added tables 143–4
learning difficulties 47, 48, 51
  see also dyslexia
left-handedness 52
leisure and tourism 181–2, 187
lifelong learning 361–4

M
marine biology 360
maths 107, 148–9, 171–3, 197–8, 351, 362–3
MBA 316
media studies 193, 214–15, 219, 226–7, 234–5, 237, 246, 309, 317
medicine 194, 198, 223–4, 263, 266–7
microbiology 331
mixed-ability classes 147
mixed-age classes 99
modern languages 194–7, 215, 242–3, 334, 363
Montessori method 326
Morrisby Test 176
moving schools 78–9, 96–7

Index

music 2, 128, 129, 176, 350
music teaching 350

N
national curriculum guides 100–1
national curriculum tests 16, 103, 104, 128–9
  after-hours coaching "128–9
  age-adjusted scores 105
  practice papers 102, 104
  thresholds 106
National Literacy Project 35–6, 117, 118, 130
naval architecture 246
nursing 342

O
Ofsted reports 7, 8, 9, 30, 94, 133, 146
Open University 272
optometry 236–7
Oxbridge 180–1, 221, 227, 229, 237–8, 239, 241, 242–3, 248, 265–6, 267, 270, 271, 272, 276–7, 302–3

P
parental choice 1–2, 11, 138–9
parents' evenings 65
performance-related pay 15
personal security alarms 81
pharmacy 240–1
PhDs 318, 332
philosophy 217–18
physical education 266, 347–8, 350
physiotherapy 345
poetry 39–40, 92
political correctness 162, 199–200
politics 322–3
polling stations in schools 13–14
postgraduate study 315–20
prep schools 97–8, 101, 102, 128, 129, 133–4
primary education 93–130
private education 7, 93–4
probation service 321
professional negligence, schools and 51
proofreading courses 358
psychology 213, 221, 224, 233, 269–70, 330–1
psychometric testing 307, 346
public relations 338–9
public schools 131

Q
Qualifications and Curriculum Authority (QCA) 103, 106

R
racism 171
reading skills 29–30, 35–6, 101–2, 112, 117–21, 124–5, 168
religious education 10
retail automotive management 325–6
returnees 358
revision/revision guides 153, 204–5
road safety 89–91
rural schools 96

S
Scholastic Aptitude Test 190

Index

school buses 91
school fees 3–4, 7
school governors 32–4
school inspections 7, 8, 9, 30, 94, 133, 146–7
school phobia 77–8, 169–70
school reports 63–4, 108–10
school transport charges 11–12
school trips 61–3, 78
sciences 152, 157–8, 193
Scottish Highers 187
secondary education 131–77
secondary modern schools 132
secretarial skills 72–3, 334–5
self-employment 333
sensory perception, careers in 341
single-sex schools 17, 134–5, 163
sixth-form colleges 183, 184, 208–9
sixth-form entry 142–3
small schools 96
sociology 327–8
soil science 332
special needs statements 48, 50
special needs teaching 349
special schools guide 51
speech therapy 342–3
spelling and grammar 30–1, 41–2, 123–4, 150–1
sports facilities 85–6, 230–1
sports science 243, 244, 307–8, 350
starting school 93, 94–5
Stock Exchange 340–1
student accommodation 298–9, 300, 301, 303
student diet 300–1

student grants 280, 282, 305
student living costs 281, 299–300
student loans 280, 281, 283–4, 286–7, 291
student part-time employment 302
student support 296, 304–5
summer jobs 294–5, 302
summer schools/holidays 41, 112, 175

T

teacher fellowships 10–11
teacher training 222, 233–4, 249, 250, 252, 270, 288, 289, 347–55, 356–7, 359
teacher/parent relations 65, 110–11
Teacher's Day 12
teaching profession 15, 16, 36–9
technology colleges 151
textbooks 34–5, 79, 80, 87, 148
theatre studies 192
theology 242
times tables 125–6
travelling to school 11–12, 55–6
tutors 205–6
TV licences 300

U

underwater science 330
uniforms and casual dress 84–5, 114, 134
universities 211–320
    A-level grade requirements 264, 273–4
    affiliated colleges 248
    American 258, 313–14

Index

changing courses 266–7, 306–7, 309
choosing a course 214, 229, 231, 242
clearing system 268, 269
deferred places 280–1
degrees 223, 310, 311–13
dropping out 305, 306–7, 308, 309, 310
'dumbing down' 247–8, 253
EU students 270–1, 284–5, 291
European 314–15
fees and other costs 257, 280–1, 282, 284–5, 286–7, 289–90, 291, 292–3, 294, 295, 297, 303
first-class degrees 223, 311–12
foreign students 289, 290, 318–20
interviews 268, 276
open days 222–3, 229–30, 238
postgraduate study 315–20
rejections 263–4, 268, 273–4
scholarships and bursaries 283, 286, 287–8, 291–2, 297–8
selection procedures 263–4, 273–5
student numbers 275, 310
subject reports 235–6
teaching hours 252–3
teaching reports 246–7
terms 254–5

V

veterinary science 269, 343–4
vocational education 174
voluntary work 255–6, 260–1

W

watch repairs 361
whistling 88–9
work experience 360–1
writing skills 121–3, 149–50, 206–7